Mia Freedman is the co-founder of Australia's largest digital media company, Mamamia. She is a writer, broadcaster, author, a former editor-in-chief of *Cosmopolitan*, TV executive . . . and a digital empire builder. Mia and her husband co-founded Mamamia in 2008 and it has established a huge national profile among Australian women of all generations, with more than 150 employees, a monthly audience of millions and the largest women's podcast network in the world. Mia hosts two of Australia's top podcasts, *Mamamia Outloud* and *No Filter* and is the author of four books.

She is the Executive Producer of the TV series *Strife* which is inspired by this book. She is married to her co-founder, they have three children together and live in Sydney.

Also by Mia Freedman

Mamamia: A Memoir of Mistakes, Magazines and Motherhood
The New Black
Mia Culpa

strife

mia freedman

PAN
Pan Macmillan Australia

Pan Macmillan acknowledges the Traditional Custodians of Country throughout Australia and their connections to lands, waters and communities. We pay our respect to Elders past and present and extend that respect to all Aboriginal and Torres Strait Islander peoples today. We honour more than sixty thousand years of storytelling, art and culture.

First published 2017 in Macmillan by Pan Macmillan Australia Pty Ltd
This Pan edition published 2023 by Pan Macmillan Australia Pty Ltd
1 Market Street, Sydney, New South Wales, Australia, 2000

Reprinted 2023

 A catalogue record for this book is available from the National Library of Australia

Typeset in 11/17 pt Freight Text Pro by Post Pre-press Group

Printed by IVE
The cover of BRW magazine is reproduced on page 59 by permission of Fairfax Syndication

The author and the publisher have made every effort to contact copyright holders for material used in this book. Any person or organisation that may have been overlooked should contact the publisher.

For Jason
Home is just another word for you

CONTENTS

BALANCE

FOREWORD TO *STRIFE*

BOOKS TAKE A long time to write. But do you know what takes longer? TV shows.

Soon after this book was released, my friend Bruna Papendrea – producer of *Big Little Lies*, *Wild*, *Gone Girl*, *The Dry* and countless other global smash hits – suggested making it into a TV show. I thought she was just being nice, because – how? But Bruna knows her shit and she saw something in the story you're about to read. She immediately identified some themes she knew would make a cracking TV series. The challenges of marriage. The challenges of starting a business. The challenges of being a Gen X woman in a male-dominated industry. And the very specific intimacy, intensity and hilarity that comes when a small group of women work closely together.

Still, it took bloody ages.

The pace of digital media suits me, always has. I can have an idea in the afternoon, bang out a story, and have it online and on socials within a couple of hours. The process of getting this book from Bruna's initial suggestion to a finished, eight-part TV series starring the iconic Asher Keddie has taken almost eight years. You will not be shocked to learn I found this an inordinately long and frustrating length of time. But the good part about having ADHD is that I kept forgetting we were doing it, as I continued to work with my real-life husband, Jason, in building Mamamia. ICYMI, we also had a pandemic. It was a time. You may have heard.

Naturally, it was also Bruna's idea that I update this book and re-release it to coincide with the show. The idea was daunting because I didn't know if what I wrote would still apply or be interesting. Good news: I can reliably report that it does and it is.

A lot has happened since this book was released, and also not much has changed. I am still married. My children are older and I think I am wiser. I have had more therapy. I've been cancelled several times. I've been diagnosed as neurodiverse, and my eldest son is now married and expecting a baby. Soon, I will be a grandmother – but that is a book for another time.

So if you've found your way to this book feeling curious about the real story behind *Strife* and the real person who inspired the fictional character of Evelyn Jones who leaves her job as a magazine queen to launch a women's website with a random group of brilliant, funny women (and one bloke) – welcome. And enjoy.

Mia xxxx

30 May 2023

AUTHOR'S NOTE
What I want to tell you before we start

THERE ARE MANY, many books written by many successful women who talk about their many successes and float their theory about how you can get some of it for yourself if you just Make a Vision Board, Live Your Best Life, Stay In The Moment and Beat Your Fear. Strive and Thrive But Not So Much That You Sleep Less Than Eight Hours. Say Yes and Also Say No. Lean In But Don't Fall Over. Empower Yourself. Practice Gratitude. Don't Lie Down, Be Mindful And Take Power Naps While Standing Up. *Be Kind But Also Assertive. Meditate!*

This is not one of those books.

You will find no platitudes here about reaching for the stars or just believing in yourself. I promise not to tell you that anything is possible if you want it enough because that's bollocks and we both know it. Also because you're smarter than that and you've bought a book (thank you), not an inspirational meme. I've always found all that you-go-girl stuff to be empty, condescending, disingenuous and most of all, incredibly unhelpful.

This book is not about my journey. It's about yours.

So why do I write so personally about my own experiences? Well, mostly because I know I'm not special. I am so very basic. I know from experience the value of being vulnerable and the power it has to help other women feel normal.

Triumphs are far easier to share. Our society is excellent at celebrations. Weddings, pregnancies, graduations, promotions, engagements, baby showers, birthdays . . . but the tough stuff of life – the strife – is far less transient than a few pinots and some congratulatory hugs.

Eating disorders. Grief. Divorce. Miscarriage. Losing a job. Losing a loved one. Losing your mind. Infertility. Most of these things don't have rituals around them. They exist secretly in our homes, our heads and our hearts. And in an age of social media humblebrags it can sometimes feel like you're the only one whose life isn't Instagram-shiney.

The way women connect meaningfully in every aspect of our lives is not by boasting about our triumphs on social media but by sharing the nuances of our failures, our disappointments and our insecurities. Quietly. Often privately. Over wine. Over text. Over back fences. In person and on WhatsApp. Female friendships and meaningful connections are forged through vulnerability, not humblebrags.

So I'm going to tell you about some of my most private failures, my most significant setbacks and my most painful vulnerabilities. More importantly, I'm going to tell you what I've learned from them. At Mamamia we call it flearning – failing and learning. Learning through failing.

In my teens, twenties, thirties and forties, I've done a lot of both and I'm ready to be brutally, unflatteringly honest about it in the hope it will reassure you that you're not alone in your thoughts, your fears or your insecurities. It's not just you, I promise.

Ready?

Let's do this.

INTRODUCTION
The #1 mistake women make

I WANTED TO call this book *Balance is Bullshit*. My publisher convinced me to go with a less sweary title and that was probably sensible. Finding the right font for the word 'bullshit' isn't easy.

But I did like the abbreviated version *Balance is* .

It's easy to text.

Work, Strife, Balance was my next favourite because it neatly sums up the three parts of this book and has the distinct advantage of not having the word 'shit' next to my face.

It's a shame in a way, though, because the balance-is-bullshit sentiment has become my mantra whenever I'm addressing this infernal modern obsession with work–life balance.

Balance really is bullshit.

And it's holding women back. All of us.

Through my teens and twenties, I noticed this one incessant question being asked: Can women really have it all? Asking a woman how she achieves work–life balance is the new version of that; yet another passive aggressive question whose very premise sets us up to fail.

Because what those questions *really* mean is this:

How do you ladies do two things at once because let's be honest, you can't and you shouldn't even try. Because there has to be a pretty big cost, yeah? To yourselves, to your employers, to your partners, to your kids, to your SANITY. Someone's gotta pay for this arrogant way you chicks want to have jobs and other things *at the same time. So WHO IS IT? Who is SUFFERING FOR YOUR CHOICES? Which balls did you drop today, lady? Who are you short-changing, RIGHT NOW?*

The 'I don't know how you do it' statement used to get my blood boiling. When I heard those words I didn't hear 'I don't know HOW you do it,' I just heard, 'I don't know how you COULD do it.' I would be feeling overworked and guilty . . . and suddenly I would be struck over the head by what felt like someone else's bullshit. It was an emotional drive-by . . . Sometimes I would fantasise about answering the question, 'How do you do it?' with quick one-word answers: 'Ambivalence.' 'Drugs.' 'Robots.'

Amy Poehler

Today, the new way to make a woman feel insecure is to ask her about work–life balance.

Originally a management catchphrase, work–life balance has become the new bar women must clear at every stage during our lives. Like most bars set for women (see: red carpets, pregnancy, thigh gaps, giving birth, bikini-bodies, motherhood, bodies after babies, breastfeeding, sex, ageing), it's placed impossibly high, setting us up to fail in myriad ways and making us feel like crap as we hit the mat with a thud.

Unless you have the elusive balance (nobody does) the implication is that we're doing it wrong. Leaning too hard one way or the other. Leaning in or out is challenging enough. Stressing about the degree and direction we're leaning at every given moment is a prescription for despair.

That's why you need to remember: balance is bullshit. It's a blunt-force instrument that women are being encouraged to use to beat ourselves around the head in the pursuit of unattainable perfection. Just like the Photoshopped, Facetuned images of women you see that don't exist anywhere other than inside the computer or phone on which they were created to digitally manufacture our insecurity.

We've all been sold on this myth, insidiously and effectively. And we're desperately hoping someone out there might just have the answer. Because there is one, right? There's a simple formula we can all apply to our lives that will magically fix them. *ISN'T THERE?*

That's why women have begun incessantly asking each other how they achieve work–life balance in the same way that sad little animal in that storybook scurried along from animal to animal asking, 'Are *you* my mother?' It speaks to our insecurities as people, not just as employees, managers, women, partners, mothers, children and friends.

I used to do it myself, ask other women about work–life balance. It's only lately I've realised how destructive it can be and made a conscious effort to stop.

Because when you ask any woman how she achieves work–life balance I can tell you what goes through her head in the instant before she opens her mouth to reply:

OH GOD, I AM THE LEAST BALANCED PERSON ON THE PLANET. I CAN'T BELIEVE I FORGOT TO SEND MY DAUGHTER TO SCHOOL WITH A SILLY HAT FOR SILLY HAT DAY, I WONDER IF I SHOULD HAVE GONE HOME TO DROP IT INTO THE SCHOOL AND MISSED THAT MEETING I CAN'T BELIEVE I WAS LATE FOR THE MEETING WAIT, I HAVE TO BOOK A PAP SMEAR DON'T I, WHEN IS MY PERIOD

DUE, WHAT'S THE NAME OF THAT APP TO TRACK IT, SHIT I HAVE TO PICK UP A NEW LEXAPRO SCRIPT I HOPE I HAVE ENOUGH REPEATS LEFT, OH NO I SAID I'D GO ON THE ROSTER TO TAKE MY SISTER-IN-LAW TO CHEMO BUT THEN I NEVER CHECKED IT I WONDER IF I CAN FIND THAT SPREADSHEET IN MY INBOX BLOODY HELL, WHAT'S MY PASSWORD, I HAVE TO TRY AND GET TO THE MAC STORE TO FIND OUT WHY NONE OF MY PHOTOS ARE SYNCING ON MY IPAD AND I WONDER IF I SHOULD CHANGE ALL MY PASSWORDS SO I DON'T GET HACKED I MUST ASK SOMEONE ABOUT THIS OTHER NEW APP ALL THE KIDS ARE ON WHAT'S IT CALLED AGAIN HOW LONG HAS IT BEEN SINCE WE'VE HAD SEX FUCK DO WE NEED TO HAVE A DATE NIGHT OR MAYBE HE CAN JUST WATCH SOME PORN SO I CAN CATCH UP ON SLEEP BECAUSE I READ THAT NOT SLEEPING ENOUGH GIVES YOU CANCER . . .

This is pretty much the narrative most of us have going on in our heads at any given moment. Our lives are one enormous exercise in triage: prioritisation and damage control. No two women ever have the exact same things laid out before us in triage. None of us even has the same triage choices to make two days or two hours in a row. There are just too many variables. The status of the patients requiring our attention – and the patients themselves – are always changing. We must assess and reassess constantly and this process in itself is draining, the endless recalibration of multiple competing needs for our time, our effort, our bodies, our headspace, our love, our physical presence, our sex parts, our concentration and our attention.

And yet we do it. Women are multi-taskers of supreme skill who have the capacity to spread ourselves surprisingly thin without disappearing altogether. Usually. It's our talent.

As if this wasn't challenging enough, though, we exponentially magnify the difficulty by comparing ourselves to the images we see of other women – not just their physical appearance but the way they seem to be living their whole lives.

This is the insidious trap of being female and it's the biggest mistake we make: comparison. By doing so, we either feel superior (which is insufferable) or inferior (which is spirit-crushing).

Nobody wins the comparison game.

Maybe men win because they're just getting on with their lives while we twist ourselves into tangled spaghetti strands of anxiety, inadequacy and self-loathing about our bodies, our parenting, our wardrobes, our careers, our grey hairs, our wrinkles and our store-bought birthday cakes. And what are we comparing our real lives and selves to? Other people's highlight reels. Their Photoshopped photos and their airbrushed lives. In actual fact, we are comparing ourselves to an enormous steaming pile of bullshit.

*

Throughout my tweens, teens and twenties, magazines were the only place you went to find information about any issue pertaining to women from relationships, breastfeeding, contraception, hairstyles, miscarriage, breast cancer, abortion, sex, career, childbirth, beauty, feminism, menstruation, hair removal, rape, sexuality, menopause, eating disorders, pregnancy, STIs, makeup, domestic violence ... there was almost nowhere else to find content for and about women, produced by women. This is now the domain of the Internet but for decades it was owned by magazines. If you're talking to anyone under 35, it can be difficult to explain the scale of influence magazines once held over women and girls back in the '70s, '80s, '90s and even the early '00s.

That's why prior to the Internet and social media, women built our social networks around our favourite magazine brands. They provided us with a sense of community, helped shape our sense of identity as girls and women, and we progressed through different magazines according to our life stage and the information we required to navigate it.

Dolly taught you what an orgasm was.

Cleo taught you how to have one.

Cosmo taught you how to fake one.

And the *Women's Weekly* taught you how to knit one.

Pretty much. For decades, and until quite recently, the editors of women's magazines held staggering power over women and in society more broadly; as did the advertising industry. Together, they defined how women were portrayed and the picture they painted of us was constricting, reductive, exclusionary and at times even damaging. Narrow in every sense.

Astonishingly, little has chawnged. The way women are portrayed by the mainstream media remains disturbingly unrepresentative. We rarely if ever see women of colour, older women, women of different shapes, sizes or ethnicities or women with disabilities portrayed in magazines, pop culture or advertising at all. And they're almost never portrayed aspirationally; that privilege is reserved almost exclusively for thin, young, white women who are presented to us as the definitive benchmark of female beauty.

In the '90s when I began my career in magazines, the models used in *Vogue* to model designer clothes costing thousands of dollars were sometimes as young as 12 and rarely older than 20. The fashion models used in the *Women's Weekly* were routinely in their early twenties, decades younger than the magazine's readers.

Models in their early twenties or late teens are still regularly cast as mothers of school-age children in ads and 'become' the parents of teenagers in campaigns well before these models turn 30.

All of this is a bigger deal than it may seem, because what advertising implies about women, and always has, is this: 'what's most important is how we look. So the first thing the advertisers do is surround us with the image of 'ideal' female beauty. Women learn from a very early age that we must spend enormous amounts of time, energy and, above all, money, striving to achieve this look and feeling ashamed and guilty when we fail. And failure is inevitable because the ideal is based on absolute flawlessness. She never has any lines or wrinkles, she certainly has no scars or blemishes, indeed she has no pores.' (Jean Killbourne 2010, *Killing Us Softly* 4, Media Education Foundation, mediaed.org) A period? A pimple? A panic attack? Don't be ridiculous.

The most twisted aspect of this is that the images of female beauty that surround us cannot be achieved without technology – nobody looks like this, including the women to whom you are unwittingly comparing yourself.

Think about that for a moment. How is it that we are surrounded by images of women's fake faces and bogus bodies that do not exist in real life?

The relentless conscious and subconscious comparisons we make of the way we look is a trap and a prison. I know how demoralising it feels because for decades I did it myself. Still do.

As much as I was enthralled by magazines when I was younger, as a reader and then an editor, I knew intimately how it felt to flip through a magazine and notice a creeping sense of inadequacy grow with every page. Even at my most devoted, I would reach the end of my favourite mags and just ... feel ... bad about myself.

For a long time, I thought I was the problem. Actually, I consciously thought nothing. I just felt. Fat. Short. Ugly.

Now, fat is not in fact a feeling. Nor is short or ugly. You can't *feel* fat. You can be fat. You can eat fat. You can look fat. But you can't *feel* fat. And yet how many times do we say this or think it because sometimes fat seems to describe exactly how we feel?

The emotion we're describing though, isn't fat, it's inadequacy born of comparison; something far more slippery and insidious than weight. Inadequacy isn't quantifiable or measurable. There's no BMI to graph inadequacy, but this is the overwhelming feeling with which women are left after being exposed to images of 'perfect' bodies, be they digitally altered or just utterly unattainable (say, a six-foot-tall supermodel, a personal trainer who exercises for seven hours a day or a 'clean' eating lifestyle blogger who in actual fact has orthorexia).

In almost every case, the women do not exist. I know this because I was there. As a magazine staffer, I watched as images of women were manipulated to the extent they were more painting than photo. When I became an editor myself, I authorised some terrible things with Photoshop, like swapping heads of the same celebrity in different photos to create a 'more appealing' cover image. On more than one occasion, I instructed my art department to digitally make a model fatter because I was worried about the message her protruding ribs sent to vulnerable women. None of this I'm proud of. Eventually,

I came to loathe the way Photoshop is used to alter images of women and began to speak out against it, earning me the wrath of many in the magazine industry. They roll their eyes at the mention of my name. They're not bad people they just don't see what the fuss is about. 'It's just art!' they exclaim. 'Just fantasy! Glamour!'

Oh, is it? Well, who decided that the only type of glamourous woman was size zero, six foot, white, blonde, young and pore-less? Who chose this singular unattainable type to be the only type of woman worth fantasising about?

Magazines and advertisements aren't the only images that are digitally altered to create fake female avatars. Celebrities and influencers routinely alter photos of themselves before posting them. You know this already. But you probably forget when you're swiping through your feed. Me too. This is hazardous.

We are swimming in a sea of visual lies about womens' faces and bodies and we're not even aware of it.

These comparisons are unreal, just like there is no secret formula for balance. We're all just trying to do our best to get through life with our pants on the right way, our jobs secure and our heads above water.

A *sense* of balance might be found in the brief pauses we have between demands or the times we quickly catch our breath before the next thing happens in our lives but it shouldn't be the ultimate prize. Because this means that *not* having it – and be honest, who has it? – indicates that 99 per cent of us are failing in some way, 99 per cent of the time.

Fetishising a teeny, tiny, almost unattainable sliver of Zen is as destructive as lusting after ripped abs or flawless skin. We will almost always fail to clear that bar. It's all part of the same destructive and inevitable cycle of comparison and failure and feeling bad about yourself. Mostly because you are a woman and society has a tendency to tell us we're doing it all wrong.

That said, I'm going to cheerfully share a bunch of my 'failures' with you over the course of this book so that you can see me falling over, getting up and trying again. But let's dispense with that terrible maxim shall we? Let's repurpose it and maybe, in the attempt, stop comparing ourselves to some saintly paragon of imagined and airbrushed virtue. Sadly, *Work, Strife and maybe-a-little-balance-but-probably-not-let's-face-it* didn't make the final cut for the title either (I remember some fraught discussions with my publisher along the lines of 'way too long how will we ever fit that over the collage of your face Mia?!'). But I did decide to structure the book this way. I'm also indebted to some very excellent women who have let me talk at length with them over the years. I've often referenced Elizabeth Gilbert and Caitlin Moran, both of whom are even more wise and delightful in person than they are on the page and who have both been hugely influential for me. In addition, there are many, many people – mostly women – who have shaped my thinking, and often our acquaintance came through working together. Sometimes we are related. Sometimes it's both. Like Caitlin and Liz, many of these women spoke with me on my podcast *No Filter*. I've cited them as I go along.

We talked a lot during the editing process about where certain chapters should sit – since it's life I'm drawing from, I think there's not always a line in the sand between events and the various life lessons I drew from them, so there you go. It's ended up more or less themed and chronological. And hey, life's a story you tell yourself different ways as you grow older and things look different through a different lens. But here's what

I know as of this moment: there's no right way to do life: strife will teach you who you really are and balance is most definitely bullshit.

See you on the other side,

Mia xxxxx

WORK

THAT TIME MY CAREER IMPLODED

THE WORST JOB you ever have will teach you a lesson. You will not know this at the time. When it happens you will be convinced that you've indelibly stained your CV and ruined your life. You will feel ashamed and devastated and possibly humiliated. You will be angry and resentful and bitter.

But it gets better. And you will learn things. Just like having an abysmal relationship helps you to recognise a good one when it comes along, so too a disastrous job will help you to learn what you do (and don't) want in your next job and the one after that.

A few months after I had my second child, I blindly walked into the jaws of a career nightmare to take an executive role at a giant commercial TV network. Over the next seven months it would devour my confidence, my reputation and my identity. It sparked a prolonged period of anxiety and was the closest I've ever come to depression.

Within weeks of starting, I was bringing my toxic work-based anxiety home and infecting my family with it like Zika, a fresh dose every night as I skulked in the door on the verge of tears and distressed to my core.

My work life had become a poisonous soup of bad decisions (mine for taking a job that only really existed on paper), bad blood (the blokes at the network who thought I should go back to magazines, home to my kids or anywhere far away from them) and bad press (humiliating articles about me sourced from spiteful leakers inside my new workplace).

The worst part was the constant fear. Fear that everyone I worked with hated me. Fear that there'd be yet another story published that made me look like a clueless fool, stupid and incompetent. Fear that I'd made the worst mistake of my life. Fear that I was trapped because leaving would create even more unwanted publicity and speculation over my disastrous tenure in TV.

Every one of those fears was well founded.

They were the worst of times.

And yet, years later, now that I've uncurled myself from the foetal position in the corner and stopped twitching, I can identify so many invaluable lessons in those seven months. Lessons that don't just apply to me or that particular job but that might also help you learn from my failure.

Here they are.

1. Don't Take a Job That Doesn't Exist

After 15 years nestled in the warm bosom of women's magazines, I'd moved to a new workplace for the first time in my adult life. The TV network was owned by the same media company that had employed me since I was 19. And yet even though my overlords were the same, the role I'd been offered was a new one that had never existed before. A different culture. Different colleagues. The same industry – media – but a different medium.

The new CEO had brought me in to bolster the female representation in the leadership team from zero to one. 'I'm sick of sitting around a boardroom table with 20 men trying to work out what women want to watch on television,' Eddie Maguire told me before I accepted the job.

His philosophy was sound, but unbeknown to either of us I was walking into a trap of our own making: a role that didn't exist.

This isn't a problem if you're taking a job at a start-up because, by definition, no pre-determined roles exist. Since Mamamia began, we have constantly created new roles in real time.

I love start-up culture because it's all hands on deck all the time and you move fast and break things. I have a propensity for doing both. Sometimes I break things and then I move fast, away from the things I just broke, hoping that nobody realises I broke them. But start-up culture is fluid and that suits me.

And it's not that new roles can't be created in established companies. Businesses do evolve, driven in large part by technology. 'Social media manager' is a relatively new job in big companies, for example.

But be aware that when you walk into a newly created role, you need to carve out a you-shaped hole *from the jobs currently being done by other people*. The politics of this can be exceptionally tricky to navigate and I did it woefully.

Another red flag: as we worked on my contract, we could not agree on a title. Nothing seemed to fit. I wasn't a consultant. I didn't have any direct reports and I reported directly to the CEO. I should have asked to see an organisational chart. I should have asked for a more detailed job description. I should have asked about KPIs (key performance indicators) and targets. I should have asked what success in this role would look like.

The fact I did none of these things came back to bite me hard because my lack of understanding of what I was being tasked with meant I was blind to all the warning signs that it would be a disaster.

They were right in front of me.

Virtually all the other men (it was only men) in the executive team didn't want me there and I can understand why. I had no TV experience. What could I offer them? As a change agent (always a fraught function), I'd been tasked with improving the network's positioning with women externally, internally and on air. It soon became apparent that nobody other than the CEO and his deputy wanted me to do any of these things.

I was impotent – or whatever the female equivalent is. My ovaries were tied. In actual fact it was my breasts not my ovaries which were giving me grief. My daughter was still only six months old and breastfeeding her had been a disaster from the start. She thrashed around every time I tried to feed and it wasn't until years later I realised she had silent reflux. Trying to stop her screams by flipping her from breast to breast every 30 seconds meant they were never emptied, which in turn led to crippling mastitis, an agonising infection inside the breast which also causes debilitating flu-like symptoms. I would collapse with high fevers, chills and uncontrollable shaking within hours of noticing a hot spot or pain in my breast and each time I had to take a 10-day course of antibiotics. It took days to recover.

By the time I started in my new job, I was up to my 70th day of antibiotics in eight months but I refused to wean my daughter because I'd been brainwashed into believing formula is poison (shut up) and that I had to keep breastfeeding my baby *at any cost* because: poison. Eventually, that cost became too high and to this day I'm furious with myself for persisting so long. It was a terrible situation for us both. There were no winners and I didn't feel smug. There's no room for smug in the bed when you're writhing in feverish agony yet again. Formula is *fine, it's fine.*

Where was I? Oh, this is a chapter about career and I'm telling you about breastfeeding. Welcome to the life of a working mother. It's all here.

2. Make Sure the Cultural Fit Is Right

As a boss myself for the previous decade, I'd been able to determine my own working environment so I'd never thought much about culture.

Culture is, in fact, everything. If you are fundamentally unaligned with the culture of the company you work for, you can't succeed. By this I mean you will not be happy. You won't fit in. You'll never be able to exhale. Every day will feel like you're pushing shit uphill because you will be. Even if you're really good at your job.

We've had some terrific people come through the door at Mamamia who we couldn't hire or had to let go because the culture fit wasn't right. Let me be very clear: I'm not talking about culture in a literal sense. This is not about whether you wear a hijab, have dark skin or come from a non-English-speaking background. It's not about being an extrovert or an introvert or what you wear or who you know. Culture in a workplace is about your attitude and personality and the way you work and interact, more than the work itself.

If you like a formal work environment, heavy on process and infrastructure, and feel most comfortable in a suit, for example, you're going to struggle at a start-up.

If you like wearing sequins, consider leopard print a neutral and have strong opinions about women, you're going to struggle as an executive in commercial TV.

And I did.

I once had a sub-editor resign from *Cosmo* because her priest told her working at a magazine that published sex information was inappropriate. 'Wait, *your priest said you have to quit your job?*' I repeated incredulously. 'Well, yes, and my bible group agrees,' she said, nodding. 'I'm sorry, I know it's awkward, but it's become a real problem for me at church.'

'What if you didn't work on any of the sex stories?' I offered, trying to salvage the situation because replacing good staff is a punish and I was disturbed by the prospect of a priest controlling the career path of a young woman.

She shook her head. 'I have to choose between my church and working here. I'm sorry.'

That, friends, is called a culture clash.

Even when I was an editor, working inside an enormous company, each magazine had its own culture which was determined by the editor. The *Women's Weekly* was different from *Dolly*, which was different from *Wheels*. I'd never consciously realised I was creating a culture but of course that's what you do as a manager by virtue of being one. You set the tone as well as the rules.

When I first became a boss at 24, I knew I wanted to work in an office that was fun, supportive, fast, passionate, positive, spontaneous, collaborative, driven, nurturing and organised. I didn't tolerate bitchiness and I discouraged drama. Nobody has time for your drama no matter where you work. It's toxic and boring. Leave it on the street before you arrive outside. You can pick it right back up when you leave but for your boss and co-workers it will always be a liability.

Parachuting into a culture that jars with your sensibilities is confronting. My experience of commercial TV culture at the executive level was that it was a hyper-masculine one: lots of middle-aged alpha men with varying degrees of talent and boundless amounts of self-confidence along with a paralysing fear of bad ratings. I've since learned that workplaces with an extreme gender imbalance are never as happy as workplaces with a more equal mix. Which is why we are always looking to hire more men at Mamamia.

Two generalisations: companies without women have a blokey culture. Companies without men have an overly emotional culture. In my research group of one, I've experienced both to be true. There's a lot of talking about feelings when you work exclusively with women, sometimes too much. Women feeeeel things. It's one of our best qualities. In a workplace or school it can be draining when it's not diluted. There is such a thing as over-communication at work; at a certain point you just have to stop talking and get shit done.

I don't find working with women to be bitchy – I never have – but it can be intense. Since women bear the brunt of domestic life, from meal preparation to being lead parents and lead children (for your ageing parents or in-laws), our lives frequently bleed into work. We're the ones fielding the calls at 11:30 am from the school, the daycare centre or the nursing home, and we're the ones whose hearts sink when we see that number flash up on our phone because we know it means disruption. There's rarely any choice but to leave and immediately attend to whoever needs us. Cancel the meeting. Fail to meet the deadline. Inconvenience our colleagues. Are we pushing our luck with the boss? Is everyone exasperated with us? How much grace do we have? We dash out the door hurling earnest apologies, trailing anxiety and guilt.

I wonder how many men know much about the families of their colleagues. As women we are often heavily invested in the lives of each other's children, partners and pets because we talk about them a lot at work. By no means is this a bad thing, I actually think it's wonderful. It's certainly a feature of the culture in any female-dominated workplace.

As I learned immediately after starting my ill-fated job as a TV executive, you cannot effect change on an entrenched culture as an individual. It's impossible.

I was a fool to even try. In my ambiguous 'women's' role, I was discouraged by the existing heads of departments from stepping remotely near their turf and everyone was relieved when I was finally given a project: to launch a women's daytime panel show.

At least I was on more familiar ground: working with a female-heavy team, able to create my own micro-culture inside a larger company culture I couldn't penetrate. It didn't last. The show didn't work, I still hated working in TV and I wanted out.

3. Don't Be Afraid To Rip Off The Band-Aid (Especially If There's Gangrene Underneath)

On my second day as a TV executive, I knew I'd made a ghastly mistake. My boss had asked me to watch a particular program and email him a critique. I did so and when a colleague found out, he went ballistic. It dawned on me that being the messenger was going to get me repeatedly shot and yet I had no idea how to leave. With all eyes on my high-profile appointment, I was paralysed by the thought of the bad press my exit would inevitably trigger. So I sucked it up. Convinced myself I was just out of my comfort zone, not that I'd made a drastic error of judgement by accepting a poisoned chalice.

Most people have a job disaster hidden in or deleted from their CV. It happens. As an employer, this doesn't faze me. I know from my own painful experience that some jobs don't work out and 'the fit just wasn't right' is usually an honest enough answer to explain why you were only in a certain role for a year or less.

At all costs, avoid the temptation to unload all the reasons *why* the fit wasn't right. Note that I've told you some things about my failed experiment in TV but I haven't dumped anyone in it by name, I've left the worst bits out and trust me, I've been enormously discreet. This is not an accident. With time, I've learned to see the contribution I made to this unfortunate blot on my CV and to willingly take responsibility for my part in it, something I can do without trashing individuals *as much as I would really love to*. So be tactful if your interviewer probes you about why you left your last job. As satisfying as it might feel in that moment to let loose, your potential new employer won't be listening to your words as much as noting the fact you're dissing your former workplace and imagining you doing the same to them.

4. Ask For What You're Owed

Once you've decided to leave a job you hate (I decided halfway between when I started and when I left, seven months later), plan your exit carefully.

Don't leave impulsively, even if it means staying a bit longer than you'd like. Be strategic. Try to leave on good terms even if you've been miserable there.

By the time I was ready to go, the situation had become toxic and for me, untenable. Having worked for the network's parent company for 15 years, I knew I was owed a redundancy.

I'd insisted on having a clause written into my contract that said I reported to the CEO and named him. Now he was gone, my role was entirely redundant. They didn't want to pay me out, though, so they tried to persuade me to quit.

I was desperate to leave. I would have happily sprinted out the door without a cent or even my handbag just to end the daily wrench of walking into an environment I hated and working beside people who were leaking about me to the media.

I was in a terrible state. Anxious, unable to eat or concentrate. I was barely functioning. It was my husband, Jason, who convinced me to stick it out. 'You're not walking away,' he said. 'Just keep your head down and negotiate.'

So I tried. I pitched my case for redundancy, which was met with an insincere plea for me to stay. 'We don't want you to go,' said a senior manager. 'But there is no job for me here,' I maintained. 'I'm redundant. What would I do?'

He thought for a moment, shuffled some paper and looked at a spot on the wall right above my head. 'You could be the head of wardrobe or hair and makeup,' he said calmly.

'I'm a journalist,' I shot back. 'Let's both pretend you never said that.'

All I wanted to do was flee and preserve the modicum of self-esteem and sanity I had left. But every night when I came home in tears, Jason would help strengthen my resolve to fight for what I was owed.

Women do this often at work and in marriages. We walk away from settlements because of the discomfort and the pain involved in pushing for what we deserve. Our fight-or-flight instinct tells us to flee, assessing the likelihood of winning a fight against someone bigger, stronger and more powerful to be remote. This might seem like the best option but only in the very short term. By standing in an uncomfortable place and holding your ground, fighting for the money, the property or the custody you deserve, you buy yourself a more stable future. Of course there are exceptions. If your home situation includes violence towards you or your children, you need to immediately do whatever it takes to remove yourself from it to be safe. And if your mental health is severely affected, staying in a workplace may not be sustainable.

Within a few weeks we had negotiated a redundancy package, and even though I was firebombed with bad press as I left, I now had the financial ability to launch my own business, Mamamia. It's not that building a website cost much money – a couple of thousand dollars to customise a free template – but giving it my full attention would prevent me from earning any income. The redundancy package meant I could continue to help pay our mortgage while I determined if a blog could become something bigger. It was suck-it-and-see time.

The story I always tell is that I started Mamamia in my lounge room in 2007. That's not technically true. It started in my head a few months earlier while I was still in the turmoil of the TV job.

Apart from my desperation to sprint as far and fast as possible from this nadir in my career, I'd realised something else: I no longer wanted to be a senior manager or a media executive.

Management was very well paid and had some delightful perks but it wasn't creative and I was spent. This was confusing because I'd always been highly ambitious and competitive. I'd always strived to climb higher, go faster, push harder, lean in further.

It wasn't that I felt burnt out so much as bummed out. The politics of senior management in any organisation are inevitably the same: endless meetings, strategy sessions, KPIs, petty dramas about who wasn't cc'd on an email, implementing processes, putting out fires, more fires, more processes, more and more and more meetings, brainstorming sessions, more fires, writing reports, doing budgets, adhering to budgets, fires, fires, fires, meetings about fires, spreadsheets, off-site meetings about strategy, writing reports about fires, meetings about processes, writing memos about people not following processes, recruitment, P&Ls, salary negotiations, learning what EBITDA means, performance reviews, having to be reminded what EBITDA means and forgetting again almost immediately, meetings about someone not being cc'd on a memo about a process and repeat until you want to staple your face to your swivel chair and file yourself in the bin under FOI for Fucking Over It.

As much as I was exhausted by the excruciating repetition and endless politics and people management involved in being a senior executive, it had always seemed counterintuitive to do anything but keep striving for promotions. The only way is up, right? A higher salary. More responsibility. Increased power and influence. A bigger team. New challenges.

Upwards is not always the right decision, though, and neither is more of everything, even if it's money. I didn't want to work less and I certainly didn't want to stop working. I love work. It feeds me. The treadmill of working inside a big company, however, was something I wanted to jump off: it was time to try being my own boss.

HOW TO BUILD A MEDIA COMPANY
FROM YOUR LOUNGE ROOM

MY EXPERIENCE OF an emotionally abusive relationship in my early twenties was a defining one in my life. When I finally, agonisingly extricated myself from it, to the soundtrack of Alanis Morrisette's *Jagged Little Pill*, I was emotionally battered, bruised and resolute about the kind of treatment and behaviour I would never again tolerate.

That relationship, as eviscerating as it was, recalibrated me, taught me the value of kindness, intelligence and respect in a partner and ensured that the next man I decided to commit to would be worth my time. The worst relationship of your life has value because it teaches you what you don't want next time.

It's the same with a terrible career move. In time, you will appreciate what it taught you. Or as cosmetics guru and businesswoman Poppy King once told me about her own experiences of falling down and getting back up, success merely confirms what you already knew about yourself. It's failure that teaches you who you are.

My career implosion taught me that I wanted to be in control of my work life and go back to building a community of women. This time, online.

On the morning after my departure, as I uncurled from the foetal position long enough to see the vast media coverage gleefully ~~celebrating~~ reporting my very public failure, a small voice in my head took a break from being Beyoncé singing 'I'm a Survivor' to observe: *Oh well. All these stories mean at least everyone will know you're currently available so they can hire you! Just wait for the phone to ring! You won't be unemployed for long!*

The phone did not ring.

To distract myself from this second wave of humiliation I had to quickly occupy my time, something I was totally ready to do. As a magazine journalist and then editor, I always based my decisions on my feelings as a reader, not a content producer. It's how you gather your most valuable insights; my advocacy around body image began that way. I knew how dispirited I felt to see nobody who looked like me or any woman I knew in my beloved magazines.

As a woman, a reader and a feminist I thought this was an appalling thing. As a businesswoman (which editors are, don't let the rest of the media mislead you into thinking otherwise with their fluffy, patronising portrayal of the women who run magazines), I thought it was a baffling one. Why make your readers feel bad about themselves after engaging with your brand? How is that good for business?

You can argue convincingly that many marketers do this deliberately precisely because it *is* good for business. In her iconic book, *The Beauty Myth*, Naomi Wolf first floated the theory that some companies marketing products and services to women use the insecurity and angst (created by them) to prompt us to buy. Create a problem then market a solution. Magazines in the '80s and '90s did this to excellent effect.

Cover lines[1] like . . .

'IS YOUR HAIRCUT MAKING YOU LOOK OLD?'

'DOES HE THINK YOUR VAGINA IS TOO BIG?'

'7 signs he's about to break up with you'

'Does your sexual history make you a slut?'

While masquerading as sisterly and helpful, these kinds of cover lines deliberately pushed the inadequacy button that made women want to buy the magazine so we could learn how to avoid being old/loose/dumped/slutty.

It worked wonderfully for decades until something shifted and women began pushing back. It was around the mid '90s when I noticed it. Women no longer wanted to be told how defective they were. And when I became an editor at *Cosmo* in 1996, I tried a different approach both with the stories and the images we published. The word 'empowering' didn't exist back then, but that's broadly what I tried to achieve with more positive articles, a less patronising tone and more diverse models.

At my Cosmo desk in 2001

---

1   I probably helped write some of those cover lines, by the way. Or similar. It took time for me to understand what I was doing and try to change it.

At first, I made some colossal mistakes. First I abolished the sex and relationships content because I thought if I wasn't interested in reading it anymore, nobody else was either. I'd recently met Jason, was embedded in monogamy and had been reading/writing/editing sex and relationship stories for at least 10 years so stories about dating and orgasms felt retro and repetitive to me. Surely there was nothing left to say . . .

My boss Pat Ingram blanched visibly when I proudly announced my idea to her but then she did something smart: she said 'Okay, try it'.

This is a boss lesson I've repeated many times with my own team. If someone you rate has an idea they passionately believe in, challenge them on it. Make them fight for it. In doing so, you'll force them to think it through thoroughly which will filter out the ideas they aren't wedded to; the ones with gaping holes. But if they keep coming back and can argue their case convincingly, so long as it's not going to irreparably damage your business, you should let them try.

On the upside, it might just work. On the slightly less but still upside, it won't work and they will learn from it in a way they never would if you'd said a flat no. Because if you simply overrule the idea, they will die believing it would have worked, if only you hadn't cock-blocked their genius.

The minute the first week of circulation figures came in, I realised how badly I'd fucked up. OF COURSE *Cosmo* needed to publish sex and relationship articles. They're the foundation of *Cosmo* and I was a fool to think I could just reinvent one of the world's most successful brands.

It was an effective wake-up call. I was in a long-term relationship, was well established in my career, and felt confident enough to flick past stories about giving better blow jobs. I had a mortgage and wasn't exactly living the *Cosmo*-girl lifestyle. I was also, aged 24, at the older end of the *Cosmo* demographic, and I was about to be pregnant with my first child which is about as un-*Cosmo* as you can get. It was yet another of the many lessons my mentors, like Pat and Lisa Wilkinson, have taught me about being a leader, a content creator and a boss.

And so after my miserable TV job, I reminded myself I had more than 15 years of experience that informed my instinct when it came to women and their media consumption. Gut instinct isn't woo-woo, you know. Whether it's the gut feeling you have about a person, a job or an idea, your 'gut' is just a term for your combined life experience. *Listen to it.*

If I was behaving in a certain way as a consumer it meant other women were doing the same thing and the mainstream would be following closely behind.

I knew I was disillusioned with traditional media. I knew I was frustrated by the way my beloved glossy magazines were published monthly[2] while I was living my life in increments of minutes and seconds.

And the three-month production time meant content created in November wasn't published until February the next year. No brand catering to young women could possibly remain current when it was months out of date by the time it hit news-stands. As the news cycle sped up and we became hungrier for more and more information, faster and for free, the magazine business model that relied on paid sales of a printed product appeared to me to be fundamentally flawed.

How could media aimed at women possibly remain relevant given the physical and practical constraints of print?

---

2 Besides magazines, the only thing occurring monthly was my period.

I had become fatigued by trying to convince my middle-aged male bosses that Armageddon was coming for our industry and the stampede of young women towards digital media had begun.

Despite my repeated exhortations in the early 2000s that we needed to pivot to digital, the online presence of magazines across the industry remained woeful.

I knew unequivocally the future of women's media was online and I wanted to be part of it – after a brief, disastrous detour via commercial TV.

*

So *this* is how the Mamamia Women's Media Company began: in 2007 I sat down at my kitchen counter and cut out letters from a magazine[3] to try and make a ransom-style logo for my blog. Or my website.

Note that my head was part of the first logo. Removing it was a crucial step in extricating the Mia from Mamamia.

I wasn't quite sure how to think of it or what it was even going to be about. I just knew that I wanted to produce content online. That was the extent of my knowledge of digital media: I wanted to be part of it, and in the months it took to negotiate my redundancy, I bought the Mamamia URL[4].

---

3 Could there be any more obvious metaphor? I was literally creating the digital logo of my future from the print medium of my past.

4 Jason and I have spent years debating whether this was a good choice. We're still debating it. No, it's not a website for mothers. No, it's not by or about Mia anymore. But back in 2007 it seemed like a great name. I never expected anyone to take it literally. It was an ABBA song.

Today, Mamamia is the largest digital company in Australia with the largest podcast network in the world. We make written, video, audio content for more than seven million poeple per month. We have 55 different podcasts with 35 episodes every week along with dozens of written articles and hundreds of social media posts.

That all feels very boasty and I'm kind of uncomfortable writing it because I want you to like me and I understand that because I have a vagina, the more successful I am, the less you will like me according to the likeability index.

But there you go. It's the truth.

What most people want to know is quite simply this: how did you get from your kitchen bench to running a media company?

In short: slowly. Building Mamamia took years, I didn't do it alone and there have been many missteps along the way.

FUN MISTAKES TO MAKE WHEN YOU'RE BUILDING A DIGITAL MEDIA COMPANY!

1. Using the wrong platform!

I had only one friend with a blog and she used TypePad, so I did too. Rookie error. TypePad was the Beta of video and WordPress was the VHS, except that is an analogy you won't understand if you're younger than 40. Are you younger than 40? Okay, so TypePad was the Blackberry of mobile phones. Or the Nokia. In short: it was THE WRONG CHOICE.

2. Not knowing how to code!

Coding is like maths crossed with Latin crossed with chemistry crossed with hell. I had to teach myself.

3. Not writing enough original content!

Bruised from the bad press I'd received in my TV gig,
I became frightened to write so at first I just republished my
old newspaper columns while feeling sick in my stomach
about how they would be received. But once I overcame my
paralysis and realised nobody in the media cared what I was
doing anymore, blogging became addictive and I started
writing and publishing six posts a day, five days a week.

4. Betraying my principles for clicks!

I once published a shot of Britney Spears with her tampon
string hanging out because I knew it would generate traffic,
which it did. This was an appalling thing to do and I had to
ignore my gut instinct to do it. My readers called me on it
immediately and I took it down within an hour, ashamed.

5. Not having a business plan! Or any plan!

Before Jason came on board, I worked day to day without
much thought for the future. To this day I don't know
how to create a spreadsheet. My audience grew steadily
thanks to a combination of the content I was producing,
the social media presence I was building for Mamamia and
the promotion I was able to give it in traditional media by
having the URL published alongside my Sunday newspaper
column and appearing each week on the *Today Show*.

6. Not having any income!

My gut feeling about what women wanted online
was paying off, but for years it didn't make a
cent in revenue. Within a year my redundancy
was gone. It was tough going from there.

The most important thing to say, though, is that I didn't build Mamamia by myself. My husband Jason is my co-founder and it took two of us to get from there to here.

Let me break it down for you because I know you probably want details.

Step 1:
NOTICE AN ITCH AND SCRATCH IT

If you observe a gap in the market for something you want and decide to fill it, you'll be guaranteed an audience of one at least . . .

In 2007, the online offering for women was very limited. Facebook and social media were not yet mainstream and the most interesting places to find content were personal blogs, often written by women.

While magazines were myopic in their insistence that women 'wanted fantasy and glamour' and the best way to do this was to saturate them with digitally altered images of impossibly flawless women and repetitive stories about sex, fashion and relationships, mainstream websites for women in the mid-noughties were just as limited.

There were women's sites about parenting or celebrities or fashion or cooking. If you were interested in news or current affairs or politics you could go to a news site, but they were all via a male lens and intimidatingly aggressive in the comments sections which were dominated by . . . men. Any dedicated women's websites were throwbacks to a very dated concept of what women cared about: kids, cooking, clothes, gossip.

This baffled me.

WTAF.

Like every other woman I know, I'm interested in everything.

News, politics, celebrities, body image, clothes, lipstick, current affairs, parenting, health, career . . . all the things, all the time. Put any two women together and in five minutes they will seamlessly traverse vast terrains from pelvic floors to politics, Trump to tampons, Syria to Snapchat, Lena to *Lean In*.

We are biologically programmed to do this.

While cavemen were out hunting, cavewomen were gathering information along with salad ingredients. Gathering and sharing information is *what we do*.

You're welcome, guys.

This is why women are compelled to share information – good and bad – about all manner of things: for the survival of our tribe. Men are different. Men need to filter out all excess information so they can focus on killing a mammoth before it eats them.

It took years for me to understand why I so often felt compelled to tell Jason a tragic story about someone he didn't know and why, when I tried, he'd hold his hands out as if to physically stop words coming from my mouth. 'Don't tell me this!' he would say, agitated.

'But why not?' I would reply, genuinely perplexed.

'Because there's nothing I can do about it and it just makes me upset.'

Now I realise the disconnect. I was sharing the tragic story to try and ensure the survival of my tribe which included him: *let's make sure we learn from this so the same thing doesn't happen to us*.

Women are forever sharing tragic stories in hushed tones with our friends and female relatives about the misfortunes of others. The underlying purpose is not gossip or voyeurism or schadenfreude (okay, sometimes it is) but more often we're simply complying with our biological instinct to learn everything we can about the dangers of the world and share that information so our tribe can benefit too. Pay it forward. Gather, learn and share. That's part of what Mamamia continues to do today.

Given this insatiable hunger for information about all sorts of things – not just 'women's things' – why in 2007 was there no single website for women that treated us like multi-dimensional people?

So I made one. Working on the basis that if I wrote about things I was interested in, other women would be too.

It was a brief that existed only in my head. No business plan. No elevator pitch. Nothing written down on paper.

'What's your tagline?' Jason kept asking me.

I'd look at him blankly. I hate that stuff. I wanted him to stop asking me sensible questions I couldn't answer.

Step 2:
WALK IN HER SHOES AND LOOK THROUGH HER EYES

'Ah, women!' exclaimed a male ad agency executive in the early days of Mamamia. 'Now that's an interesting niche!'

Facepalm.

My intention in starting Mamamia had been to take back my voice. Blogging has helped so many people – so many women in particular – express themselves. I was already a published journalist and author but blogging was the first time I had a direct line of communication to my audience.

Writing my monthly editor's column at *Cosmo*, even though I signed off my own copy, I still had to stick within the boundaries of the brand and company I worked for. Same with my weekly newspaper column, which for years I would self-edit. While for years I'd been fortunate enough to have a degree of success that gave me power over what and how I wrote, I was still building my own brand inside much bigger brands who had their own constraints which in turn impacted on me.

This is what everyone does when they work for someone else.

Like so many millions of bloggers before and after me and now anyone with a social media account, I became quickly seduced by the ability to have a thought or an opinion, bang it out, hit publish and reach my readers instantly. From thought to audience in moments. As someone who used to have to write my editor's letter three months before it was read and my newspaper column a week to 10 days in advance, this was a revelation[5].

Suddenly I had the ability to write about things that had just happened or were still happening. I could update my posts in real time. It was intoxicating.

Mamamia was founded on the principle of 'what everyone was talking about' because I've always been preoccupied with the zeitgeist. I'm a creature of FOMO. Curious and reactive, I want to know things first and be part of the conversation. With Mamamia and the Internet, I could finally indulge my twin passions: speed and currency.

Not that it happened immediately. It took me much longer than I expected to find my groove. But my guiding principle then was something I learned in magazines, and what was reinforced by those early posts; it's a maxim we now repeat daily at Mamamia.

WALK IN HER SHOES
LOOK THROUGH HER EYES

---

5 The 24-hour news cycle suits my temperament, and by temperament I mean the concentration span of a small yappy dog in a park full of sausages.

Too many people make the mistake of looking outwards at their audience. Wrong. Turn around. Look back at what *you're* doing through *their* eyes. It's the only view that counts.

This is how I came to move into the digital space years before our competitors even understood what a powerful commercial force women were, responsible as we are for 51 per cent of the population and 85 per cent of household purchasing decisions.

I cannot emphasise this concept enough: Understand who you are talking or selling to and use that knowledge to inform everything you do.

No matter what business you are in, you must master this skill or you will fail.

In our business, we have two groups to understand: our audience and our advertisers. The editorial team walk in the shoes of our audience and the sales team walk in the shoes of our advertisers.

If you're not able to do this from inside your business, I don't believe you can succeed. Because if you're relying on the behaviour of others – to consume your content or buy your goods or services – you need to see yourself as they see you and modify your practices to appeal to them.

Step 3:
BECOME FAMILIAR WITH THE DEEP TROUGH OF PAIN

This is a phenomenon well known in start-up culture. As a business owner/operator, you will fall into the Deep Trough Of Pain many, many times and it's as bleak as it sounds. It's from the depths of the trough that I have tried to quit my own company more than once. I have despaired and insisted I couldn't stand another day. At various trough times I've felt burnt out, fed up, fucked off. It always passes. When you tumble into the trough, you need to pull yourself out. When you want to quit? Don't.

Often I'm asked if I'm surprised by how big Mamamia has become and I'm never quite sure how to answer. It's true I've always had big ambitions for it and I've always chased big audiences in whatever medium I've worked.

It takes the same amount of work to create something consumed by one person or a million people. I like mass very much, thank you. I've never been a niche girl.

Having left a big status job to go start-up, I was warned about Relevance Deprivation Syndrome and it kicked in for me when Mamamia was about nine months old. I felt restless even though I was enjoying watching the website become a fast-growing online community where real-world friendships were being formed.

Within a year there were meet-ups in various cities around Australia as commenters and readers followed the ins and outs of each other's lives, particularly via a regular Friday post I did called 'Best & Worst', where I shared the highlight and lowlight of my week and encouraged readers to do the same. It was an ideal way to build a community and it became part soap opera, part therapy session as we all gathered to hear the latest about each other's love lives, divorces, infertility issues, medical diagnoses, mental illnesses, job promotions and losses, financial hardships and all the various plot points of suburban life. Some weeks there were more than one thousand comments.

Working at home was lonely though, and the pace of growth wasn't fast enough for me. I'd had fantasies of someone calling me up six months after launch and offering me a million dollars to buy Mamamia. When that didn't happen, I was disappointed.

Which shows how naive I was. I had nothing to sell. It was just me and my laptop making no money for 18 hours a day.

The best part about working from home: you never have to go to the office. The worst part: you're always at work.

I missed real office life. I missed getting dressed every morning and putting on makeup and having a desk to sit at and an office door to close. My kids were then nine and two and we had a wonderful nanny called Mel who was my wife. She came four days a week to look after Coco so I could work and in some ways we were a workplace of two. The flexibility and freedom of not having to answer to a boss or be involved in office politics was dreamy. But I missed working with a large group of women and being part of something bigger. I live for the warmth and camaraderie of working with women. It's life-affirming. Fun.

For that first year at home, I'd wandered around our house schlepping my laptop from surface to surface like a cat, looking for just the right spot to settle. Eventually I found it in the lounge room where I erected a makeshift desk behind the couch. Six days a week (Sundays off), I spent most of my waking hours sitting there, long after my family had gone to bed.

My 'office' for the first two years. Note: this photo was taken by a newspaper and is not how I ever looked.

Balance? Hahahahahaha-hahahahahaha!

After 10 years as a media executive, I was struggling with my new life as a blogger. It wasn't the PA or the fancy invitations I missed, it was ... I couldn't really put my finger on it, but it was tied up with my identity. Since I was 19 I'd been able to say I'd worked for a well-known brand at a large media company and suddenly I had no status in my industry, despite having worked my arse off for more than 15 years.

It felt like starting my career from scratch and it was my first plummet into the Deep Trough Of Pain. Thankfully I had no idea how much deeper I would tumble in the future and how many more times. This was a very shallow trough. A baby trough.

Just when I began thinking I might knock on some doors and explore the idea of returning to a big media company in a senior role, I got knocked up again. I was thrilled.

I'd been begging Jason for a third child and he'd been resolute: NO MORE.

We were both having major changes in our careers so I made a vision board to help nudge the process along and I snuck in a tiny photo of me pregnant in a bikini in the corner where I thought he wouldn't notice. It worked, aided and abetted by a lax attitude to contraception admittedly.

And that's how our third child and another accidental-on-purpose pregnancy saved me from a reactive backwards step into my old corporate life that would have been an epic mistake. Pregnancy meant I had to persevere with Mamamia. I couldn't – or didn't want to – take on a new job and prove myself to a new employer while pregnant.

So I stuck it out, grew my baby, wrote a book called *Mamamia: A Memoir* to draw a line under my magazine career and open up about motherhood and pregnancy loss, and really committed myself to building the site.

Giving birth while running Mamamia posed new challenges. It was still just me and my laptop at the kitchen bench and with traffic growing, I knew I couldn't simply take maternity leave as I had with my last two babies.

The idea never occurred to me, frankly. Once you start a blog or a business (I use this term loosely, as I was still losing money), you can't just . . . stop.

I mean, of course I could have stopped publishing posts, but I was terrified of losing the audience and momentum I'd worked so bloody hard to build.

Practically, though, I knew there would be at least a week post-birth in which I wouldn't be able to create new content. And I wanted to give myself that time to immerse myself in the baby bubble. Those few days are always one of my favourite parts of giving birth, where I mentally disconnect from the world in a way I've never been able to replicate without pushing a small human out of my vagina first. Not even when I went on safari in Africa with no wifi.

In the months leading up to my due date, I stockpiled content, pre-writing and loading posts into the back end of the site and scheduling them for the week around that day. I scheduled four posts a day for two weeks. It was a little less than my usual output of six daily posts but I figured my audience would understand.

On the day I went into labour, 10 days early, I spent the first hour frantically amending the scheduled dates of posts between contractions in order to accommodate this unexpected change of plan. Jason happened to be doing tuckshop duty at Luca's school for the first and last time in his life and 25 minutes after arriving, having made one sandwich, I called him to come home. He ~~apologised~~ bragged to the tuckshop mums who gave him a hearty round of applause as he jogged out the school gate towards his car. Men are heroes.

The birth went splendidly – a corrective experience after my daughter's birth when no epidural was available and I was left with a mild case of post birth trauma where I was tormented by flashbacks – and I lost myself in Remy for a full 10 days before venturing back online. We stayed mostly in bed.

I felt ~~blessed, grateful~~ relieved that I worked for myself and could control the hours I worked.

Except that work was out of control. I'd never worked so hard or for so many hours in my life. I was delirious. Each day started at 5 am when I'd wake with the baby, having already been up with him three, four or five times during the night. (I never have sleepers. All my babies woke half a dozen times a night in those first six months until I brought in Elizabeth Sloane, the 'Sleep Whisperer', for in-house sleep training[6].)

Self-employment meant maternity leave wasn't an option but at least I didn't have to change out of my pyjamas, commute further than my lounge room or speak in sentences. As soon as Remy woke up, I'd feed him while checking the comments that had been posted on Mamamia overnight. This was becoming increasingly fraught.

I needed help.

On January 1st a few years ago, I wrote this:

This is my year of saying no. No to requests from people I don't know to do things that matter to them but which will take me away from my family, my friends and my work. It took me a long time to realise that saying 'yes' to avoid a very brief moment of discomfort or awkwardness or disappointment for someone else just bought a much bigger problem for myself in the future. Now I am a No Machine.

---

6   Years later, Elizabeth and I, along with Bec Sparrow, would write an e-book together – *The Gift of Sleep* – for women who couldn't afford her services but who desperately needed help.

My year of saying no was born from the previous year when I'd said yes way too many times and ended it feeling drained and overwhelmed. I'd found myself regularly drowning in a clusterfuck of commitments that I'd agreed to in a(nother) weak moment. I was on a plane every week, sometimes twice a week. I had speaking engagements, client presentations, charity work, MC gigs, TV and radio commitments on top of my day job at Mamamia and my 24/7 job as a mother of three and wife of one.

What had I been thinking when I'd said yes to so many people? Some of the commitments were non-negotiable – things I had to do for our business – but many of them weren't important. I could have said no. But I didn't because like so many women, I am inherently a people-pleaser. I want to be liked, even by strangers who want me to do things that benefit them enormously and me in no way whatsoever. If you too are a people-pleaser, these steps will be familiar to you:

1. Someone asks you to do something. You do not know them very well. There is not much in this for you. Saying yes will cost you time that will have to be stolen from someone or something else in your life. The only winner will be the person who asked you to do something.

2. You say yes anyway because it seems easier and avoids an uncomfortable exchange or confrontation.

3. By doing so, Today You avoids a few moments of discomfort. The person asking is thrilled. You feel a fast flush of relief that you didn't have to disappoint them and a sugar hit of gratification from their gratitude. This is the happiest time in this shitty process. It will be fleeting. Seconds, maybe. Enjoy it. Because you've just bought a problem for Tomorrow You. She won't mind, you think. She'll be fine with it.

4. When Tomorrow You becomes Today You and it's time to go and do whatever it was you agreed to in that weak moment, you will suffer. Things and people in your life will need to be sacrificed. Essentially, then, you've put the wants and needs of someone you don't care about ahead of people you do. Ahead of you. You curse Yesterday You. When will she learn?

Remember what they say on planes about putting your own oxygen mask on first otherwise you'll pass out and be of no use to anyone? Do that in your everyday life. Self-care is a term I like even though it sounds a little bit like something that happens in a salon where there's whale music playing and everyone is barefoot and speaks softly; a scenario I find enormously anxiety-producing.

By learning to say no, I began putting my own oxygen mask on first and prioritising the needs of the people who rely on me – family, friends, colleagues – over people who aren't important in my life. Often, these people aren't even in my life. They're strangers asking for favours. Or acquaintances asking for time.

By saying no, I know I've disappointed people and I've missed some appealing opportunities. How do you make peace with that?

I've grown comfortable with disappointing people too because the pay-off is enormous. I now have a more consistent routine in my life and the lives of my family and staff. I am a much more constant and predictable presence in my own life because I function best when it's the same most days. I like the predictability of it and I find it gives me more mental space to be creative instead of anxious or overwhelmed. You really don't want to be around me when I'm overwhelmed.

There's another way to look at saying no: it's simply setting boundaries. Generally, I find people with lax boundaries are more stressed, resentful, bitter and generally unhappy than those who can say no.

Step 4:
KNOW YOUR STRENGTHS AND HIRE (OR MARRY) AGAINST YOUR WEAKNESSES

If you try to do everything yourself, you will fail. Understanding what you're good at is helpful. Understanding what you're bad at is crucial . . .

Mamamia was like a small bar in those days. Like the bar in *Cheers* where everyone knew your screenname. Many of the commenters became mini-celebrities themselves and three volunteered to help me behind the scenes, moderating comments, giving me advice about content and eventually writing and editing posts themselves. Lana, Kerri and Amanda quickly became friends and were a lifeline when I was drowning. Lana eventually became one of our first paid employees and was my right hand for several years while Kerri and Amanda went on to develop their own thriving careers in the media.

Other regulars went on to start their own blogs or create private groups on social media where they could talk about other commenters. There was lots of gossip and a few dramas. It was part bar, part high school, part support group.

And still, I was earning nothing.

Mamamia was about 18 months old and traffic was growing rapidly. I'd had a few approaches from venture capitalists but not to buy Mamamia. Most of them hadn't even heard of Mamamia. It was still very small. They were looking to start their own digital ventures and wanted me to come on board as a partner.

I took a few meetings and Jason came along to advise me but nothing appealed. It made no sense to help someone else build their business when I could do it myself.

Except I couldn't do it myself.

I was working 18-hour days, six days a week on Mamamia. I'd maintained this pace for more than a year with a new baby, a pre-schooler and a tween.

Two years earlier, Jason and I had sat down to discuss our future. I wanted out of the TV executive hell I'd got myself into and he had built, run and sold a business over the past decade.

While I'd never worked for myself before – and never wanted to – Jason had always been his own boss. These days it's called being an entrepreneur but when he did it, it was just called self-employed.

We were both often stressed by our jobs but in different ways and for different reasons. I was stressed by the politics of working in a big company with no control over my working hours, conditions, pay or holidays.

'But why don't you just work from home if you're getting nothing done in the office?' he once asked me after I'd called him to whinge. 'You don't understand!' I hissed down the phone. 'I can't just do that. It's not just about how busy I am, it's how busy I *look*.'

However, I slept much better than him. I knew that no matter how much I cared about my job, at the end of the day if something really bad happened to *Cosmo*[7], it didn't impact on my personal finances; the bottom line was my employer's responsibility. When you're a business owner, all roads lead to your bank account which is a much higher and deeper level of stress.

With the proceeds of his company sale and my redundancy, we had both gained a precious commodity: time to breathe. Naturally, I didn't want to breathe because I knew I needed to be busy. So by the time we left, I'd already launched Mamamia. The breathing space for me came in having a financial buffer. My income had dropped by 95 per cent overnight but I was able to ride out the next year without putting pressure on my fledgling blog to pay any bills. I could invest my redundancy in myself and the idea of a website for women.

Jason took more time to decide on his next move, enrolling in a business course at Harvard where he spent several months studying intensively.

---

7 Like the time I published a sealed section the supermarkets weirdly deemed too risqué and pulled the issue off sale, forcing us to print and hand-apply 150,000 stickers over the offending coverline 'Oral Sex Lessons' which cost the company a fortune.

One night, as he looked around for an investment opportunity to which he could turn his entrepreneurial mind, he noticed me working behind the couch at 2 am yet again. Writing, coding, loading, publishing, editing, spruiking, repeat.

I was burning out. Jason could see it. He could also see an opportunity. Right there in his lounge room.

'What if I come on board and we try to monetise Mamamia together,' he suggested one day. 'If we can't do it in a year, it might be time to get a real job.'

I had nothing to lose and everything to gain. I couldn't make less money or be more overwhelmed than I currently was. And I had no money to hire anyone so the idea of having a partner who was also working for love sounded sublime. I felt cautiously thrilled.

Our areas of responsibility split naturally. I continued producing the content while he took over the tech side, the financials as well as the advertising and the strategy – of which there was neither (and this was the problem).

From those first days in 2009, the differences in our styles were apparent and caused huge friction until years later when we would understand how useful they were and how to harness them to propel us forward.

Jason is a strategist. A big thinker and planner. He's always been the one with the vision for our business while I remain immersed in the weeds. I like the weeds, I feel at my safest and most creative there and I become incredibly irate if anyone tries to drag me out, which is what Jason does, damn him.

It started in the first week we worked together.

'The problem with this business,' he told me calmly as we grabbed a quick bite at our local cafe, 'is that you're the single point of failure.'

I chewed my toasted sandwich and bristled. It's every woman's dream to hear her partner to call her a 'single point of failure' and I was living it. Foreplay is overrated.

'What does that even mean?' I snapped irritably.

One of the things I'd most loved about working on my own, apart from everything I hated, was not having to consult anyone before making a decision. This suited me because my style is fast, loose and sometimes inconsistent. I don't enjoy being slowed down or made accountable; qualities which are vital in business.

This partnership thing was already annoying me.

'It all rests with you,' he pointed out, correctly. 'All of it. You write and edit every post. You're the face and you do everything. You're not a business. You're a person. And a person can't be scaled.'

I winced and bristled some more. He continued.

'There's a limited amount of content you can produce each day. And if you fell over tomorrow, Mamamia wouldn't exist.'

Jason was right and I knew it. He'd accurately identified one of my biggest frustrations, not just from a lifestyle or business point of view but from an editorial one. I'd always wanted Mamamia to be a platform for lots of different women's voices, to tell a range of stories. I was a middle-class, straight, white girl from the suburbs. My window on the world was intrinsically narrow and I didn't want Mamamia to be narrow.

Lately I'd begun experimenting with guest posts from other women who wanted to share their stories or writing with my audience. But I was torn about this. Even though most of the posts I wrote were not about me personally, I felt that my readers expected every post to be written *by* me. That's why they were coming to Mamamia, right? For my writing? What if I lost them by writing less?

The alternative was far less appealing. I was exhausted and bored by the sound of my own voice. And I was lonely.

'Mamamia needs to be a women's website edited by you with many different voices, not just yours,' Jason insisted.

He was right but it still made me feel oddly pissed off. Maybe it made me feel oddly pissed off *because* he was right. I am highly competitive. I like to be right all the time.

This working dynamic between us – Jason pushing us forward and me resisting – was established early and it exists to this day. At first it was polarising but once I saw that he was right – and right again and right again – in his vision for Mamamia, I accepted that our different styles were in fact the unique key to our success.

Jason has always been the one looking over the horizon and mapping the path we need to take to get there. I'm the one dragging my feet, grumbling, 'BUT IT'S TOO FAR AND I'M TIRED AND THIRSTY AND THAT PATH LOOKS SCARY AND FAR AND HARD AND WHAT IF WE GET LOST AND IT'S COLD AND HOT AND I JUST WANT TO SIT DOWN IN THE DIRT AND PLAY WITH THESE SHINY THINGS I FOUND.'

When Jason tries to make me strategise, it triggers a physical sensation I can only describe as being like when someone tries to drag a mule forward against its will. So many times, when we've reached crossroads for our business on the way from personal blog to media company, I am that mule. I now recognise the feeling and know to ignore it. *Ah, the mule*, I think, and try to dislodge my hoofs from the earth.

This is where I've learned how important it is in a start-up to partner with someone different from you and to do it as soon as you can. You'll notice most start-ups are founded by people who already know each other; as friends, partners, spouses or family members.

Before you commit to starting a business with anyone, make sure you're bringing different skills. A girlfriend recently told me about her plans to start a business with a close friend in the same field. 'You're too alike,' I warned her. 'We're really not,' she assured me, and went on to explain in detail the ways in which they differed. It wasn't enough. She was talking about how they had distinctive personalities and took diverse approaches to their current jobs, which was true. But their skills were essentially the same, which is the groundwork for failure.

In a start-up, you can rarely afford to hire anyone so you must do everything yourself. As soon as you can, though, hire or partner with someone who knows things you don't, who can do things you can't, who can give you a perspective you don't have.

Jason and I were a classic example of this and our worst clashes have always come when he's tried to make me be more like him or I've tried to make the business more like me.

If Mamamia is a mixture of art and science, I'm the art and he's the science. I'm the maker and he's the planner. And for the first six years or so until the business could afford to appoint a senior management team, we were both the doers. We hired, we sometimes fired, we were HR and PR and we answered the phones and bought the toilet paper.

Start-up culture is wildly intense and more demanding than you could ever believe. Having Jason come on board as CEO was the moment Mamamia went from a very time-consuming passion to a business.

Step 5:
GROW FAST BUT NOT TOO FAST

The rules of engagement are different for start-ups. Simply put, there are no rules except you must do everything, earn nothing, shelve your life and work insufferably long hours. That's not sustainable long-term and if your company is growing, you have no choice but to evolve your structure.

There are some fantastic things about starting a business in your lounge room. You get a thorough understanding of every part of what you're doing because you're doing all of it yourself.

You must also decide when you need to pay for expertise and how much you can afford to spend. When you have momentum, start-ups move so brutally fast it can be hard to keep up.

Jason and I moved Mamamia out of the house soon after he came on board so we could start hiring staff. After almost two years of working at home and living at work, it was time.

Some of our interns have gone on to do great things . . .

We relocated to what seemed like a large office (it was in fact the size of a small apartment) on the outskirts of the CBD and at first it was just the two of us, sitting at desks at either end of the space. For the first few months we didn't even have a landline or wifi[8].

Slowly, cautiously, we began to hire. Editorial assistants, sales reps, developers.

---

8   Actually we did. We stole it from the office upstairs. Sorry, guys, and thanks.

The recruitment never stopped and it still hasn't. Our leadership team is always interviewing because when you employ more than hundreds of women and you work in digital media, there's inevitable churn and you always want succession plans.

Within a year, we were sardined into that space with 35 of us sharing a single toilet. I'd gladly given up my own office as more people joined the company and by the time we left, I sat around a large desk in the editorial room with 12 other women. It was the best fun.

Step 6:
LEARN TO LOVE THE THINGS YOU HATE
(OR AT LEAST IDENTIFY THEM)

As Mamamia grew, I was schooled daily on my failings. For example, the word 'brainstorming' is the fastest possible way to delete from my head every idea I've ever had. Poof. Gone.

My tolerance for meetings is also low. They make me behave very badly. Ditto anything with the word 'strategy' or 'planning' in it. They are my kryptonite.

Not that you always have a choice about what aspects of your business you participate in; opting out of them is a luxury that comes later or never. But even at the start it's helpful to know your enemies. Strategy, meetings and planning are mine. I loathe them and yet they are crucial for business.

Knowing your strengths and weaknesses at work is the foundation of your career self-awareness. Once you've identified them, there are a couple of different options. You can either strive to improve the areas where you're weak or abandon that playing field and consolidate your talents. Either way, understanding your abilities and liabilities is essential.

As Jason worked to monetise Mamamia and we became

profitable, we got really rich
and went on fancy holidays.
Hahahahah. No. Not how
start-ups work. We poured
all our profits straight back
into the business so we could
hire more people and keep
growing. Over the next few
years, I slowly clawed back
the ability to do more of
what I was good at and less
of what made me want to
stick a fork in my eye.

You can literally see the moment
Jason came on board.

2015 was one of my most miserable years at
work and at the end of it, I finally realised this was because I
was doing less 'making/creating' and more managing. I was in
back-to-back meetings, looking at reports and spreadsheets and
I was miserable.

My enmeshment in management was at first fuelled by ego.
I wanted to be the co-boss! Until I admitted to myself that
I didn't really want to be the boss because what Jason's role
involved did not appeal to me even remotely. Realising this was
a relief and it improved our relationship markedly both at work
and at home. The pressures I had as the face of the company
were unique, as were the pressures Jason faced as CEO. It
wasn't a competition, it was a partnership. Divide and conquer.

While Jason remained CEO from that first day in the lounge
room in 2008 until 2016 when he became Executive Chairman,
I've had half a dozen different titles from publisher to editorial director and now creative director as I've bounced around
moulding myself in and around our growing editorial team.

I'd been trying to step away from editorial management and hadn't edited Mamamia for quite a few years but in your own business you have to be prepared to jump back in when necessary. You must constantly recalibrate your role and adjust it according to the needs of your company and your staff. In 2015, some staff shuffles meant I'd been dragged back to the frontline and I was frustrated.

This wasn't just a time of growing pains for me, the business needed to change too. The seat-of-your-pants culture of a start-up was no longer appropriate when we had more than 100 employees, multiple websites, a rapidly growing podcast network, a women's marketing consultancy and now a US business with the impending launch of our sister site for American women, Spring.st.

We needed infrastructure and an HR department and travel policies and org charts and a leadership team and KPIs and development plans and we needed to articulate the core values of our business and implement 90-day plans and forecasts and report timetables and a thousand other things that made me want to vomit. What I wanted to do and how I wanted to work was irrelevant, however. This wasn't about me. For Mamamia to continue its rapid rate of growth, we had to evolve from start-up to scale-up, and Jason knew this long before I did.

At first, I resisted the idea of scaling up in the same way I've resisted almost everything else our business has required. But quickly I saw that I just needed to get out of the way and facilitate the process. Once I began to do that, things clicked into place and became remarkably easier. By 2016 we'd realigned my role to Creative Director, reporting to no one and with no direct reports. This is my happy place. I keep my meetings to a minimum and try to contribute to the business in the way that suits me – and it – best. Creatively. I host podcasts, write posts, present to clients and instigate bigger editorial ideas. I ensure the Mamamia brand stays on point and I recalibrate it often. As a website for women, we are indexed to women's needs and wants which are always changing. I need to ensure we are just slightly ahead of those changes, so we're providing what women want before they even know they want it, like podcasts.

One of the most challenging parts of a growing company is when it grows out of people you love working with. You hire someone for a reason or a season until they're unable or unwilling to meet the growing demands of the business. Not everyone wants to work for a company our size. For some, we're too small but for others, we're too big. If I weren't a co-founder, Mamamia would have grown out of me too. It has, many times. I've adapted my role to suit the business and it hasn't always been smooth, but quitting or being fired isn't an option[9].

What you need to know is this: running your own business, no matter how big or successful, is absurdly hard work. It's stressful, terrifying and it devours your life. It can also be hugely rewarding, energising and the best fun you've ever had. There are days I dream of walking away and days when I can't ever imagine doing anything else. There are days when my children complain that all I ever do is work[10] and days when they get to come and shake hands with the Prime Minister in our office.

There have been some memorable moments. Like the day Jason had to write a company memo pointing out that nobody

---

9 Actually, in the early days, I used to quit often. Every time Jason and I had an argument it would end with 'I quit!' 'No, I quit!' and then we went back to work.

10 They never say that to their father even though he works longer hours at the office than me. Go figure.

was allowed to do drugs or drink alcohol in the single toilet we all shared due to a former staff member getting very sniffy in the bathroom. The day when a client arrived for a meeting to see me on my hands and knees on the office balcony cleaning up my dog's diarrhoea; the day when an editorial assistant had to send Jason an email asking if he could approve us buying a sanitary bin for our (one) toilet because certain staff members (me) didn't know you couldn't flush tampons and it kept getting blocked; the day when Jason raised in a management meeting that he'd noticed all the women carrying our little toiletry bags to and from the bathrooms and wondered out loud why we didn't just supply free sanitary items to all Mamamia employees. The next day our bathrooms were stocked with free tampons and pads. There are days when we have reality TV stars or celebrities popping by to record interviews, with everyone from Nigella Lawson to Leigh Sales, Andrew Denton, Annabel Crabb, Rosie Batty, Turia Pitt, Magda Szubanski and Julia Gillard walking the floor. Kasey Chambers sang for us standing next to the office fire extinguisher. It's never dull.

I've also met some of my favourite people and closest friends through Mamamia. And I've been able to use the platform we've built to advocate for causes I feel passionate about like vaccination, marriage equality, domestic violence, child safety and body image.

Our establishment of an annual Pregnancy Loss Awareness Week across Mamamia in mid-2016 crystallised everything I ever dreamed of when I started a website. The isolation piled on top of the grief I felt after losing my baby late in my pregnancy back in 1999 seared itself into my heart. I resolved to build a place – and then a company – to make the world (and Internet) a better place for women and girls. A place where they could go to feel normal and reassured. A place of empathy, emotion and empowerment. By creating an entire themed week of content at Mamamia, including podcasts, written posts, videos and a private Facebook group for women who had suffered miscarriage or stillbirth to come and find solace with each other, I felt this embodied everything I'd set out to achieve by starting Mamamia.

Today, it still surprises me when people say Jason and I have built a media company. But we have. And against a huge amount of competition and enormous odds. We are underdogs with giant competitors who took almost a decade longer than us to realise that women and girls matter and whose motivations are embedded in a bottom line rather than any desire to make the world a better place for women. Mamamia remains the only women's media company in Australia and the only media company to be digital-first and women-first. And Jason and I are still married. I'm proud of what we've achieved and the fact we've done it together with a genuine goal of supporting and promoting women. We've made mistakes and missteps, we've had setbacks and slip-ups, no question. We've moved fast and broken things. But overall, I know our hearts have been in the right place and I'm proud of that too.

MIXING WORK AND MARRIAGE – A USER GUIDE

Whenever I tell anyone I work with my husband, this is the response I get:

'I could never do that.'

'Oh my God, we'd kill each other.'

'I don't know how you do it.'

'That's my worst nightmare.'

Only the women say this.

The men just nod and look thoughtful and I know this is what they're thinking:

Wow, if I worked with my wife there'd be so many more opportunities to have sex – like, during all of the hours of the day! I wish I worked with my wife.

Soon after Jason and I began working together at home, I was a guest speaker at a corporate lunch. Afterwards, a couple of old school friends came over and we quickly caught up.

'I've just started working with my husband in his accounting business,' one told me, rolling her eyes. 'But because we have a home office, he thinks it means we can just have sex while the kids are at school.'

Her friend nodded until her head fell off. 'I work with my husband too and it's the same.' She grimaced. 'Every time he says we need to have a "meeting", I wince. Honestly, it's impossible to get anything done.'

The exponential increase in couple time can certainly be a shock. The constant closeness was a massive problem for me at first and not just the complete dissolving of sexual boundaries. (It helped enormously that we had a nanny and baby in the house, sometimes also a toddler.) It was the quantity time: being together all day as well as all night.

Jason didn't seem to mind. I was climbing the walls[11].

So how have we worked together for more than a decade without getting divorced? Well, of course, we did separate before we started Mamamia so we got that out of the way early. But there are four very clear rules we've always had:

1. **We've never, ever shared an office.** I've always located myself as far away as possible from Jason during work hours.

2. **We drive to and from work in separate cars (sorry, environment).** We don't keep the same schedule and even if we did, I crave time alone in my car where I can listen to podcasts in peace.

---

11 This is a common feature of retirement, apparently. The men want to spend every second with their wives but the women? They go nuts. 'I married you for dinner, not for lunch' is a common refrain among claustrophobic women whose husbands just want to . . . hang out with them.

3. **We work in very separate areas of the business and respect each other's expertise.** It's not always possible to give each other autonomy because every decision impacts elsewhere. But we tread lightly.

4. **Separate bathrooms at home.** Enough said.

In one of our early meetings with an agency we appointed to sell advertising on Mamamia before we could afford to employ our own sales people, Jason and I were having coffee with the two women who ran the business. At the end of the meeting, one of them said, 'So, what's the connection between you two? How did you come to work together?'

'Um, we're married!' I blurted, much to their surprise.

'Oh! We had no idea!'

Our different last names had thrown them.

Afterwards in the car on the way home, Jason and I decided we either had absolutely no chemistry or were just really, really professional.

THE GRATITUDE PLATITUDE

GRATITUDE HAS BECOME grating. I'd very much like to punch it in the face and I suspect I'm not alone. The ubiquity of grateful women (always women, only women) is impossible to avoid on social media. There are so many women feeling so #grateful about so many things and we know this because they broadcast it, often along with a shot of their pert bum in a bikini or their kid holding a trophy.

These women are #blessed and also #grateful except they're neither blessed nor grateful. Not really. They're thirsty. Thirsty for praise, acknowledgement of their beauty, their body, their success. Thirsty for compliments. This is very different to being grateful.

The Gratitude Platitude has bastardised gratitude in a uniquely female way that leaches it of all real meaning.

Consider the kinds of things women are grateful for on social media.

Finishing PhDs:

> Looking forward to finally getting out of these tracksuit
> pants after just submitting my PhD. #Grateful

Signing book deals:

> Feeling #soblessed to be writing a book for the
> wonderful people at PanMac. Thanks to the team for
> having faith in me!

Winning awards:

> This baby is going straight to the pool room! Lol!
> #Gratitude

Acquiring vast numbers of social media followers:

> Can't believe I got to 10K! #sograteful you guys!

Being named on lists of successful people in their industry:

> Wow! #Grateful to everyone who voted for me. You guys
> rock.

Their children doing things. All the things:

> So excited to be here with my daughter at her first ballet
> concert. #Blessed

Business successes:

> Just about to give a speech to an audience of 2000
> people! Love my life! #Blessed

Promotions:

> I have a new job! New York here I come. #Gratitude

Looking ~~good~~ skinny in a bikini:

> Glorious day in paradise #holidays #blessed

When women say they're grateful and blessed on social media, what they usually mean – what they WANT to say – is that they're proud. Proud of their hard work. Proud of how they look or what they've done. Proud of their kids' achievements. Proud of themselves.

But if you're female, to be proud is to invite backlash.

For women, pride is perceived as boastful. Vain. Or being up yourself. And nobody likes a woman who's up herself. There's nothing less attractive, less conventionally feminine, less socially acceptable than a proud woman who knows and speaks her worth, right? That's certainly what we're told.

As women, we're encouraged to tow the gender line of self-loathing. That's our narrative. Stick to your lane, ladies, or risk ridicule, humiliation and purgatory.

Women learn to fear the Tall Poppy Syndrome early and it's reinforced throughout our lives: don't toot your own horn. Don't big yourself up. In fact, put yourself down. Stew in self-doubt and self-loathing because you're so much more adorable that way. Prune your own poppy before someone lops it off.

On the off-chance you *do* do something impressive, make sure you're modest and demure, self-deprecating and humble. Don't fly too close to the sun, little girl, or you'll get burned by your own ambition[12].

The reason we are so averse to descriptors like 'proud' and 'ambitious' is ingrained in our desire to be liked.

---

12 Oh, PS: don't ever say you're ambitious. That's a word that's only ever used as a compliment for men and an insult against women. 'She's very...ambitious' is always said with a metaphorically raised eyebrow. If the woman has children and a career, it's usually code for 'bad mother'. Sometimes it just means 'bitch'. I can't think of a single woman I've heard use the word 'ambitious' about herself, even when it perfectly describes her desire to progress her career. Its negative subtext is ingrained in our psyches. I know I use the word 'competitive' about myself instead of 'ambitious'; it's more socially acceptable, perhaps because it's rooted in sport. This is the closest I get to sport and I remain comfortable with that happy distance.

It's crushingly simple: as a woman, your likeability is inversely proportional to your success. The higher you rise, the brighter you shine, the more people will dislike you. For men, it's the opposite, of course. Powerful men are immensely popular. Success amplifies male likeability.

Men are openly encouraged to showcase their wins and achievements and they can do this without seeming like arse-holes. They're encouraged to brag freely without consequence.

Oh wait, there *is* a consequence for men who brag about their success: ~~they become President~~ they're more likeable!

What a great guy! And smart too! Handsome!

Humility is not expected of men, ever.

Women, however, eschew humility at great personal and sometimes professional cost. We must actively talk ourselves down if we wish to remain unthreatening and likeable not just to men but to other women.

We need not only be careful to avoid mentioning the goals we kick and the mountains we climb, we must constantly work against the perception that we've ever actively sought success, money, power, influence or fame. It just came to us, right? We are so blessed. Such gratitude.

So instead of saying we feel proud, we use weasel words like gratitude and blessed, infusing our achievements with pseudo-spiritual meaning, making them seem fated or like aw-shucks-golly-gee gifts from God or the universe. Feeling lucky, fortunate, blessed and grateful are exceedingly passive states. They imply effortless privilege, selective good fortune and they reinforce the idea that women must never strive to achieve things and, if you do, you must obscure all evidence of your hard work. Call it luck! Make it sound random! A bit woo-woo!

What a disingenuous crock. Women do other women a huge disservice when we make it seem like our lives are perfect, our triumphs merely big-hearted gifts from the universe like stumbling unexpectedly upon a $50 note in the cleft of Ryan Gosling's bare buttocks. Blessed!

This is the Gratitude Platitude and it is informed by this principle: you have to make everything good that happens to you seem like a miraculous bequest. You must never out yourself as the architect of your own success. Society only wants to see the beautiful swan gliding across the lake, not the furious paddling underneath the surface that propels it forward.

'It's kind of weird – I never took modelling very seriously,' demurred Miranda Kerr when asked about her exceptional rise to the top of her industry in an interview with *Stellar* magazine[13]. As if her years of hard work – and modelling is hard work despite its glossy exterior – just happened by accident.

Some of the most polarising women in public life are those who refuse to hide their effort, their ambition and their desire to succeed. Hillary Clinton, Sheryl Sandberg, Taylor Swift, Kris Jenner, Julia Gillard, Kara Swisher, Jacinda Ardern, Julie Bishop, Gwnyeth Paltrow . . . they're all hustlers. And they're all excoriated for it.

'She just tries too hard' or 'she just wants it too much' is an insult only ever hurled at women.

---

13 Patently and demonstrably untrue. As detailed in the same article, Kerr has moved across the country and across the world numerous times to further her career as a model. For many years she was a Victoria's Secret model, one of the rarest and most lucrative jobs for any model in the world, and she has maintained her weight, stamina, face, skin and reputation in a way that has earned her millions of dollars. She has worked incredibly hard and achieved incredible things and yet like so many famous successful women, she plays down the role of hard work and shrugs off any suggestions of ambition or effort.

The terms 'blessed' and 'grateful' aren't just passive, they throw a smug, moral layer over something that isn't remotely moral.

Being blessed suggests you were chosen by some external force who decided you deserve good fortune. Oh, really? How come you were chosen for these wonderful blessings and not that kid with cancer or that woman whose husband beats her?

Perhaps this is why men never talk about feeling blessed or grateful for things they have done; because it reduces their perceived power and influence. Men own their achievements in the real world, as they should. They don't flutter their eyelashes and say, 'Oh golly, I don't know how this amazing thing happened to me, what a blessing it is.'

Gratitude is different from luck and relief and joy and pride. It can include components of all these things but it's deeper, more profound. Often, it's about things outside of your control.

This is what actual gratitude looks like:

It's sitting in hospital cradling your newborn son a year after your daughter was stillborn and crying hot tears onto his perfect little face because you can't quite believe he is pink and breathing and kicking his little legs against you instead of lying lifeless in your arms.

It's hearing from a doctor that you're in remission after a double mastectomy and six months of chemotherapy.

It's holding your loved ones tight when the news is full of yet another terrorist attack and the faces of other people's sons, daughters, mothers, fathers, husbands, wives and friends who will never come home.

The Gratitude Platitude does women no favours. It keeps us passive, reduces our power and obscures our wins. We must own our emotions and our achievements like men do. We must start using words like ecstatic and satisfied and proud and joyful because they're the truth. We must show our work and be honest about how much of it is involved when we achieve things. We must lift up other women and celebrate their successes and not demand they put themselves down or be coy and disingenuous to win social acceptance.

Be proud, be loud. You earned it.

A CONVERSATION WITH MY
MOTHER ABOUT FEMINISM

My mother Kathy never sat me down to teach me about feminism. She didn't have to. She lived it and I learned by osmosis. As a first-wave feminist, she was heavily influenced by icons Germaine Greer, Gloria Steinem, Eva Cox, Erica Jong and Betty Friedan. As a second-wave feminist I was heavily influenced by her. To give you a sense of what that looked like, I persuaded my shy mother to sit down and let me interview her.

Me: I have written about feminism a lot and I consider myself a feminist because of you.

Mum: I am absolutely delighted by that. It is one of the happiest things about my relationship with you, is that you as a contemporary woman are proud to call yourself a feminist, because feminism has had such bad press over the past couple of decades. And I have an incredibly strong, positive feeling about feminism. And I guess that is partly why I imparted it to you over the years.

Me: Well, it could have gone the other way – with you and your hairy armpits – I could have rejected feminism in order to rebel.

Mum: You could have.

Me: Your hairy underarms could have scarred me – which they did a little bit.

Mum: Look, I can't even bring myself to say sorry about it because I'm actually not.

Me: We will get to the armpits in a minute because they were clearly a formative thing for me as far as feminism goes. But I want to know what was your awakening as a feminist because you were just a regular suburban Aussie girl.

Mum: Sure, a regular suburban Aussie girl of the early '60s. In a way we weren't aware that we were suffering because our lives were pretty good, but still even then I was aware of being very constrained by what it meant to be a good young woman. It was about the way you behaved and there were very constricting and constraining values to being feminine.

Me: Like what?

Mum: Well, I remember making a very clear decision when I was about 14 to quit gymnastics. It certainly seems ridiculous now but even though I was very keen on it, I knew I either continued on that path and became more athletic or I tried to get a boyfriend, and the two would not go together.

Me: Really?

Mum: So I deliberately pulled myself back from something I loved and chose a boyfriend instead.

Me: So the idea of having a boyfriend while also being successful in what you wanted to do, that didn't exist?

Mum: Not at all! Well, that's how I saw it and I think a lot of my friends saw it that way as well. I was brought up middle class so the philosophy was, work only if you had to; the normal thing for a woman was not to have a career path in any way. Getting married was your career path, even if you had a temporary little flirtation with work or a career.

Me: Like being a teacher or something?

Mum: Yeah, in fact that was one of the three occupations open: teacher, nurse or secretary.

Me: Seriously? Just those three things?

Mum: Yes. And maybe an air hostess if you were really glamorous. And even then, none of those jobs were careers because you had to quit them as soon as you got married. Being married meant that you didn't 'need' a job because your husband would support you and anyway, you'd be pregnant in a minute. No employer wanted to deal with that and they didn't have to. In the public service in the '60s, women were just sacked when they got married to make room for a man or an unmarried woman who needed the job more.

Me: What did you actually want to do?

Mum: I didn't know exactly, but I knew one thing – and this was a very strong feeling I remember having – I wanted my father's life and not my mother's life. My mother was at home looking after us and supporting my father – as you know your grandfather was a GP, and before mobile phones and answering machines, someone had to sit by the phone after hours to take calls from patients. That was what the doctor's wife did. From a really young age I looked at the difference in their lives and I wanted to do something with my life that was out in the community, that was making a difference. I wanted to work outside the home. As a child I didn't see how important my mother was to my father's ability to do his job. He probably couldn't have done it without my mother looking after the phone and everything at home and that was a very common thing. Wives did a large amount of unacknowledged work – they still do. But I was very clear in my mind that I wanted a career and I wanted children as well.

Me: You knew you wanted children?

Mum: I knew I wanted children.

Me: What about your friends? Did they share that? Or is it something you talked about together?

Mum: Not really. Look, in those days, if you went to university as a woman it was quite unusual. I wasn't clear what I wanted to do. But my parents encouraged me to get a university education so that's where I went. Then I found myself pregnant at 18 and there was severe social stigma attached to that.

Me: There still is! I can't imagine how bad it would have been for you in the '60s.

Mum: Horrendous. And I guess that began my awakening to feminism. Because I suddenly encountered these incredibly prescriptive attitudes about unmarried pregnancy. There were no supporting mothers' benefits in those days, so your choices if you fell pregnant were very, very narrow.

Me: Was there contraception?

Mum: Not really. There was very little emphasis on contraceptive education, so my friends and I would talk about it and we would exchange notes. It's not as if we were even particularly sexually active at that time, but we had our boyfriends so we would talk about it, just as girls do today. I got some bad advice about a contraceptive sponge and found myself pregnant.

Me: When the Pill came out it was more for married women, wasn't it? You couldn't just get a script.

Mum: Oh no, you couldn't just walk into a doctor. Right up until the '70s, the Pill was only prescribed to married women.

Me: So, you got married?

Mum: I got married. There weren't many options. Abortion was illegal. And there was no government support for single mothers. So I got married when I was 18. I was still at university.

Me: What were you studying?

Mum: I was studying an arts degree – majoring in psychology – and I was reasonably clear I wanted to be a psychologist at that stage. So that was kind of derailed with my pregnancy. The father was also at uni and both our parents agreed to support us to finish our degrees. So in fact we were very lucky.

Me: Was abortion even an option?

Mum: Well, it was illegal and if you wanted to do that it was incredibly risky. You could die or be arrested. I knew a few people who'd had backyard abortions and their stories were horrific. It was surrounded by shame and it was regarded as a criminal act. I didn't want to go down that path. But if it hadn't been for my parents supporting me financially, I would have had to give up my education or have the baby adopted. Not that it wasn't a crisis in my family or the family of the baby's father. It was! But our parents agreed to support us so we could keep the baby. So I feel incredibly grateful that I did not have to take that option. And I feel desperately sad for those women who were forced to give up their babies against their will just because they were single. It could have been me. It could have so easily been me.

Me: Did this galvanise you towards feminism?

Mum: Yes. Feminist writers of that time like Germaine Greer, Betty Friedan and Gloria Steinem . . . they were my lifeline. They were what I held on to as I encountered roadblock after roadblock in my life. I ended up getting married before the baby came and obviously the marriage was doomed under those circumstances. Two years later I left the marriage and my next big feminist wake-up call was when I got legal advice about divorce. It was because I had been the person who had left – there was no other party involved and it was amicable at first. But I was not able to start divorce proceedings because I was the 'guilty' party and I had left.

Me: Because there was no such thing as a no-fault divorce.

Mum: That's right, there had to be fault. Someone had to take the blame, legally. And for women with children, the major risk was that if you were shown to have committed adultery, you would usually automatically lose custody of your child. That proved you were an unfit mother and they took your kids away and gave them to your ex-husband.

Me: So after you split with your husband, you had to live the life of a nun pretty much for how long?

Mum: I remember sitting down in front of a lawyer, a young man who seemed to be quite embarrassed talking about it.

Me: Because you were 21 and a single mother.

Mum: Yes. He explained I was legally dependant on my ex-husband's goodwill and permission because the earliest we could divorce was in three years' time and my ex would have to institute divorce proceedings, I couldn't do it. If he became hostile and didn't file for divorce, I would have to wait five years until I could do anything. And so this lawyer sat me down and said, 'You won't want to hear this but my advice to you is that you do not have a relationship with anyone for the next five years.' And I was 21. Anyone I had sex with during that time would be considered adultery which meant losing custody of my son. Then he said, 'Now I also need to tell you that pictures are not necessary as evidence of adultery; all the evidence the court requires is that you spent an hour in a house alone with a man.'

Me: That was considered proof of adultery?

Mum: Yes, and he said, 'You have to be very careful, so for the next five years, you must live your life . . .'

Me: Like a nun? Because if you had a boyfriend in that time or even had a guy over for coffee, you could lose custody of your child?

Mum: Yes. And yet a man could do anything! Have as many girlfriends as he wanted. Spend as much time alone with as many women as he liked because none of that affected his ability to be a good father, according to the law. It was like Anne Summers' book, *Damned Whores and God's Police*; women were held to such ridiculous expectations of how they would behave.

Me: And so where did Germaine come into it?

Mum: Germaine, as I say, was a lifeline. It's funny because all this was happening to me in the mid to late '60s. *The Female Eunuch* only came out in 1970. But I think she must have spoken out a lot beforehand and written things because I remember feeling incredibly galvanised. I had this feeling of being an outsider in my own culture. As a woman often it felt like you were an outsider and suddenly the Women's Liberation Movement came with Germaine as a spokesperson. And it was really a call, not to arms, but to revolution. It was nothing short of revolution. And it was a sense of, claim your own lives! Claim your power! And by that stage I had felt powerless for years, completely constrained in any choices I might want to make as a woman. In my work, I was lucky enough to have a mentor who spoke up for me when I applied for a government research job. I was a single parent at the time and nobody wanted to hire me because it was assumed I'd get married again quickly and then I'd leave my work. But he argued for my appointment and I got the job.

Me: The idea of single women being unreliable was really used to deny women jobs?

Mum: Oh yes, all the time. Say you went to an interview panel and say there might be four people interviewing you and if they were men (they usually were), three of the men would say, 'We can't possibly have her because she is a young woman and will get married again, so it will just be a short-term employment because once she gets married she won't want to work.'

Me: And didn't women in the public service have to give up their job once they got married?

Mum: Women in certain jobs did, I think maybe in banks, you had to give up your job for a man. But there was very much an attitude of – well, of course she is not going to stay because she might get married again. While I was supporting my child, they regarded me as a safe bet, but they said as soon as I have other means of support, I'd be out of there. So the idea of me wanting work and career was completely foreign. It was a battle in every sense.

Me: No wonder feminism felt like a lifeline.

Mum: Yes. In my late teens, early twenties, it was like – wow, I can now make sense of my experience. That's why a lot of women of my generation feel indebted to Germaine and love her even though I haven't agreed with everything she says. She literally saved our lives.

Me: That sounds dramatic. Why?

Mum: Her clarion call was, 'Get together with other women! Talk about it.' It was obviously before the Internet and we didn't really have a vehicle for communicating. The media was owned and run by men for men so there was nowhere except in books about feminism where you could read about women's lives and challenges. It was very much our own personal little lives we were struggling with, alone.

Me: So she made the personal political.

Mum: Absolutely, and I don't know any women who weren't at some level struggling, not necessarily the struggles I was dealing with but struggling with the discrimination and feeling like an outsider in your own culture because it was a male culture. And so she made sense of it and she made it political and she urged us to make it political, simply by getting together in groups. Unfortunately, I was always too busy to get together in groups because I was a working mother which made me unusual. But I remember just the ideas of feminism being so inspirational and suddenly it was like breathing a great sigh of relief. It was a little bit like a cult and a little bit like a religion. And I must say I experienced it as that, certainly I experienced the good side of that, in that it was inspiring and you felt like you were following a very important cause.

Me: How did you reconcile feminism with the way you looked during those years? Because you have always been a hottie – you still are. You have always been very feminine, very beautiful. But the stereotypical feminist in the '60s and '70s, and even '80s, did not look the way you looked with your long blonde hair.

Mum: Look, I didn't wear lipstick. To make a statement. And later on, as you know, I stopped shaving under my arms.

Me: How did the lipstick and the armpits come into it?

Mum: I delighted in my hairy armpits.

Me: As your daughter, I did not delight in them. No delight from me.

Mum: [laughs] I don't think anybody in my family did. I think I was a source of great embarrassment to my family. But I could not have cared.

Me: But you didn't reject every aspect of conventional femininity, did you?

Mum: No. I revelled in my hairy armpits but I kept shaving my legs. For me it was very much an aesthetic choice; I thought my hairy armpits were beautiful. I liked smooth legs so I shaved my legs. So I chose things that fitted with how I felt. And that in itself was so liberating even though it sounds a bit ridiculous today. It was, 'No, I won't wear lipstick or paint my nails!'

Now I do both because it doesn't seem as important as it did then and I want to. Now women have a choice, but then it felt so subversive and powerful to reject all those signposts of femininity. Whereas always before it felt almost compulsory to conform to the female ideal of the lipstick and the neat hair and the smooth shaved body.

Me: Right, so it was hairy armpits as a statement of choice.

Mum: Yes, it was a statement, it was a badge.

Me: It certainly was a badge when you came to pick me up and called out 'Darling!' and waved your arm in the air while wearing a singlet top.

Mum: [laughs] I can't think that I did that deliberately but perhaps there was some pleasure in it.

Me: Not every aspect of Germaine Greer's feminism sat well with you in the '70s, though, did it?

Mum: No. There was a point in her book where she wrote that the only way to be truly free is to walk out of your marriages and walk away from your children. She's since said she exaggerated and perhaps she didn't mean it literally. But she wrote that the only way to truly be free and really be yourself might be to leave your kids. She said something like that you may have to rethink and re-evaluate your role as being indispensable to your child.

Me: That from a woman without kids.

Mum: Yes, yes. I remember throwing the book across the room and I was like – absolutely not! And it was a shock because up until that point I'd been so on board with everything she'd said. It was like yes, yes, yes, yes, and then suddenly no! On a very basic, fundamental level, leaving my children was never an option for me or a lot of women. And I think there was a backlash to those attitudes. And a lot of ideas about feminism became quite prescriptive. It's like – you don't wear makeup, you don't wear a bra.

Me: Did you wear a bra?

Mum: No I didn't for a long time, I didn't wear a bra.

Me: Was that comfortable?

Mum: Yes! I mean I didn't have a great deal of . . .

Me: Well, you've got enough.

Mum: Well, I've got a bit more now but I didn't have as much then.

Me: Right, so it wasn't a problem?

Mum: No, no, no. It was totally liberating.

Me: So then why did you start shaving your armpits again in the '80s?

Mum: Funnily enough, I remember the night. It was so significant and I was wearing a little black dress and I was going out to a work dinner with Dad.

Me: How old were you?

Mum: I was in my forties, I think. It was purely an aesthetic decision. I looked at myself in the mirror and I had a little black dress and little puffy hairy armpits and I think I had something around my neck and I just thought – *Nope, doesn't look good.* So I shaved them off.

Me: How did you feel when you did that?

Mum: Good, I didn't regret it.

Me: Because it didn't have that weight anymore?

Mum: It didn't have significance. And I mean I must have worn little black dresses before but suddenly it was just a stage in my life where maybe I was feeling comfortable and wasn't fighting any battles and so I could afford to just look at it and go – hmm, doesn't look good with that dress. And it was 100 per cent my decision. I think after 10 years of my entire family telling me to shave my armpits it was like I had proved my point. It was just for me.

Me: I want to ask you about how you raised me as a feminist. Was it a conscious thing?

Mum: Um, I can't remember thinking that I've got to make this little girl a feminist.

Me: Because I feel a lot of, not pressure, but responsibility to teach Coco about feminism.

Mum: Yes, look, I remember the two of us getting incredibly excited the first time Julia Gillard was acting Prime Minister. And there was a photograph of her behind her desk and we cut it out of the paper and I remember you put it on the fridge for Coco to see. And that was such a revelation to me because I could see how my granddaughter was safe, in the sense that when I was growing up, I would read the paper and have this very conscious thought that I am not part of this culture because week after week, month after month, on the front of the paper there would only be men, men in government, men in sporting teams, military men, men in business. Page after page of men telling stories about men. The whole discussion was about men and men's lives, never about women's lives. So there were no role models for young women. And I think maybe by the time you were growing up, I didn't necessarily think so much about it because by that stage I felt like I was living my life as a feminist.

Me: That's why it never occurred to me that I couldn't work and have a family, because you were my role model and you did and the idea of doing anything else was not even on my radar. You lived by example, you taught me by example.

Mum: Yes! Where I look back and feel so sad is that my mother didn't have the benefit of that because she was the generation before. So hence I had to go through the thing of saying – I want my father's life not my mother's life. He was my example, not her. I was very lucky that I was able to convert my job into a part-time job and I was able to spend time with you growing up as a child.

Me: Yes, and I watched you navigate that balance.

Mum: Yes, it was tricky but it was enormously fulfilling. I wouldn't have wanted one without the other.

Me: No, I don't want one without the other.

Mum: I could never have given up the option of having children or of having my career. So it's lovely, I feel fantastic that women do not have to make those sorts of choices anymore.

Me: Thank you for being my feminist role model and just my role model for how to be a woman. It's only sometimes when I speak to friends that I see that other people didn't have that kind of feminist upbringing and that feminist education and that role model and that gift that you did give me.

Mum: That is lovely. So it was worth being embarrassed by my armpits.

Me: No one tells you how fun it is to embarrass your children. Now I totally get it.

STRIFE

THE TIME I LOST MY VIRGINITY

SO THE FIRST time I had sex, the condom broke. While this was not an auspicious start to my sex life, I don't know many people who lost their virginity in particularly edifying circumstances. At least I was sober, consenting, and in my boyfriend's bed instead of a park. Not that the bed improved the outcome but it was without doubt more comfortable.

I was 15 years old.

Like every other Gen X teenager, I knew nothing of emergency contraception and I blame the woeful inadequacy of school sex education programs for this. I hope to God they've improved. If only they were mandatory instead of the choose-your-own-adventure-or-opt-out-altogether approach taken by schools to an activity that can change your life in a far more permanent way than, say, French.

My high school was non-denominational so religion wasn't a barrier to us learning about sex and yet still we didn't, not really. All I can remember was putting a condom on a banana and learning about the horror of sexually transmitted diseases.

Of course now that kids are exposed to porn as early as eight, the whole idea of a-penis-goes-in-a-vagina-to-make-a-baby type of sex education seems hysterically quaint.

By the time they hit high school or even finish primary, most kids will have been exposed to pornography well before any formalised sex education so perhaps combining Sex Ed with Maths is the way of the future:

If Jenny has a foursome with Graham, Barry, Steve and Phil, how many condoms will they need to safely practise triple penetration? And how many penises will be left without a corresponding hole?

Mary and Margie want to have a threesome with Matt. How many orifices do they have between them and how many possible penetrative combinations could they perform?

Back then and also now, teaching teens about the existence of emergency contraception would have been extremely helpful; almost as relevant as (1) 'Each condom can only be used once' and (2) 'No, you cannot use Glad Wrap instead'.

We learned both these things in sex ed and thank heavens we did because otherwise I may have confused a penis with leftovers. No Glad Wrap. Writing that down.

When sexually inexperienced teenagers (often drunk) have sex (often outdoors), accidents happen! Condoms break! Or aren't put on properly! Or at all! That's why girls need to know about emergency contraception well before they become sexually active.

My Catholic school friends had it even tougher; their sex education began and ended with: Keep-your-legs-together-until-you're-married-or-you'll-go-to-hell-now-girls-let's-all-praise-the-lord-Jesus-Christ!

So there I was, alone in my bed crying quietly the morning

after losing my virginity; hymen broken, sexual confidence shattered, future uncertain, life ruined.

In a clusterfuck of unspeakable irony, it was Mother's Day. And so I woke up to the grim reality that next year I might be receiving a gift[14] as well as giving one.

I was distraught. My most urgent need was to confide in my mum so she could tell me what to do. We have always been close, although I was certain she would be pissed with me. Suddenly I didn't feel quite as mature as when I'd decided to have sex just a few hours earlier. I was in trouble and I needed my mum to help me. Better still, I needed her to fix it.

Oh also, my mother's own mother had died just a few days before.

My father and brother were away so I'd been tasked with comforting Mum in her grief on this difficult day. The plan was for me to make her breakfast in bed and lavish her with flowers, gifts and a poignant card.

Instead, I would be gifting my mother with the fact her 15-year-old daughter probably needed an abortion.

Hallmark? Please put that on a Mother's Day card and save me an awkward conversation next time, okay?

My timing was exquisitely awful.

Around 8 am, Mum walked quietly, tearfully, into my room with her cup of tea to say good morning. I sat up in bed and burst into tears. 'I had sex last night and the condom broke,' I blurted between heaving sobs.

'I mean, Happy Mother's Day.'

I wish I could say I was wracked with guilt and shame for

---

14 By gift I mean an actual Mother's Day gift from my own human child, not the euphemistic 'gift' of a baby so often referred to by anti-abortion zealots. No woman considers an unwanted pregnancy a gift, especially when they're 15 years old.

pulling focus on a day that should have been about my mum, but I was 15 and teenage girls aren't big on guilt or shame, so.

Inventively, I'd used my grandmother's death as an excuse to skip the overnight portion of my school music camp that weekend. 'I really need to be with my mother in her dark time of grief,' I'd murmured to my teacher.

The school had allowed me to return home overnight to comfort my mum. Instead, I'd snuck over to my boyfriend's house and broken a condom with my vagina.

I wouldn't have sex with him again for nearly two years.

He was a lovely guy, my first love. We'd been together for almost six months and we'd been steadily progressing towards this moment. We were committed. His parents were out. We had the house to ourselves. I was ready.

Oh my God.

I wasn't ready. Not for the consequences of failed contraception. Not for the terror now gripping me.

I called a cab and fled home, my stomach knotted with fear. I crept quietly into my bedroom and cried myself to sleep.

The next morning, after I told her, Mum sat down on my bed and we both looked at each other for a while, waiting for me to stop crying, thinking about what it all meant.

Reminder: my mum fell pregnant the first time she had sex.

Given how little she'd known about conception and contraception before she'd lost her virginity in the '60s, Mum had been determined to right this wrong by informing me early and in detail about baby-making.

When I was around eight years old, I recall us sitting on a picnic blanket in the backyard one sunny day as she talked me step by step through the whole process from penis-in-vagina to labour (which in those days routinely included an enema so you wouldn't poop as you pushed) and finally childbirth.

I listened attentively.

'Any questions?' she asked.

No, just a comment. 'I think it all sounds okay except for the penis-in-vagina part and the enema. Those bits sound disgusting.'

Fair enough, she said. 'Although you might feel differently when you're older.'

Less than a decade later, I did indeed feel differently and the penis-in-vagina part had landed me in a wildly unoriginal predicament. Enema notwithstanding.

As if it wasn't harrowing enough to have your sexually formative years in the '80s. Pregnancy wasn't even our biggest worry. Unlike our free love, sexually liberated, baby boomer parents, Generation X and all those who came after us have never experienced sex in a world without HIV/AIDS. We'll never know how it feels to be sexually active without some degree of fear and guilt about not using a condom and the ever-present risk of catching a disease that could kill you. Because back then and until fairly recently, HIV/AIDS could kill you.

This was certainly the public health message.

As treatments and life expectancy have improved dramatically, there's far less hysteria about HIV, but in the '80s, AIDS awareness campaigns were the stuff of nightmares, with disturbing Australian TV commercials featuring the Grim Reaper hurling bowling balls at women, men, children, babies and little old ladies, who were depicted as human pins.

The voice-over was a terrifying man with an inexplicably English accent who boomed:

'At first only gays and IV users were being killed by AIDS. But now we know every one of us could be devastated by it [*close-up of a six-year-old girl crying before she's knocked over by the bowling ball to lie dead among all the other bodies*]. The fact is, over 50,000 men, women and children now carry the AIDS virus [*close-up of stricken-looking young mother holding a crying baby as voice-over gets louder and shoutier*], THAT IN THREE YEARS OVER 2000 OF US WILL BE DEAD [*mother and baby are knocked over by another ball and the Grim Reaper keeps hurling them faster and faster*], THAT IF NOT STOPPED IT COULD KILL MORE AUSTRALIANS THAN WORLD WAR II. But AIDS can be stopped and you can help stop it. IF YOU HAVE SEX, JUST HAVE ONE SAFE PARTNER. AND ALWAYS USE CONDOMS. ALWAYS . . .'

And this, my friends, is how sex and death became inextricably linked in the '80s, the most traumatic time in history to get laid.

The sex–death connection was even stronger for us than the sex–pregnancy one had been for our parents.

Nothing like thinking about the Grim Reaper mowing you down with a bowling ball to help you have an orgasm.

As a result, like many girls, I was cautious to the point of paranoia about sperm and its potential to kill me.

I believed sperm could fight its way through multiple layers of fabric including underwear, possibly outerwear, even across a doona. I believed it could swim through jeans and fly through the air like teeny tiny triathletes who ran, swam and cycled their way defiantly towards the finish line of my eggs. It didn't even have to be in the vicinity of my vagina. I convinced myself that sperm could somehow be absorbed through my skin. Oh God. The bowling balls.

Even dry-humping wasn't safe.

I was enormous fun to fool around with.

And yet despite my extreme caution, I was possibly pregnant because no matter how careful you are (and we were), sometimes contraception fails. Write that down, Religious Pharmacists Who Refuse To Dispense Emergency Contraception And Anyone Else Who Wants To Take Away Women's Reproductive Choices.

Yes, condoms break. Water-based lubricant and being sober enough to put one on properly will reduce the risk of condom breakage for sure, as will making sure you're using an actual condom, not a plastic bag or Glad Wrap, but unfortunately accidents still happen.

Whether you're a teenager or married or rich or poor or smart or dumb as a box of hair . . . contraception sometimes fails.

And so, like generations of women and girls before me, I hurtled into a prospective hell. Along with my mother. And, presumably, my boyfriend, although who'd know. I was so freaked out I hadn't spoken to him since I ran screaming (in my head) from his house. But of course he was panicked. I don't know many teenage boys who are gung-ho about becoming dads before they can legally have a drink at their own baby's head-wetting.

'I just wish you'd waited until you were ready,' sighed Mum as she sat on my bed looking distraught while I wept. I couldn't tell if she was angry or disappointed. She sounded a bit angry but disappointed is far worse and parents know this. As a parent myself now, I often deploy disappointment as a weapon with my own children. Works every time.

'Having sex involves consequences and I just don't think you were ready for them,' she said wretchedly.

I've considered it many times in the years since and I think she was right. And wrong.

Is anyone ever ready for the consequences of a condom breaking or the Pill failing? Can you ever be entirely ready for an unexpected pregnancy? That's why it's called unexpected.

My boyfriend and I had known each other for years and I believed then – and now – that he was the right guy to lose my virginity to. We loved each other. He never pressured me. He was considerate and patient and responsible and loving. Also he was super hot.

Our relationship was my romantic and sexual awakening and, looking back, nobody could have told me I

Me and my first love, two years after we broke up. We remained close friends and took each other to our respective formals.

wasn't ready. I didn't sleep with him because I thought it would make him like me more or stop him dumping me. I was certain he would wait as long as I wanted but I didn't want to wait anymore. It was not a spur-of-the-moment decision. We were safe, we were ready and we were careful.

And none of that was enough.

*

The few weeks after I lost my virginity were tense. Mum decided not to tell my father that his teenage daughter might be pregnant, sparing us both from a mortifying conversation.

We had my grandmother's funeral to organise. Life and death went on.

Here's the smartest thing my mum did: she forced me to find out how to get an abortion. I was deeply shocked by this.

Obviously I was going to have one if I was pregnant, that was clear to us both. But how could she not help me? How could she leave such a mind-bendingly ADULT situation to me? Why wouldn't she just . . . *tell me what to do and fix this shit*?

'I'll come with you and I'll pay for it but you have to do the research and make the appointment,' she said.

Her thinking: if I was old enough to have sex, I was old enough to organise my own abortion. Good parenting.

It was hard to argue with her logic even though I felt like a little girl who just wanted my mum to make it better. That's clearly why she didn't.

Google was decades away so to research abortions, I did what we all had to do whenever we needed information: I used an enormous book to look it up. Depending on what you wanted to know, your choices were encyclopaedia or phone book. So I grabbed the *Yellow Pages* and looked up 'abortion services'.

I was shocked to find abortion clinics listed there with architects and attic restoration nearby. Discovering that something so taboo was sitting there in plain view is how I felt when I found out condoms were sold at the supermarket. Or that the word 'penis' was in the dictionary. *No way.*

Over the next fortnight I spent hours staring at the phone numbers and locations of different abortion providers, paralysed at the prospect of calling to make an enquiry, let alone an appointment. My teenage brain was struggling with the consequences of my actions. Biologically, the part of your brain where consequences live doesn't even develop until your early twenties. Remember this if you ever have a teenager. It won't make their behaviour any less infuriating but you'll understand it better.

As real as shit was getting, though, having a baby at 15 was never a consideration. I still was one.

Mum made me promise not to tell anyone I might be pregnant, not for reasons of morality – she was stridently pro-choice – but because she was worried I'd be expelled from school.

When my period eventually came – more than two weeks late – I was weak with relief. Not just because I wasn't pregnant but because I'd been spared from dealing with something that seemed way too adult.

The whole experience certainly threw a spanner into my nascent sex life. Having always been afraid of pregnancy and AIDS, I was now a human ball of sexual anxiety. It would take me a long time to regain confidence in condoms enough to relax and enjoy sex and I didn't try it again for about a year, which probably wasn't a bad result, all things considered. The age of consent is 16 for a reason. That's about right.

My boyfriend and I split up without giving sex another go. The damage was done. We hooked up a few times years later though, as friends with benefits, and those experiences were corrective. Learning the fallibility of condoms was useful, ultimately, and so was the realisation that sex and having babies are adult things with serious consequences. It was also a reminder that I wanted both in my life – on my terms.

A LETTER TO MY SONS ABOUT PORN
(TO BE READ AT AGE 13)

To My Darling Boy,

I realise a conversation about sex is not one that any boy wants to have with his mother at any age because even having the words 'mother' and 'sex' in the same sentence is deeply upsetting.

As a gift to you, let's agree not to talk about this face to face. That's better than a PlayStation, isn't it!

We do have to discuss sex though, or more specifically porn, because as your mother and as a woman, I would be failing in my duty of care if I didn't share some crucial information with you. You won't find it on porn sites or in conversations with your mates. Your future sexual partners probably won't tell you, not for years or decades.

Disclaimer: as a woman, I am giving you advice pertaining to heterosexual porn because I am a straight woman and straight sex and porn are my areas of expertise. Obviously, whether you are gay, straight or anywhere on the LGTBIQ+ spectrum, I care not a jot.

Oh happy day! My mother is now talking to me about gay porn. THIS JUST GETS BETTER.

Look, the information I'm about to give you has the power to transform your future sex life. And your relationships. It's that good.

So listen carefully.

This is really important.

First of all, I know you've watched porn. Probably a lot of it. I struggled with this at first. Nobody wants to imagine their child watching strangers having sex, let alone porn-sex, which is something else entirely.

The age most boys are first exposed to porn is somewhere between 9 and 11 which I can't even get my head around because that's the age when our parents used to have the clumsy sex talk with us, which made it sound vague and clinical and like a long way off. Like space travel or flying cars or a computer tiny enough to carry around in your pocket. One day. The future.

But I've come to accept your world is different and exposure to porn is just something that happens to kids, usually well before they become teenagers. This makes me sad and worried, but not for the reason you might think. There's nothing wrong with sex and there's nothing wrong with being interested in it.

For me, this is not a moral question. If you've been watching porn I'm upset *for* you, not *with* you, because I think it has the potential to affect early sexual experiences in a really negative way.

It's not just me. This is a proven fact. Guys who watch a lot of porn can often have trouble enjoying real sex with real people. And men who watch a lot of porn are usually pretty bad at sex. They are more likely to do things their partners find disgusting, demeaning and painful – just because they saw them in porn.

You don't want to be that guy.

I don't want you to be that guy either – not for yourself and not for your future sexual partners. They won't come back.

In my heart, I wish your generation could have been free to embark upon your sex lives without the hardcore, soulless, sexist imagery of porn. I wish you could all have had the chance to explore sex organically, with all the surprises, the thrills and the spills (sorry). Without expectations, preconceptions or distorted ideas of what sex looks, sounds and feels like. That's the way it used to be. For us, sex was a cool, often awkward experience of discovery. Lots of fumbling and working it out as you went along.

I'm sure you're riveted by your mother reminiscing about how sex used to be for her and you want to hear much, much more about that. Are you still even reading?

Today, though, by the time your generation embark on your sex lives, you'll have seen hundreds of hours of porn stars doing it in hundreds of ways. They will all be in your head in bed with you and their influence will explicitly fuel your actions, if not your desires.

But look, I get that the porn genie can't be put back in the bottle. Your generation is a product of our time and you're all in the same porn boat. So I guess you'll all figure it out together. You'll have to. Good luck. Remember to wear a condom and don't try to use Glad Wrap instead.

Also, while I've got your attention, remember that it's crucial women have cheap, safe and legal access to contraception and abortion because without these things, there's every chance you will end up with half a dozen kids before you turn 30 and you will have to pay for all of them, okay, so make sure you march alongside women whenever they are worried about their reproductive rights because you should be too.

Do you like how I slipped that in there? #women #mumjoke.

Okay, there are a few other important things you need to know. Remember them. Tell all your friends.

1. *Porn is not real sex.* There's a saying that old people like to post on Instagram, you may have seen it: *Dance like no one is watching.* Sex is the same. Whether it's commercially produced porn or a sex tape, the way people behave in front of a camera is different from reality. Most of what you see online is people having sex for money. It's their job. Just like Kardashians aren't representative of what regular women look like and *Call of Duty* isn't representative of actual war, neither is porn the same as sex. Porn is to sex what Formula 1 is to driving: an extreme version best left to professionals.

2. *Never compare yourself to the men you see in porn.* Male porn stars are chosen for their giant penises and their ability to maintain erections for a really long time. Often they use drugs like Viagra to do this. Other times, the video is edited to make it look like one continuous sex session when it's not. They also usually have hairless bodies and no pubic hair. This is a porn thing, it's not because all women prefer it. Just like women, men come in all shapes, sizes, skin colours and degrees of hairiness. Not all men have sixpacks. In fact, most women have never had sex with someone who has a sixpack. Sixpacks are not standard and they have no bearing on your ability to be good at sex.

3. *Never compare your partner to the women you see in porn.* This may seem obvious but I need to spell it out in explicit (sorry) detail. The women you see in porn usually have fake boobs that are much bigger, higher, harder and rounder than natural boobs and which point to the ceiling no matter what position she's in. Real breasts don't look or move like that, they fall towards a girl's armpits when she's lying on her back. That's normal.

   Often, women in porn have also had surgery on their vaginas to make them look a certain way. Vagina surgery.

It exists. Keep reading. So the vaginas you see in porn look very different from real-life vaginas, which are far less 'neat' and contained. Just like faces, vaginas all look different. Be prepared for that. There are all sorts of other things female porn stars do to change the way their genitals look, everything from lasering off their pubic hair to bleaching their anuses. Yes, I know. You never expected to be discussing anal bleaching with your mum and you'd really rather die than know this but here we are and it's for your own good. You need to know that there's nothing remotely natural about the women's bodies you see in porn.

4. *Women in porn are faking it.* Female porn stars are paid to look like they enjoy everything. All of it – no matter how uncomfortable, awkward, humiliating or painful. These women are paid to fake pleasure even when they're being degraded or abused. Even when they're scared, in agony or subject to violence. The more humiliating, painful and dangerous it is, the more they are paid. And the harder they must fake their pleasure.

   Think about that for a moment. If you have to pay someone more to do a particular act, it's because they don't want to do it. That's why you must never be fooled into thinking the female responses you see in porn are real. They're not. Women in real life do not respond the same way to those things. Women in real life generally take much longer to warm up than women in porn, who are paid to be instantly, convincingly theatrical and whose 'pleasure' is a transactional performance for money.

5. *Porn sex is not indicative of mainstream female taste.* Within a loving, consensual sexual relationship, there are no rights or wrongs. Different strokes for different folks (sorry). But there are two very common acts in porn that are portrayed as wildly

enjoyable for all women when in fact many women are not okay with them.

Coming or spitting on her face is one. Anal sex is another.

Did you know that female porn stars are paid twice as much to have anal sex on camera as they are for vaginal sex? Now you do. And remember what I said about women being paid more for certain types of sex – it means they need extra incentive because they don't want to do it.

The same goes for spanking, hair pulling or any kind of rough treatment; not all women like these things. Just because you've seen it in porn, don't assume it will fly in real life. Always ask first. *Always*. Never, ever make the mistake of thinking that a girl is into something just because you saw someone online 'enjoy it'.

6. *Porn is made by men for men.* That means what you see is what men want to do – not what women enjoy. It's almost impossible to speak in absolutes here because sexual tastes are highly individual but let's compare porn to food.

    There are certain foods which have a limited fan base – say, brains and brussel sprouts. Sure, there are some people who genuinely enjoy eating those foods (Good for them! No judgement!) but these people are not indicative of mainstream tastes. Now imagine if every TV cooking program featured these two ingredients in every meal that was cooked. It would be weird, right? But if you watched lots of cooking shows, all featuring these two ingredients, you would be convinced that everyone loves brains and brussel sprouts. EVERYONE. ALL THE TIME.

    They don't. And porn is the same.

    By making things like anal sex, double and triple penetration and coming or spitting on women's faces standard in most porn, you could easily be fooled into thinking every woman liked those things. NOT TRUE.

Think of them as the brains and brussel sprouts of sex. An acquired taste. Loved by a few. Loathed by most. So always ask your guests before you try to serve them up.

I'VE PROBABLY GIVEN you enough to think about at this point. I know it won't stop you from watching porn but I hope it will make you smarter when you do. And don't watch too much of it. Go for a walk.

Sex with the right partner is awesome; when you're ready to go there, you're going to love it and you should. Just don't confuse it with what you see online.

And always, always, always make sure your partner is sober, awake and able to consent.

Love,

Your mum xxxxx

PS: THERE'S A great website you should check out called makelovenotporn.com which has lots more information about this from a cool woman called Cindy Gallop who gave a great TED Talk about it which you should also watch. Google it.

AND ALSO: YOU know that 'tea and consent' video I showed you on YouTube? Send it to 10 friends. Thanks. Love you.

NOT ALL SELFIES ARE CREATED THIRSTY

WOMEN AGED 16–25 spend five hours per week taking selfies. This, friends, is why the world is going to hell. Except we won't notice when it does because we'll all be pulling duck faces into our phones. All this thirst – for praise, for likes, for validation – it has to stop.

The above is a highly unoriginal rant. A woman in her forties griping about how appalling it is that young women are taking photos of themselves at funerals and in the aftermath of terrorist attacks and during labour and when they wake up and go to sleep and get out of the shower and during their pap smear and that this is the defining trait of a generation of self-obsessed narcissists . . . this hot take is stale and predictable.

Nevertheless, it was my view until recently.

I relish having my mind changed. The term back-flip, when it's used pejoratively against politicians who change their views, can be unhelpful. Attitudes evolve and so can our opinions as we learn new things. It's a mistake to confuse stubborn intransigence with consistency-as-virtue[15].

---

15 Look at how I seamlessly justified my philosophical selfies back-flip while also giving myself a backhanded compliment: I changed my mind about selfies because I'm so intelligent.

The evolution of my u-turn on selfies came slowly and then suddenly.

Like so many people who aren't millennials, the obsession with taking selfies used to infuriate me.

And yet I still took them myself sometimes, albeit with myriad justifications as to why I was different from those selfie-takers who were simply vain tossers.

I awarded myself smug points for the following:

- I never use filters, Photoshop or autotune to alter my appearance.

- I never try to look sexy or 'thirsty' – I never use selfies to elicit compliments or validation.

- I take photos of what I'm wearing because clothes are a form of creative expression. Unlike, you know, my face (getting borderline here, I know, I never said I wasn't a hypocrite).

- I deliberately take photos of myself looking unattractive. This is a radical act of helpful feminism.

My loathing of 'thirsty' selfies was clearly a sign I needed to understand this activity better, so I took a deep dive. I wanted to hear from people who loved taking selfies about why they did it and what it gave them.

None of my friends could help me. Nor could my peers. At best they tolerated selfies, at worst they loathed them too. They dabbled, sure, everyone does, but my friends weren't advocates. Rachel Syme is a millennial reporter who wrote a 10-part essay on Medium.com (called *Selfie*) exploring her devotion to taking and sharing photos of herself. This is what I learned from her:

- Turning your camera around to capture your own image is not intrinsically a bad thing or even a vain thing.

- It's not always about saying 'I look great'. It can just be about wanting to be seen. Wanting to inject your image into the public realm.

- I am a hypocrite for sneering at women who think they look great, because I've been railing against the alternative – women feeling bad about themselves due to the unrealistic images portrayed by the media.

- Just like I use words to anchor my thoughts and feelings, some people use selfies to literally put themselves in the picture.

- Selfies are the ultimate democratisation of women's power in reclaiming agency in the way we're portrayed.

- Selfies have usurped mainstream media as the main source of female imagery – created by women of ourselves. This should be encouraged and celebrated not castigated or mocked.

- You want diversity? How much more diverse can you get than allowing every woman with a phone to capture and distribute images of herself in the way she chooses?

- Taking selfies isn't just vanity. Or doesn't have to be. It can give you joy, power, visibility, control and agency. Since I've spent my career advocating for women to get more of all those things, what's my goddamn problem if some of them find it through taking, posting and sharing selfies? (Let's park the subject of nude selfies to the side for a moment, because they exist on a different level and are more fraught from a safety point of view, and a political one.)

My u-turn was underway but here's the single thing that crystallised it: ISIS.

A few weeks later I read an unrelated article about the radicalisation of young Muslim men in Australia. The story included quotes from the friends of one particular young ISIS recruit, chronicling his radicalisation. One incident – a tiny one – stayed with me.

Apparently, the young man had sent his sister a text angrily demanding she stop posting selfies on social media. The photos she was taking of herself, mostly with friends in social situations, were not remotely sexual and she was wearing a hijab. But still, these tame photos horrified her brother. It was immodest, he ranted. She was disgusting for 'flaunting' herself like that.

I sat quietly for a moment after reading the story to let it sink in as I felt the moral ground shift beneath me. The idea of taking a selfie suddenly took on new meaning for me: it could be an act of feminist rebellion. Because any act that was opposed by the radical oppressors of women had to be a positive thing for those women, right? The enemy of my enemy is my friend.

Finally, I could understand the concept of a selfie as a positive expression of self.

It was a freeing realisation and I take selfies more often now, posting them or sending them to friends without hesitation. Often, among girlfriends, they're a visual shorthand when you can't be bothered to text. An emoji but using my face. Pull a silly expression, snap, send. Capture yourself crying with laughter after watching a video they sent you. Snap, send.

I give little thought to the selfies I post on social media and yet I give them enormous thought. In taking photos while I go about my daily life, I make a conscious effort to shrug off the shackles of my innate vanity.

This doesn't always come easily. We are deeply conditioned to seeing ourselves through the male gaze which has become synonymous with the wider gaze of society. It's a powerful pull to appear sexually and aesthetically desirable at all times.

Oh no, my hair is dirty. I have a pimple on my chin. Bags under my eyes. No makeup. Pad Thai on my t-shirt.

Rarely is it all these things at once but sometimes it is. And so what? This is how I look today, in this moment in the world, and that's part of my story. More broadly, it's the story of women. You can't be what you can't see – well, you can but you can't feel normal about it. By putting myself out there, zits, wrinkles, grey hairs, stomach rolls and all, I'm deliberately seeking to widen the spectrum of 'how a normal woman looks'.

I make a deliberate decision to never Photoshop myself or my life. I write about the ugly bits. The embarrassing bits. The vulnerable bits. I take pictures of myself looking terrible as well as when I look nice. I tell the truth about my age. This is important. For me.

Because if anyone is going to compare themselves to me, I must not present myself as a lie. That's deceptive and unhelpful; a betrayal of women.

Of course you must make your own decisions about how you wish to portray yourself. This is the glorious freedom of a democratised media when we are all editors of our own social networks while also being the stars of them.

Magazine editors, photographers, TV programmers and advertising casting directors no longer have a monopoly over the way we're portrayed. Women have stormed the barricades of media power and overthrown the ruling class with a tidal wave of selfies that portray our faces, our bodies and our lives in myriad different ways.

And yet.

There are aspects of selfie culture that trouble me.

Comparisons are one of them. The blurred line between self-empowerment and self-objectification is another. A generation of young women have grown up marinating in an objectifying sexualised culture that has confused for them the act of feeling sexual with looking sexy.

Self-objectification is not power. Nor is feeling sexy. Feeling sexy is great, no arguments there. But so is eating cookie dough. Not empowering. Just delicious. Different things.

One is about physical pleasure, the other is the ability to effect change in your life and in the world. They're both terrific but don't mistake one for the other.

For many young women, sexuality and the culture of selfies that feed on it have become a performative act done for the benefit of men.

There is a term for this: the Patriarchal Bargain.

'Patriarchal bargain' is a term coined by Turkish author and researcher Deniz Kandiyoti back in 1988 which describes the act of taking a tool of female oppression and using it to get ahead. A bit like climbing higher by walking over other women. You rise up, they're squashed down by your ascent. On *Geek Feminism Wiki*, feminist Lisa Wade explains it like this: 'A patriarchal bargain is a decision to accept gender rules that disadvantage women in exchange for whatever power one can wrest from the system. It is an individual strategy designed to manipulate the system to one's best advantage, but one that leaves the system itself intact.'

Did someone say Kardashian? They are a perfect example of women who have made a patriarchal bargain. So are the supermodel businesswomen who make their fortunes out of modelling lingerie or selling skincare. So are the women on Instagram who post selfies of their abs or their bikini bodies.

So are the celebrities who pose for 'body-after-baby' photos weeks after giving birth.

All these things are good for them personally. They derive power through the societal praise, attention and validation their self-objectification generates. They are usually then able to convert this into money via products or endorsements – the Kardashians have adroitly built a multi-million-dollar empire this way. And so when these women say it's 'empowering', they're right. *For them.* It enhances their personal power in a system rigged against women. Instead of allowing others to derive money and power from objectifying them (for example, Hugh Hefner or Donald Trump both profited from objectifying women in magazines and beauty pageants), they are sharing in the spoils by objectifying themselves.

Is this good for them? Sure it is. In the short-term, at least. Long-term it's never a good idea to index your worth to your appearance because it's an asset that reduces in value over time. Is it good for other women? Not at all. Objectifying yourself in a way that conforms with sexist ideals about what a woman 'should' look like harms other women. It holds us all back by reinforcing these gendered and incredibly narrow ideals about 'hotness' in the guise of empowerment.

It's the reason my heart sinks a little when I see a women's sports team strip off to promote their sport and hopefully attract the attention of sponsors.

Or when a blogger posts a photo of her flat stomach after giving birth.

Or when I saw a sexualised image of myself on the cover of a magazine that I'd agreed to be photographed for, wearing leather hot pants, smoky eyes and fuck-me boots.

The goal of the talented, all-female creative team behind this cover shoot had not been sexist but merely to portray me in a way I'm not usually seen. Tick. However, I'm not usually seen like that for a reason. I agreed to the styling without complaint because I didn't want to be a diva and I was happy to help fulfil their creative vision.

But when the magazine came out, I felt uncomfortable and not just because I had a UTI at the shoot (that 'sexy' expression on my face is actually 'Oh God, I need to wee again'). Men I knew well – and women – remarked on how incredible I looked and this made me feel worse. I didn't want my kids to see it. I felt vulnerable and clichéd.

It's not that being sexy is not a part of who I am but wasn't I just making my own patriarchal bargain by conforming to a very stereotypical portrayal of sexy? Are there not enough images of women in the world looking like this? Couldn't no makeup be sexy? Couldn't my soft tummy be sexy? I would have been totally up for that but nobody suggested it. Not even me.

*

Stuck on the wall in front of my desk at home as well as all around our Mamamia offices in every city are images of women – famous and not – who inspire me.

Among them are images of feminist Caitlin Moran and in every photo she's pulling a funny face. For a long time I've done the same in photos and it's something I never noticed until my husband pointed it out. 'Why do you pull faces like that?' he asked. I had no idea.

Then I read an essay called 'My Muppet Face' in Moran's book *Moranthology* where she writes about being asked about her silly photo faces. 'Stop it. It's profoundly unattractive. Why do you persist in it?' they tweet her. She's not pulling a silly face, she tells them. She's pulling her cleverest face. It's the face of cultural critique and political statement.

When women are being photographed, she explains, they're expected to make a 'calm, emotionless expression' that's 'serenely impassive'. A face of repose. And Caitlin Moran argues that she does not feel that way inside. She feels excited and crazy and interested and interesting; the opposite of repose. 'I want to project how I feel on the inside: like a Muppet being fired out of a cannon onto a large pie. On Christmas Day. I want to look alive . . . Like I'm having fun.'

She goes on to point out that by posing in that passive, sultry way women are expected to, you're silently agreeing to something. 'I don't want to enter that competition – for that's what it is, when a woman dresses, and poses, like that. She gets rated. Rated against all the other women posing like that and doing those things with her face. I'm not trying to project some sexy authoritativeness *at* the world. I'm being amused *by* the world, instead. I'm not *transmitting*. I'm *receiving*.'

And this is why I feel my spirits lift when any woman does something to push against restrictive expectations of women, whether it's running to be the President of the United States, being made CEO of a publicly listed company or proudly displaying a body that society tells us is unattractive like Lena Dunham joyfully does.

Or when Caitlin appears in glossy magazines in her own clothes having done her own hair and makeup, pulling a Muppet face.

And that's why women respond so positively whenever I share photos of my grey regrowth or my soft tummy or my post-laser skin looking like it's covered in coffee granules. The response is one of resounding relief. *Phew, me too.*

For famous women, women like Lena and Caitlin, it can be harder. They risk being attacked, ridiculed or abused. Sometimes I am too. But how else can we change the terms of the patriarchal bargain if we don't do anything other than objectify ourselves? How else can we change what it means to be and look like a woman in our society if we don't try to widen the goalposts? And sometimes the best way to do this is in a selfie.

THAT TIME FOOD NEARLY DESTROYED ME

I DON'T REMEMBER the first time I made myself throw up. But I know I was in my first year of high school so I must have been about 12 or 13.

It wasn't a weight thing, not at first. I had no particular issue with my body beyond being desperate to shave my legs and not being allowed to. This was upsetting but I stole Mum's razor and got it done.

No, it wasn't about weight, it was simply wanting to have my cake and eat it – all of it – too. Or so it seemed.

I was one of the 'latchkey kids' of my generation; in the '80s we were the minority who came home to an empty house because both our parents worked. My mum was a psychologist and my dad was a fund manager; I didn't know exactly what that meant but he worked in the city. Kids care remarkably little about their parents' lives outside of them being parents. They exist to meet our needs, the end.

My routine was well established from around age 10 when Mum no longer had to pay a babysitter to stay with me after school.

I'd walk home from the bus stop, call Mum to let her know I'd arrived safely and then my dog and I would walk up to the local shops. My first stop was always the newsagent where I'd spend my pocket money or surreptitiously browse the magazines for as long as was acceptable without buying one. I didn't limit myself to teen titles; I was so in love with magazines I read whatever was available. Where else could I learn about my life as a girl and my future life as a woman? I was a sponge.

I also bought snacks. Hot chips, potato scallops, chocolate or a packet of Twisties . . . eating was something to do. A way to pass the time while treating myself. Nurturing myself with food? Comfort eating? All of it.

When I was 12, my parents decided to renovate and we rented a house nearby while the builders came in.

It was the year I started high school and it was an awkward, false start. I switched schools just two weeks into the term when a place suddenly became available at a private girls' school and my parents decided to move me. New house, new school, puberty . . . with the combined wisdom of therapy and hindsight, it was an obvious time to develop an eating disorder.

I was the first person in my family to go to a private school after generations of co-ed public education and I was distraught at the prospect in the way only a hormonal 13-year-old girl can be.

'It's going to be a pack of snobby girls standing around talking about what kind of Mercedes their dad drives,' I wailed to my mother, who was also tortured by the idea of abandoning the public education system she'd always championed. But our local high school had some deep-rooted academic problems and Mum was concerned. Later, she told me she'd also been alarmed by the fact my best friend's boyfriend was 21. She was 13.

Mum promised I could return to my old school after a year if I was still miserable. Well played. Of course I wouldn't want the upheaval of moving again after a year. Her gamble paid off[16].

It was ugly at first, though. The majority of girls had known each other since kindergarten and the newbies had all started together at the beginning of term, so by the time I arrived new friendship groups had already formed and I was in none of them. Twelve and 13-year-old girls can be terrifying if you are one. And even if you're not.

I couldn't find my tribe, not for months. Mortified by my conspicuousness, I spent every lunchtime in an empty classroom doing my homework. I didn't want pity. I just wanted friends.

After school, I started to eat more junk food and the connection between my mouth and my stomach somehow frayed. I ate until I was overly full and the way I was eating began to change. It was less pleasurable. More hurried. When my mother came home from work and served dinner to the family, there would be cross words if I didn't eat what was served. I felt bad. I wanted to be hungry for dinner. But I also wanted to eat junk in the afternoon when I was by myself. So almost by accident one day, home alone, I stumbled upon the way to eat my fill of junk and still be hungry enough to eat dinner. Vomiting.

I was a great vomiter. Still am. I haven't been bulimic for decades but if I throw up now due to illness, I'm untroubled by it.

---

16 As a parent, I would have moved me too for all the reasons she did. And I'm grateful she didn't let me decide. I've seen too many parents give their children the ultimate say in what school they go to, even if they're as young as eight. This is absurd. Unless your child is begging to change schools due to bullying (in which case, listen to them), you need to decide. By all means, take their views as a comment, but remember: you're the grown-up, make the call.

Most people hate vomiting. I have one friend who had to seek cognitive behavioural therapy to treat her anxiety about it which is apparently quite common. Even if your fear of throwing up is not that extreme, you likely see it as something to be avoided under every circumstance. I understand this. Uncontrollable vomiting is horrendous because you're invariably sick or drunk and it's a violent, involuntary, out-of-control process. For bulimics, however, vomiting is the ultimate control. A bulimic never feels as in charge of her body or her life as when she's sticking her fingers down her throat.

This mirage of control is the appeal of purging, although it's absurd to use the word 'appeal' to describe a bodily function so convulsive, solitary and ugly.

Of course you can't control it. Not really, not for long. Blink and you're in the grip of an eating disorder.

And then I was.

In our rented house, my bedroom had a tiny bathroom off it, and I found this new luxury intoxicating. The novelty of bathroom privacy enabled me to refine my appetite-creation trick. That's how I thought of it. The idea of being able to eat anything you wanted and never feeling too full was some kind of awesome Willy Wonka shit.

Why didn't everyone do this? I wondered.

Pretty soon I was throwing up every afternoon quite happily until one day, Mum came home early from work and caught me. Concerned, she spoke to our family GP and the following week she took me for an appointment. We were left alone, the middle-aged male doctor and me, to talk about my vomiting. The word bulimia was never mentioned and I wouldn't learn it until years later. I just thought this was a handy trick I'd discovered to manage my appetite. No big deal.

The doctor assumed I was throwing up to avoid gaining weight and I didn't disavow him of this because I had no idea why I was doing it. So I just sat there and listened.

It was kind of embarrassing.

'You know if you eat a Mars Bar you can work it off by running up and down the stairs 20 times,' he assured me kindly. 'Then it's just like you never ate it.'

I nodded, thanked him for the information and the vomiting promptly stopped.

In the weeks that followed, I ran up and down the stairs half-heartedly a few times after eating chocolate, taking his advice quite literally and trying to apply it, but the disruption of having my secret out in the open was enough to cause a shift and break my habit.

For a time.

A few years later, it returned, sparked by some unsuccessful attempts at dieting. During high school I watched several girls I knew battle anorexia or skirt dangerously close to it. Dieting and weight had become highly competitive sports. I recall a particular fallout between two friends who had agreed to eat a single Smartie each when they got home from school. The first girl ate hers but the second girl abstained. When the first girl learned this at school the next morning she became hysterical, insisting she'd been betrayed, freaking out that she would now get fatter than her friend.

Teenage girls are intense.

Dieting was a frequent topic of conversation in the play-ground as we all tried to make sense of our changing bodies and compared them unfavourably to the models we saw in *Dolly* magazine, one of whom, cover girl Sarah Nursey, thrill-ingly went to our school and could be gazed at in the library.

If we weren't getting drunk in parks and pashing boys, social activities often revolved around 'pigging out' at someone's house while watching a video.

The word 'binging' didn't yet exist and neither did the word 'obesity'. The most famous campaign of the '70s and '80s around exercise was called 'Life. Be In It', which featured a cartoon character called Norm who was a middle-aged dude with a big gut who sprawled on the couch watching sport. The catchy jingle involved whistling and Norm getting off his couch and being more active. Norm. Get it? I know.

None of this felt remotely relevant to women, let alone teenage girls.

Eating disorders weren't mainstream back then and pigging out sounded as harmless and fun as it felt. I hated organised sport and loathed the idea of being in any kind of team. Aerobics was peaking, though. It was all very Olivia Newton John in 'Physical'. Gyms were social places, the daytime equivalent of nightclubs. My friends and I joined a big fitness centre where the instructors had cult-like followings and everyone got to class early to nab a spot up the front near the mirrors. We were shameless. Step classes, grapevines ... I used to go to aerobics semi-regularly, wearing a cutting edge 1980s outfit of Lycra tights with a g-string leotard *over the top*, big white scrunchy socks and Reebok high-tops. I wanted to be thinner, of course.

Pre-selfies. My mum took this shot. So teenager.

Everyone did. Taller too. And blonde. Blonde would be nice. Like the models in *Dolly*. Like Alison Brahe and Sarah Nursey and Sonia Klein. I got streaks and sometimes used a crimping iron.

At school, I waged a personal war against PE and would do anything to escape our weekly swimming sessions. I became adept at forging my mother's signature and most weeks I would stand in line with the other malingerers and present my fake note to the PE teacher. *Mia is unable to swim this week because she has her period*, it read.

Four weeks out of every five, my PE teacher would read my note and regard me with a mix of scepticism, exasperation and profound disappointment. The phrase 'harden up princess' had not yet entered the lexicon and her job didn't permit her to snap, 'Have you heard of a tampon?' but that's what her eyes said as she reached for her red Texta and wrote a big capital P next to my name.

Again.

My bulimia returned for a few months when I was about 16 and this time it was absolutely about my weight. There is no creature as narcissistic or insecure as a 15-year-old girl, and like every other teenager I was struggling to cope with the tsunami of hormones, sexuality, rebellion, self-image and identity that churned through me and would do so for years with little respite.

I didn't recognise the pattern then but it was emerging. At times in my life when I felt out of control, when the waves of uncertainty and emotional turmoil were washing me off my feet, I would try to block those uncomfortable feelings with food. At least I could control the food I absorbed into my system, I told myself, and for a long time I foolishly believed that to be true.

It was a perverse form of comfort and – like any addiction – I quickly began to use the rituals of binging and purging to numb my emotions and give me some relief from my own thoughts, even if it was only temporarily.

Unlike other addictions, though, food addicts can remain fully functioning in the world. It rarely impinges on your ability to live your life and, specifically, to care for other people.

It's also far, far cheaper, easier to access, simple to hide and legally available no matter your age, making it particularly appealing to teenagers.

This is how so many people with bulimia or binge-eating disorder are able to abuse themselves in plain sight for years or even decades. The external markers of anorexia or obesity don't apply. You'd never know if you passed a bulimic in the street. And every day you do.

In a conversation I once had with Eve Ensler, iconic feminist and author of *The Vagina Monologues*, the subject of eating disorders came up. She told me she'd had anorexia and I confided in her that I'd been bulimic years earlier.

'I picked you as a former bulimic,' she said, smiling.

'How?' I exclaimed.

'There's a type.' She shrugged and we both laughed because it's true. You can't pick a bulimic from their size but sometimes you can pick a personality. Bulimics and anorexics are polar opposites. Anorexics view bulimics with horror and disdain for their lack of control (while secretly envying them their ability to eat forbidden food). Bulimics, meanwhile, roll their eyes at what they see as the smug piousness of anorexics (while secretly envying them their extreme discipline).

Anorexics are repulsed by the thought of food at volume. Bulimics wonder why anyone would starve themselves instead of having their cake and eating/vomiting it too.

My phases of bulimia during high school and afterwards

were only ever brief. A month or two every few years and then I'd get a handle on it as I began to spiral and pull back from the brink of serious illness.

When I was 19 years old, though, I returned from a gap year in Italy and descended into a full-blown eating disorder. For six months, I'd lived in Florence with three girlfriends where we'd enrolled in language school while eating, drinking and partying our way through each day and night.

In theory, we were meant to study at an Italian language school for foreigners, and we did that for a few months before deciding to dedicate ourselves full-time to drinking tequila and visiting bars and clubs all night before popping into the local bakery for hot pastries at 5 am. We'd return home by about 6 am, make ourselves a giant bowl of pasta and crash out until about 4 pm, when we'd inhale giant mugs of espresso before getting dressed and going out for pizza, wine and tequila followed by gelato, dancing and pastries again at 5 am. Repeat. Seven days a week.

Not surprisingly, I put on 10 kg in a few months. We all did. The tiny one-bedroom apartment my girlfriends and I were renting had no full-length mirror and we were too poor to turn on the heating so we'd make our nightly dash to the shower, stripping off at the last second. Any sex we had occurred furtively in our boyfriends' cars because all Italian men under (and often over) 30 seemed to live at home with their parents. As a result, we didn't see ourselves naked for months, and since it was 1990, most of our clothes were made of Lycra anyway. There were no belts, buttons or zips to alert us to our rapid expansion.

It wasn't until we took a weekend trip to London where we hopped on the scales at the Natural History Museum for a laugh and suddenly realised how much weight we'd gained. We reeled with shock, but it didn't stop us from popping into KFC on the way back to our hostel to ruminate on this while eating deep-fried chicken and mashed potato with gravy.

Weeks later, I flew home from the depths of a European winter into the glare of an Australian summer to begin my new life as a journalism student at university. Without the camouflage of winter clothes and the confidence boost of men who called you *bella* simply for existing as a woman, I could no longer hide from myself.

For the first time in my life, I decided to go on a crash diet or what might now be called a DIY detox.

All I permitted myself to eat was apple, passionfruit, steamed vegetables and herbal tea. Immediately, I was starving. Predictably, within a week or two, I began to binge. If you'd asked me, I'd have said I wanted to be thin, but of course the root cause ran far deeper. I was lost and deeply unhappy and it had little to do with my weight.

My gap year was over and I'd begun a course I hated almost immediately. Journalism was the only thing I'd wanted to pursue as a career so I'd applied for an arts/communications degree. At the time it was one of the only degrees pertaining to media that was available so I was happy to land a spot and excited about what I might learn.

But I loathed it. Again, I struggled to find my friendship group and my tutors sparked no passion in me.

For the first half of the year, I maintained a relationship with my boyfriend back in Italy, which gave me an excuse to avoid any social life at home. When I eventually gave that relationship the green needle and broke up with him, there was a boyfriend-shaped hole in my life that I didn't know how to fill.

It wasn't about him, it was about having a relationship. I had no experience of being single, traipsing as I had from boyfriend to boyfriend from age 14. To numb the discomfort of being alone and unhappy at uni, I descended further into bulimia, my days consumed with buying food, binging on it and then purging. It was an expensive, time-consuming, physically exhausting, shameful addiction that was rapidly devouring my life and compromising my physical and mental health.

Very quickly, I became incapable of eating normal meals. Within just a couple of months, I lost the ability to regulate the amount of food I ate and I felt panicked at the prospect of having to eat in public without immediately throwing up afterwards. I became increasingly solitary. The feeling of being full or even having food in my stomach became intolerable. It was like I could feel the calories being absorbed. Making me fat. Losing control.

The only things I deemed 'acceptable' to digest were fruit, herbal tea and steamed vegetables. I swung between this kind of maniacally puritanical eating and the repellent, magnetic gluttony of binging on enormous quantities of 'forbidden' foods.

It was lonely and isolating and all-consuming. Princess Diana had not yet confessed her bulimia to the world and the Internet wasn't around so I had no way to connect with other people going through the same thing. I knew nobody else who had bulimia and so I existed inside this pervasive, toxic cloud of isolating humiliation.

There is nothing sexy about vomit.

I became adept at throwing up quietly and quickly. I knew where the 'best' public toilets were for maximum privacy. And I had my favourite foods and ways to binge, none of which I will detail here because this is not an eating disorder instruction manual. What I will tell you is that the quantities of food I could consume in a single binge would shock you. A loaf of bread. Half a dozen cupcakes or doughnuts. A whole tub of ice-cream. An entire cake. A bowl of raw cake mix.

At first, each binge was carefully planned. I would drive to a particular shop to buy the food, my heart beating rapidly, my eyes slightly glazed, my pupils dilated in anticipation as if I were about to have sex. My emotional switch would automatically flick off and I'd have an adrenaline rush of excitement mixed with extreme focus. Everything faded away but the food. Often, I'd consume it in my car, not able to wait until I got home.

Whether or not anyone ever suspected what I was doing is hard to tell. When a young woman is buying a large quantity of food, your first thought is probably not that she's going to stuff it all in her face and then throw it up. There was so little awareness of eating disorders back then, it would have taken a sufferer to recognise another.

Perversely, I took very little pleasure from actually eating all this food. I was in too much of a frenzied, altered state. Bulimic binging is not a pleasant thing to observe.

I'd usually eat with my hands, hunched over while standing up at the kitchen bench and at terrific speed; this was crucial because I didn't want anything to absorb.

In fast, out faster.

An enormous quantity of food would be stuffed into my body in the space of a few minutes. Rarely more than that. There was a ritual about it but not in the slow, deliberate sense that word implies. There were things I did to ensure the food wouldn't be absorbed in the short time it spent in my stomach and would come up easily. Things I won't detail for reasons you now understand.

That done, I would stuff myself until I was in physical pain. This was the only indication that the binge was finished: pain. In an altered, binge state, you don't really feel anything. Physical sensation is obliterated by the intense focus applied to the frantic task at hand.

In fact, the ability to switch off your senses is crucial to getting it done. If you were in any way present in your body, your stomach would send urgent signals to your brain to stop this madness.

That's why the short duration of a binge is paramount – you must try and trick your body into accepting vast quantities before it realises it's stuffed to bursting point. This makes the period between finishing a binge and throwing up desperately uncomfortable in every respect. Physically, it can be hard to walk and even breathe – imagine a volume of food large enough to fill two grocery bags stuffed into your stomach which is the size of a fist.

Far worse, though, is the overwhelming mental panic. Every second is crucial. Every second more calories are being ingested.

Being disturbed or somehow prevented from completing a binge is a bulimic's worst nightmare. Decades later, occasionally I still have actual nightmares about being prevented from purging after a binge; the anxiety wakes me. The purging part brings not only physical relief but a mental release that's far greater. It's absolution of the most dysfunctional, fucked-up kind.

Even today I have a Pavlovian response to nausea or feeling too full. It triggers a low-level panic within me and a nagging desire to throw up. I'm not sure this learned mental connection will ever recede completely. I'm stuck with ignoring it and waiting for it to pass, which can take anywhere from a few minutes to an hour.

Ironically, I rarely get stomach bugs of any kind. I've had food poisoning only once or twice in my life; not even when

I've travelled to India, Papua New Guinea or Vietnam. I barely suffered any morning sickness during any of my pregnancies. After so much practice at vomiting, my stomach is cast-iron and the prospect of throwing up holds no fear for me.

*

By my twentieth birthday, my bulimia was becoming severe. I'd gone from binging every few days to every day, to five times a day. Sometimes I would binge consecutively. Stuff myself, throw up. Stuff myself again. Throw up. Until I was an exhausted husk, my knuckles swollen, my throat raw. It was also getting expensive. I was spending everything I earned on food, sometimes as much as $50 or more a day.

My eyes were sunken. My skin was grey. My bathroom stank. My world had shrunk monstrously to binging and purging. Bulimia had consumed me. I was never far from a toilet bowl.

My close friends guessed what was going on – it wasn't hard to work out when we were out to dinner and I'd gorge myself and then leave the table repeatedly. They tentatively tried to intervene, to talk to me. Nobody knew much about bulimia or eating disorders in the early '90s. There were no help lines. No online resources. No celebrity survivors.

I dismissed their tentative concerns, chirping brightly about food poisoning or just flat out denying there was anything wrong. I pushed down the shame and pretended to myself they believed me but I knew they didn't and I didn't care. The space in my life for anything other than food and receptacles in which to vomit was shrinking. I became adept at surreptitiously purging into plastic shopping bags if I was unable to discretely access a bathroom. The madness was escalating.

Just a few months into my degree, I was already flailing at

university. One of my classes was Women's Studies and I was exposed to academic feminist theory for the first time. I baulked.

'My lecturer told us that lipstick is a tool of patriarchal oppression which is then sold back to women to enhance latent feelings of inadequacy,' I complained to my mother. 'But I *like* lipstick.'

Conspiratorially, we rolled our eyes at the absurdity of this kind of polarising feminism which seemed to diminish women and set us against each other more than it expanded our lives or our power.

The feminist police who patrol Twitter in search of petty transgressions now serve this function expertly.

It wasn't just the extreme rhetoric that soured me on my degree nor the soul-crushing ugliness of the campus which wasn't a campus at all, just a squat concrete building on the outskirts of the city. I was also struggling with the laidback pace of university life after attending a strict high school and being cosseted within the snug confines of its myriad rules. The course I was doing was pass/fail with no exams and it was almost impossible to fail. This should have delighted me but instead, complacency popped the balloon of my competitive nature. I deflated.

Since my university hours were so minimal compared to school – a paltry 20 hours per week – I was able to work several part-time jobs. As a waitress, a promotions girl – handing out flyers and alcohol samples at Motor Shows and night-clubs – and at my mother's photographic gallery.

But my bulimia was making my waitressing job impossible. I was losing the ability to control my binging at work and some-times during my shift I would smuggle food from the kitchen into the toilet where I'd binge and purge before rushing back to the restaurant floor. Like every other aspect of my eating disorder, I thought I was being highly discreet. I wasn't. My boss eventually twigged to what was going on and fired me. Fair enough. I was literally flushing his money down the toilet.

As the months passed, I was rapidly spiralling downwards and I knew I needed help. Numb and desperate, I finally told my mum how bad things were and agreed to see a counsellor at my university. As I waited for an appointment to become available, I looked into the support group OverEaters Anonymous, which is based on the 12 Step program of Alcoholics Anonymous and applied to people with food addiction.

I was envious of alcoholics and drug addicts. Even gambling addicts. Their lines were clear, their boundaries well drawn.

They simply had to give up whatever they were addicted to; success or failure was absolute. No doubt it wasn't simple at all, because no addiction ever is, but almost all other addictions are binary: you drink or you don't. Smoke or don't. Put money in the pokies or don't.

Notably, none of those things are life affirming.

But what if you're addicted to food? You can't stop eating altogether. So? I was overwhelmed, perplexed and despairing when I thought about trying to navigate normal eating. I didn't even know what that looked like anymore.

*

Hesitant and anxious, I attended my first meeting on a Monday night at 8 pm in an inner-city community centre where I appeared to be the youngest person there. My fellow food addicts were mostly women but there were a few men too and everyone seemed to fall into one of three categories: bulimic, anorexic or compulsive overeaters; those who binged but didn't purge. An outsider looking through the window would never have been able to glean the common thread of our experience: an inability to consume food in normal ways.

The basic premise of these meetings was the same as at all 12 Step meetings. Anyone was welcome to come along and it ran for a couple of hours. People stood up and told their stories without comment or judgement and at the end, you would say the serenity prayer out loud together.

> 'God grant me the serenity
> to accept the things I cannot change;
> the courage to change the things I can;
> and the wisdom to know the difference.'

There was no 'teacher' or professional counsellor. The meetings were led by a fellow addict who was currently 'clean'; the idea was to derive support from those who were further along their recovery journey than you, and to learn from each other's mistakes and successes.

As communicators, this is a way of learning I've always found women in particular are drawn to. We like to connect through stories of vulnerability and learn lessons in a passive way via others, almost by osmosis rather than having didactic lessons thrust onto us from an expert.

The meetings were a revelation.

Pre-Internet, it's hard to overstate how tough it was to find anyone who shared your problems. Whether it was people who couldn't manage food or people who wanted to have sex with plush toys or people who had bladder cancer or people who cared passionately about the rights of caged chickens or people who were interested in American politics. There was no way to find and communicate with others who shared your interests, kinks, challenges or afflictions in real time.

For the first time in my lonely, shameful experience of bulimia, I felt like I was among a group who understood its complexities, its pain, its appeal and its secrets.

Everyone was encouraged to have a 'sponsor', someone who had been doing the 12 Steps for at least a year and who you could call privately when you needed support or advice such as when you were tempted to slide. OA was a free service; you paid with your time by helping others when you were further down the road.

In that first meeting, I learned the rules. You weren't allowed to mention foods by name in case it triggered in someone else the desire to binge. It was my first exposure to the term 'trigger' and I understood it completely.

I attended maybe 10 meetings over a few months and it was certainly helpful to hear other people's stories and feel less alone. There is so much shame involved with bulimia – as with any addiction – but vomiting and our culture's disdain for gluttony, overeating and loss of control emits a particularly pungent stench. I felt a surprising sense of belonging.

Something about going to those meetings troubled me, though. When my fellow sufferers stood to tell their stories, they would often speak of being 'clean' for months and even years, meaning they no longer binged or starved or purged. This was puzzling at first. They'd been free of their addiction for years and yet still they were coming to meetings?

I was impatient to be free of this horrible addiction as soon as possible and I didn't want my life to be defined by bulimia after I'd recovered from it. Was I really going to be here in this room telling my story of how 'back when I was 20 I used to binge and purge five, six times a day and my life was unmanageable. That was 10 years ago . . .'?

The thought was unbearable to me. When I beat this soul-sucking affliction, I wanted to move on.

How little I understood of addiction.

Now I know better. Now I know that you're an addict for life. You're vulnerable to it forever. Now I understand why there are people who attend AA meetings and still call themselves an alcoholic despite being dry for decades. It's a bit like having a peanut allergy. Whether you eat peanuts or not, you still have the allergy.

When you have an addiction, by definition you are unable to control it. It controls you. And you must remain mindful of your recovery and vigilant against relapse your whole life.

For many sufferers of addiction, going to NA or AA or OA or GA meetings is a crucial part of staying straight. For them, attending a meeting is a very real substitute for going to a bar, a casino or their dealer's house. Not everyone can afford therapy. Not everyone can just recover and move on with their lives.

For almost all addicts, some degree of maintenance is required because at its core, addiction isn't about a substance or activity. It's about using those things to block your feelings. It's about relying on them as a way to deal with stress or discomfort or anger or boredom or grief or frustration or any of the other complex negative emotions life gifts you. Attending meetings and having some kind of ritualised practice is, for many, a crucial part of staying well.

One day at a time.

THERE IS NO RIGHT TIME TO HAVE A BABY

THE DAY I told my boss I was pregnant was a puzzling one for us both. Just three months earlier, I'd landed my dream job as editor of *Cosmopolitan* and my feet were barely under the desk when I weed on a stick and saw two lines.

Blink. Blink blink.

It took some time to process. How could something so enormous as having an entire baby, with all the seismic aftershocks that would reverberate through my life because of it, be reduced to this small white stick?

I didn't tell my boss until the 12-week mark and by then, I'd had time to work out my approach to the upcoming collision of work and a baby: ignore it. I saw no reason why it would affect any aspect of my life other than perhaps my wardrobe. God, these jeans are tight. Motherhood wouldn't change my career path. No need. It would be business as usual.

Some may describe this as denial but it wasn't. To deny something you have to know what it is and before you have your first baby, you have no idea. It's a batshit crazy cocktail of naivety and optimism.

10 DUMB THINGS WOMEN AND MEN SAY BEFORE HAVING THEIR FIRST BABY

1   'I think a baby should fit in with your life not the other way around.'

2   'We're not going to become like those baby-obsessed couples who can't talk about anything else.'

3   'We're going to just put the baby in one of those strap-on things and travel. How hard can it be?'

4   'I'm only going to take a month or so off work.'

5   'We are going to share all aspects of parenting. It will be totally equal because we're both feminists.'

6   'I'm going to be so bored on maternity leave. I need to use my brain. Maybe I'll do that MBA.'

7   'Please can you make sure you all keep cc'ing me on emails so I can stay across everything.'

8   'I refuse to buy any maternity clothes. I'm just going to make do with what I already own.'

9   'We've decided to get the baby into a routine straight away so we can still plan our days.'

10 'Our dog will always be like a child to us.'

To these ridiculous sentiments I say: BAHAHAHAHAHA HAHAHHAHAHAA!

If you want to make a baby cry incessantly and for no apparent reason, tell it your plans.

Actually, you don't even have to bother because a baby will cry anyway.

I probably said all of those absurd things when I was pregnant the first time but none so laughable as during the meeting with my boss when I told her I was knocked up and then presented her with my plan for maternity leave. It was a short plan.

'Look, I won't really need any,' I announced dismissively as she tried to keep a straight face.

'I'll work right up to the birth and then take a few weeks off, but I'll come into the office during that time and I'll be available every day from home and everyone can come to me for meetings. You won't even know I'm gone!'

I truly believed this. I was not clucky. I knew I wanted to be a mother one day in theory but I'd spent no time with babies and I did not delight in the company of kids. They irritated me, frankly. I had no nieces or nephews. No godchildren. No clue.

What I did delight in was my job. My career. The office. I'd been in love with magazines since I was 12 years old and at 25, I was finally an editor and it was Disneyland.

What the hell would I do at home with a baby? Learn another language while it slept all day?

If you don't have kids but plan to, you will be nodding internally right now. You'll be thinking: *Yeah, that sounds sensible, I'm totally going to download the Duo Lingo app and I'll be speaking fluent Spanish before my baby is on solids.*

Logistics aside (babies literally eat time), what I hadn't factored into the equation was how deeply I would fall in love with my son and how that would upend everything I thought I knew about my identity, my career and my priorities.

I quickly extended my three months of maternity leave to four and that still wasn't enough. I actually contemplated not going back at all and floated this with my mum, who wisely told me, 'Darling, there's a big difference between being at home on maternity leave from your job and that being your actual life.'

NOT JUDGING.

This is the part where I have to make that disclaimer so as not to antagonise stay-at-home mums who are feeling totally judged right now because being at home with their kids every day *is* their actual life *and what's wrong with that?*

Nothing! If it works for you and your family and your finances, then go for it. There is genuinely no moral judgement here. Choosing to stay home with your kids full-time or part-time when they're little doesn't make you less feminist, less intelligent, less successful, less anything except maybe less financially independent than you would be if you were earning money.

Once again, I will point out that it's dangerous for women to disconnect from the workforce entirely for long periods of time – like years. But you know that. The short version is this: lean in, lean out, but don't lie down permanently by removing yourself from the game.

So back to my mother's wise advice for maternity leave: Enjoy this time in the baby bubble but don't make any rash decisions because you're all milk and hormones.

Indeed, I was. Throw in sleep deprivation and the slow-dawning realisation that my life – our lives – would never be the same, and it's a miracle new mothers can remember which end of the bottle the wine comes out of, let alone make any meaningful decisions about the future.

The future? I could see pretty much up until the next feed but only because – demand feeding! – that was probably only 40 minutes away. After that it was anyone's guess.

Very soon, I realised I didn't want to go back to my job full-time after four months even though I'd promised my boss, my staff and myself I would. This perplexed me. Who even was I? I loved my job and my career was everything to me. I was ambitious and competitive and I relished almost every moment of being the boss of *Cosmopolitan*. I'd wanted to be an editor since the first time I'd picked up a magazine. I'd only just got there. Where had this bizarre career ambivalence come from?

It would be decades before Sheryl Sandberg would put some words around how I was feeling. At that time, the only terminology around work and women was 'having it all', which implied a level of greed and smugness that made me want to make like that emoji with the screaming face. Or the poo. Sandberg's philosophy perfectly described what I'd done since I walked in the door to beg for a work experience gig at *Cleo* when I was 19; I had leaned in.

Now at 25 and with a baby in my arms, I wanted to . . . well, if not exactly lie down, at least lean back for a little while longer.

In the lead-up to my maternity leave I'd been unable to comprehend how the magazine would cope without me. Or me without it. Leaning in was all I knew. All I'd ever wanted. When you enjoy your career and have built it with loving care over many years, leaning back can be disorienting and confronting because it raises questions of identity.

Who would I be if I wasn't my job?

And yet before the placenta had even left my body I was all, 'Magazine? Shmagazine.'

This was great news for my son. Despite being convinced I would suffer postnatal depression because that's the kind of optimist I am, I didn't. And much to my surprise, my focus was singular even if the love took a few days to kick in. Like most mothers – especially first-time mothers – I think I was in shock. This baby is mine? Like, mine-mine? I made this person? I'm responsible? Hang on, what?

It was a happy shock, though. I loved diving so deeply into him, into motherhood.

It wasn't until a couple of months later that I noticed something. Or rather the absence of something.

Where had my ambition gone? My drive? My passion for work? I contemplated this as I climbed the vertical cliff of new motherhood, hoisted upwards by unwitting ignorance. I didn't know what I didn't know; the Internet was, like my son, in its infancy; and I had no friends or relatives with babies who could give me advice.

So I just bumbled merrily along while feeling faintly sick about the prospect of having to tell my boss I was freaking out and wasn't remotely ready to leave my son and return to the office.

The relief was unspeakable when she cannily sniffed my angst and proactively suggested a phased return, two days in the office and three at home for the next six months. This wasn't just an altruistic move on her part. Like other smart bosses who understand the enormous benefit in retaining women they've invested in, she understood the short-term pain of not having me back full-time meant a significant long-term gain: she wouldn't have to find a new *Cosmo* editor and start over. I was lucky. I know a lot of women aren't so fortunate. And that is criminal. Because there is *no right time* to have a baby.

I could have kissed her. I probably did.

I've always been an inappropriate kisser.

THE BABIES THAT COULD HAVE BEEN

'HOW MANY TIMES have you been pregnant?'

Ask this question to a group of women and we will fall silent, if only for a moment. The calculations we are making in our heads and our hearts are deeply personal and some of the information we require is not easily accessible. So we reach back through years and tears and regrets and relief as our thoughts turn to the babies we desperately wanted and lost and to the pregnancies we chose to end. The babies we knew we couldn't have.

Not at that time.

Not with that man.

Sometimes it's our bodies that end a pregnancy and sometimes it's our minds, notes Caitlin Moran in *How To Be A Woman* of her own experience of miscarriage and abortion, 'I don't believe one's decision is more valid than the other. They both know me. They are both equally capable of deciding what is right.'

Miscarriage, neonatal loss and abortion. It's a slippery sense of loss for babies we never got to hold, children we never got to know, future lives of our own that we never experienced. Choices we made and choices that were taken away from us. Sliding doors through which we never walked. For those who oppose abortion, this sentiment of loss, reflection and grief; this delineation between different types of pregnancies is contradictory. Hypocritical. How can women grieve the loss of some pregnancies and not others? All embryos are babies waiting to be born, aren't they?

No. Not to the women inside whom they are conceived. There's a lifetime of difference and a chasm of despair between a pregnancy you want and one you don't.

The choice to continue with a pregnancy or terminate it is a deeply individual, complex and contextual one.

It's different for every woman and every pregnancy.

Sweeping generalisations about the reasons women choose to end pregnancies, how they feel when they do so and how they reflect on it afterwards are impossible to make.

The one thing all abortions have in common: every woman who's had one sees it as a sliding doors moment in her life.

What if I'd had a baby, that baby . . . What if I'd become a mother then? Irrevocably changed course? Tethered myself to that man forever? Impacted upon my family, the father, other children, my education, my future children, my career, my health, my financial security, myself?

For every choice you make, whatever life you choose for yourself, there's another one you discard. A termination is never, ever just about a baby, no matter how fervently anti-abortionists try to make it so.

It's also about the life of the mother, who she will and won't be, what she will and won't do, to whom she will and won't be forever shackled.

It's about the lives we don't choose, the lives we don't want, the lives we cannot endure. The babies to whom we can't be mothers.

For many of us who have had abortions, we imagine our lives had we continued with an unwanted pregnancy and we feel a tremendous sense of dodging a bullet.

Lena Dunham began a project to help women learn more about what life was like before abortion was legal.

'Ask your mother about her abortion,' they urged young women.

And young women did.

In having these one-on-one conversations with their mothers, millennials learned more than they could from any opinion piece shared on Facebook or any famous feminist.

It's hard to galvanise people to fight for something when nobody wants to admit having done it.

In many countries, reproductive rights are not a theoretical issue but an urgent and immediate one. Even in first world countries like the US, it's not until a woman needs an abortion that she discovers how difficult it can be to access this basic health procedure.

Unless you are wealthy or live in a big city, abortion services are slipping ever further from the grasp of desperate women who just want control over their own bodies and their own lives, which is surely a basic human right. As Germaine Greer writes in *The Whole Woman*: 'To become a mother without wanting it is to live like a slave, or domestic animal.'

The ask-your-mother approach opens up a conversation at the most grassroots level. Talking across generations helps younger women see how common abortion has always been, personalises a procedure that's deliberately demonised and 'othered' by zealots who want to ban it, and gently educates millennials about what can happen when women's reproductive rights are restricted or removed.

Ask your mother. Ask your aunts. Ask your grandmothers and your godmothers. Ask any older woman in your life. In a quiet, appropriate moment, ask if she's ever had to end a pregnancy. Or, if a less direct approach is required, ask how many times she's been pregnant.

This idea of asking older women about their abortions resonates more strongly with me than the #shoutyourabortion movement, which encourages women to be loud and proud about their terminations on social media.

If you want to shout your abortion, go ahead. I support your choice. I don't wish to shout mine, but after 25 years I decided I should write about it because how can we combat the stigma surrounding abortion if we choose never to share our experiences of such a common procedure? By talking about our pregnancy mistakes – just like our career mistakes and our relationship mistakes and all the other missteps we make as humans – we give the gift of reassurance and normalise it for other women who have experienced or will experience an unwanted pregnancy in the course of their lives. There are millions of us. There will be millions more. Accidentals happen and no amount of moralising or abuse will change that. You know what will? Sex education and access to cheap, reliable birth control. How helpful that anti-abortionists also usually oppose all the ways in which unwanted pregnancy can be avoided in the first place.

There is a spectrum of emotions and circumstances on which every abortion sits. Just because I don't want to shout it and turn it into a hashtag doesn't mean I've spent the 25 years since my termination consumed with regret or sorrow, guilt or shame. None of the above, actually. There is no one way to feel after an abortion, no right way. You may feel 10 different ways in an hour.

As I entered my forties, I noticed a loosening of the bonds of shame, stigma and guilt around sharing abortion stories. We've made peace with our choices; it's the wisdom gleaned from distance and from seeing how our lives turned out. If we have children after a termination, we think about the pregnancies we lost and the pregnancies we ended and we are quietly thankful to those souls for making room in our lives for the children we hold in our arms and hearts today.

Perhaps there are women who look back and say they regret their decision. I'm sure there are, although I've not met them. Sadness is not the same as regret.

Gloria Steinem dedicated her book *My Life on the Road* to a doctor who risked his licence to refer her for an abortion in 1957. When I met Gloria, I had to ask if she felt the weight of those sliding doors.

'Oh yes, absolutely,' she exclaimed in her caramel voice. 'I had left the States partly because I was engaged and trying to get unengaged . . . and I was in London . . . working as a waitress, waiting on my visa to India. I was pregnant and I kept hoping that I was not. And I did all the dumb things you're not supposed to do like going horseback riding and considering throwing myself down the stairs. And I just happened to be at a party where there was a dreadful American theatre producer who was complaining about having to get an abortion for someone in his cast . . . and it was the first time I knew that was even dimly possible . . . so I found his name in the telephone directory . . . and went to see him. And he was a lovely old man . . . he signed for the abortion which was the great risk; it was actually a woman physician who did the abortion but it was he who was taking the greater risk.'

Just a few minutes earlier, she'd slipped silently into the interview room at her hotel, wearing a wine-coloured turtleneck, black pants and boots and a leather jacket.[17]

It can be disconcerting to meet icons, especially if they're yours. When the spectre of someone's influence on society looms impressively over multiple generations, how can they be anything other than a little lacklustre in person?

Oh, but Gloria was glorious. A dame. A broad. A kick-arse woman even (and especially) at 82. All angular cheekbones and golden skin and gentle dark brown eyes full of curiosity and lived wisdom. Great hair. If I had to choose one word to describe her, it would be elegant. And magnetic. Sexy. Gentle. Glides when she walks.

As iconic as Gloria Steinem is to my generation of feminists, to my mother, she is a hero. Her influence on my mother's life is both specific and manifest. She'd been thrilled to accept my invitation to come with me to meet Gloria. On one condition.

'I don't have to be part of the interview or anything,' she'd asked anxiously. 'I can just sit in the corner, can't I? *Can't I?*'

'Of course you can just sit there,' I reassured her. 'Just come and bask in the glow of Gloria. Meet your hero.'

---

17 As we warmly shook hands, I asked, half joking but also half serious, if I could curtsey. She laughed self-deprecatingly in a way that spoke to humility while also being very used to women genuflecting in her presence.

So she did. And it was more emotional than either of us expected.

When I asked Gloria what the most important thing she took away from her abortion was, my mother was sitting in the corner of the room and I sensed her energy heighten as Gloria spoke.

'I think we ought to give birth to ourselves before we give birth to someone else,' Gloria said. 'And at a minimum we have a right to decide what we do with our own bodies. And besides that, children have a right to be born, loved and wanted. And it's connected to everything. Forcing women to have children they don't want is a major root cause of global warming. Having children against their choice and too early is a major cause of death amongst teenage girls.'

An hour later, Gloria slipped elegantly from the room like smoke and Mum and I stumbled blinking outside the hotel and into the sunshine. As we walked to my car, she confided how moved she'd been when Gloria spoke about unexpected pregnancies and sliding doors moments. There had been no Dr Sharpe for my mum in Australia, where abortion was also illegal when she was a pregnant teenager around the same time as Gloria.

Mum had given birth to my brother, been forced to marry his father and her life had swerved in an unexpected direction.

Just like Gloria, though, she looks back on her sliding doors moment, feels its enormous weight and just like Gloria, she has no regrets.

In many ways, both women were defined by unplanned pregnancies early in life and branded as feminists in the fire of that experience. Both women were radicalised by their pregnancies and both went on to fight for the right of every woman to control her reproductive system and her life. I have marched through the street for abortion rights beside my mother.

It's been a long fight. It continues.

The poignancy of their shared circumstance was deeply moving to me in that moment as I thought about the generations of women before me, all of whom had choices made for them. And choices taken away.

Later that night, at Sydney Town Hall, flanked by my mother, my daughter and thousands of other women, I listened to Gloria Steinem share more of her wisdom with a rapt audience.

My daughter was 10 at the time and it felt like an important feminist moment for the three of us as we sat together grasping hands and squeezing them every so often.

Later, in the car on the way home, I asked my daughter what she thought of the evening.

Her eyes were bright even though it was late. I'd been so proud to have her by my side, absorbing the energy, the stories and the shared courage of her elders.

'I really loved it although I didn't understand what was so funny a lot of the time when people laughed.'

'Yeah. There were some jokes that were hard to understand for a kid.'

'Totally. And some words I didn't understand, like, what's an abortion?'

I knew this question would come at some stage and tonight I felt ready for it. I'd spent the day thinking and talking about abortion with Gloria Steinem and my mother. I was as prepared as I'd ever be.

'An abortion is when a woman gets pregnant except she doesn't want to be so in those first few weeks she has a procedure or takes some medicine to remove the baby – well, it's not actually a baby, it's just a few cells and it's called an embryo.'

'Oh, that's sad.'

'The embryo is really tiny. Sometimes it is sad, but the alternative is for the woman to have a baby she doesn't want or can't take care of and that's sadder.'

'Yeah.'

Pause. I'm bracing myself for the next question.

I'm waiting for my daughter to ask me if I've ever had an abortion.

In an instant, I decide I'm going to tell her the truth.

She looks up at me. I breathe in. 'I'm hungry,' she says. 'Can I have toast when we get home?'

I laugh. 'Sure you can.'

The moment is gone. And with a flicker of surprise, I realise I'm disappointed.

A FUTURE CONVERSATION WITH MY DAUGHTER ABOUT MY ABORTION

SO. YEARS BEFORE I met your dad, I was dating this guy. We hadn't been together long but I already suspected he was a bit of a jerk. Later, I'd discover he was a massive one. I'm pretty sure he cheated on me. He lied all the time. There were lots of red flags I missed. And lots I ignored. I used to cry often and feel terrible about myself. Remind me to tell you more about those red flags another time because they're important. True love, real love, shouldn't be overly dramatic and it should never make you miserable for long periods.

Anyway, a few months into our relationship, I got pregnant by accident because sometimes that happens no matter how careful you are with contraception. I was really young and I'd just started my career and I knew this was not a guy I wanted to have kids with. He wasn't responsible. He was a liar. He was addicted to drugs.

Here's the kind of thing he did: on the way to the abortion clinic, we had to stop at the ATM. It took two of us to get pregnant so it was only fair we pay half each, right? He pretended his ATM card was broken but he was totally lying. He apologised. Promised to pay me back. Then when we were in the clinic waiting room, he put his head on my shoulder and started crying. Him! He didn't want to have a baby but he still made it all about him when I was the one who needed the support. That's the kind of guy he was.

Oh, and he never paid me back.

See why I didn't want to have his baby? Because when you have a child together, even if you split up, you'll always be co-parents. Stuck in each other's lives until forever.

The best part about breaking up with someone is that you never have to speak to them again. If you have kids, you don't have that luxury.

Besides that though, I knew I just wasn't ready to be a mum. Not every pregnancy is planned of course and not every unplanned pregnancy is a bad thing. Your two brothers were surprises but with each of them, I knew straight away that I wanted to be pregnant. Just like the time I had an abortion, I knew I didn't.

Was it an easy decision to end the pregnancy? Yes and no, but mostly yes because there were so many reasons not to have a baby at that time, with that person, in that way. Remember when we went to see Gloria Steinem? She had an abortion at about the same age as I was – even though it was dangerous and illegal back in the 60s – and she said that she needed to give birth to herself before she could think about giving birth to anyone else.

She meant that having a baby changes you in every possible way. In a million wonderful ways but also some really challenging ones and you can never go back to how you were before. It's important to have a life of your own and know who you are before you become someone's mum.

One of the hardest parts about deciding to have an abortion is that even in the early stages of pregnancy, your hormones are all over the place and you can often feel changes in your body. It can be hard to make one of the most important decisions of your life when you're feeling emotional, which is why it's so crucial to get advice and support from people you trust. If you ever get pregnant by accident, make sure you tell me straight away so I can help you work out what to do, okay? I promise I won't be angry. But that's a long way in the future and hopefully it won't happen. But if it does, tell me, okay? Okay. We'll work it out together. Promise? Okay. Yeah? Remember.

So after I found out I was pregnant, I flirted a tiny bit with the idea of having the baby but never seriously, more just as a way to avoid having an abortion because I was scared about that. I knew in my heart it was a bad idea to have a baby but when faced with a big decision, you need to let yourself think something all the way through with every single one of its consequences so you can find the answer you need.

My answer was that I had to have an abortion. I told my parents and they were very supportive. Relieved actually, that I wasn't going to have a baby at such a young age with someone I barely knew. My mum offered to come with me but I thought it might be awkward if my boyfriend was there too and I just wanted to get it done.

I was nervous though. I didn't know what the procedure would be like and I felt sad because I knew I wanted to have kids one day, just not then. The physical thought of it was upsetting but then I spoke to the doctor at the clinic and she reassured me that it was very early – just a few weeks – and it wasn't a baby or anything even like a baby. It was just a few tiny cells clumped together. I'll be honest with you: there's nothing fun or easy about having an abortion but it didn't hurt and it wasn't traumatic. Not for me. The whole thing took just a few minutes and they gave me a needle so I wasn't awake during it and I can't remember anything about it. When it was done, after having a cup of tea and a biscuit, I went straight home.

The procedure I had was called a surgical abortion but there's another way to do it now by taking some pills prescribed by a doctor – not a GP but a special doctor at an abortion clinic – that cause the embryo to come out of your body like a heavy period. It looks nothing like a baby because it's not a baby. It's an embryo. It happens at home and no surgery is involved.

Anyway, my mum came over with cake afterwards and we drank tea and had hugs and I cried a little bit but mostly with relief that it was over.

I wish I hadn't had to have the abortion but that's different to regretting it, which I never, ever did. Not at the time, not imme-diately afterwards and not now, looking back. Never. Having an abortion did not define my life. Not having one would have.

If I hadn't ended that pregnancy, I wouldn't have the children or the life I have today. I wouldn't have you. And that's unthink-able to me. There are many, many countries like Ireland and Brazil and parts of America where abortion is illegal and this is a terrible, terrible thing. It means women will either take grave risks by trying to end a pregnancy themselves in distressing, hazardous ways or they'll be forced to get backyard abortions – which means unsafe operations done by people who aren't medical professionals and who have to perform them in dangerous, unhygienic places – or have babies they don't want or can't take care of. This is dreadful for the women and horrendous for the babies they are forced to have who will often be neglected or abused by parents.

There are many men (I know, right?) who want to change laws, or uphold current ones, that stop women from controlling our own bodies. These same men are against contraception too so basically, they want women to be baby machines and spend our lives at home being pregnant, and taking care of all children we're forced to have. That's the endgame when female choices are taken away.

This is why your grandmother and I have protested in the streets when there have been any moves here in Australia to restrict women's access to abortion.

Here's what you need to know: it's always better to avoid becoming pregnant in the first place if you don't want to have a baby. That's Plan A. Contraception is crucial. Protect yourself. And if something goes wrong with your contraception you can get a pill from the chemist the next day that will stop you becoming pregnant. Because as a woman and a feminist, I believe women must always be in charge of our own bodies, including who grows inside it and when. If we don't have the right to decide that, it's impossible to have control of anything else in our lives.

THAT TIME MY MARRIAGE ENDED

'WHY DID YOU and Dad split up?' my son asked me when he was seven. We'd been talking about his friend whose parents are divorced. Against my natural impulse to speak first and reflect later, I paused briefly to gather my thoughts.

I usually enjoy the mental challenge of answering hard questions under pressure. Like the ones my children ask when I'm driving where I must instantly wrestle my face into a neutral expression instead of a surprised emoji one while trying not to veer into oncoming traffic. I always imagine the moment being re-enacted in their future therapist's office as she gets that aha glint in her eye which means she's identified the root source of some serious life crisis.

'Ahh, finally! This explains your meth addiction and your attempts to join ISIS. This right here. When your mother explained divorce/ homosexuality/how lesbians make babies/depression/Caitlyn Jenner/ God/plastic surgery/death/sex/diets/feminism/rape/eating disorders/ Hitler/racism/cancer/veal/September 11/misogyny/pornography/war/ gravity/Donald Trump/refugees/sexual harassment/Kim Kardashian to you as a kid, it changed the course of your life and led you down this

terrible path. It's going to take A LOT of work to undo all that damage. I'm not sure my decades of psychological training and my two PhDs are up to it but I'm willing to give it a red-hot go. Get comfy on that couch, we're going to be here for several years.'

Under the weight of this imagined dystopian future, I invariably flub my lines and spend the rest of my life wanting to go back for a redo.

I'm a writer and an editor. Rewriting words and massaging copy is what I do. So it's a source of ongoing frustration that I can't do this with conversations and it's a big part of why texting is my preferred method of communication.

It's also why I try to fight the impulse to blunder into big answers whenever I stumble into a Teaching Moment. Get it wrong and your kid will end up in a gutter with a crack pipe hanging out of their pants, if they're even wearing pants.

Life ruined.

No pressure.

Deep breath.

It's not a secret in our family that Jason and I separated when Luca was about two years old and didn't get back together until he was almost five. Coco and Remy were born after that but they know we had two houses for a while and that we dated other people. It's part of our history and we've never hidden it.

But none of my kids had ever asked *why* we split up before. This was new. My answer was important. This was something I couldn't undo if I fucked it up. This was a Teaching Moment under klieg lights.

'Well, do you know what foundations are?' I asked my youngest child. He nodded, snuggling in closer.

This better be good.

'Like what you have to put under a house. You can't build a

house just on sand, can you? You need solid foundations made of concrete so that when the wind blows, the house doesn't fall down.'

Another nod, more tentative.

I pushed on, brightly.

'Well! Lots of things in life, like your career and marriage – and all relationships really, even friendships – are like houses. You need to lay down strong foundations before you build something on top otherwise they can fall over just like a house in a strong wind. Dad and I didn't lay down the foundations very well when we first got together. We built our relationship too quickly. So then when the wind blew, everything fell down and we decided to separate.'

I silently congratulated myself for my simple yet illuminating analogy to help explain a complicated concept to an impressionable child. I'm good at analogies. They're my thing.

He made sure I was finished talking, that there was nothing more to come.

'That's the cheesiest thing ever,' he sighed, rolling his eyes.

We both burst out laughing.

And this is the problem. Right there. When I try to tell you how important it is to have foundations – in your job, in friendships and especially in relationships – you will roll your eyes too.

You're probably doing it already. You may have even decided to skip the rest of this chapter due to cheese, in which case you won't be reading this and *don't come crying to me when your house falls down.*

I know foundations are cheesy. They are neither sexy nor exciting. They sound boring and like too much hard work and hard work is boring and I don't want to.

But my God they're crucial.

There is nothing in our instantly gratifying culture that teaches us to invest time in building foundations, let alone revere them.

If fast is good, instant is better. Love at first sight; overnight success; instant fame; instant messaging; apps for food delivery and sex; everything immediately on demand . . . it's all about short cuts to the finish line. Better still, finding a way to win without even having to go to the effort of running the race. Can't I just text the race while I lie in bed and flick through Instagram?

And I get it, because you've never met anyone who loves a fast track and a short cut more than me. At our wedding, my father gave a speech that described my relationship with Jason as a case of, 'Fire, aim, ready.'

This has always been my approach to life.

Why get bogged down in the boring details, the time-consuming research, the dull due diligence of *anything* when you can just jump in and deal with the fallout later?

Slow and steady is anathema to me.

And yet . . .

Fast never works. Oh, it may feel like it does at first. It's certainly intoxicating, all that adrenaline. It can be appealing on many levels. But fast up, fast down. Fast on, fast off. Remember that.

Think about all those times you've instantly clicked with someone. It could be a romantic click; it could be a friendship click. The person is GREAT, you think. This person GETS ME. I am at my BEST SELF when I'm with them. I want to text them ALL THE TIME. I want to be with them AT EVERY MOMENT. We should be BEST FRIENDS. Or we should HAVE SEX RIGHT AWAY MAYBE TONIGHT.

Nothing wrong with this. But it will rarely last. The headier and more intense those first days and weeks and even months (never years), the more difficult it can be to transition to that next stage of deeper, less adrenalised intimacy.

When the initial buzz wears off (it must), when you stop having sex multiple times a day (because you have a UTI and chafing) or stop WhatsApp-ing constantly – and that has to happen if you're going to function in the world – you want to be left with something more substantial and solid where the adrenaline used to be.

Or, maybe that never happens. Maybe you stay in that can't-get-enough-of-you phase, both of you at the same level (again, rare) and everything's great and you're rollicking along but uh-oh, some bad shit happens. Maybe it's something involving the two of you or maybe it's something external. If it's a relationship, maybe you can't get pregnant. Or get unexpectedly pregnant. Maybe it's a miscarriage. Or an illness. Or one of you loses your job. Maybe you buy a house together and there's sudden financial pressure. Maybe you discover – or develop – an addiction.

If it's a fast friendship, maybe one of you starts a new relationship. Or one of you ends one. Maybe you have a fight about something seemingly dumb like putting an unflattering shot on Instagram or cancelling a dinner and it escalates. Maybe one of you moves interstate or reveals she 'doesn't believe' in vaccination.

When the wind blows – and it will because life is inherently windy – will your house fall down?

If it's not built on solid foundations, yes, it probably will.

*

I married a man who shared a name with my first love, who was a dog.

I'm not being euphemistic here. He was an actual dog called Jason and I loved him deeply.

Decades later, Jason the man would become my husband. At our wedding, my mother handed around this photo of me with Jason the dog, recounting how as soon as I told her the name of this new guy I was dating, she knew

Me (5) and Jason (6)

he had a significant advantage over anyone I'd dated before. His name gifted him a short cut to my heart.

I don't believe in love at first sight but when I first saw Jason, I had a feeling unlike any other I'd experienced. It was like a feeling of coming home, of already knowing him on some deep level.

Things moved fast. We went to see a movie straight after the BBQ and by the following weekend we were essentially living together. Inseparable. Until we separated, but that devastating time was still some years away. We bought a house within months. I became a magazine editor and I was pregnant by the time we celebrated our one-year anniversary.

We renovated.

And the milestones kept coming.

Right before my 26th birthday, we had our first child, a boy we named Luca.

Our lives were bright and brilliant until he fell suddenly and dramatically ill when Luca was just four months old.

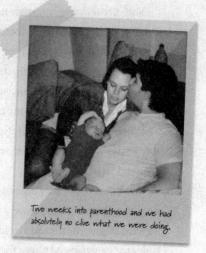

Two weeks into parenthood and we had absolutely no clue what we were doing.

Cue: wind.

Jason couldn't work, couldn't sleep, couldn't concentrate. Could barely function. An eventual diagnosis of chronic fatigue syndrome was a relief in some ways, redundant in others because there was no treatment. We couldn't have friends or family visit because as part of his illness, Jason found all sensory stimulation to be intolerable, even soft music and conversation. Watching TV or reading was impossible because his attention span was obliterated. He didn't have the strength to carry our new baby or even look after him for any longer than an hour. Some days he couldn't climb the stairs to our bedroom.

The wind blew and our house shook.

With his tiny reserve of energy, Jason searched hard for a cure and tried every conventional and alternative therapy. Imagine looking for something that specific pre-Internet. Without Google, searching for a cure, a treatment or even basic information meant an exhausting and exhaustive stream of phone calls and referrals and word-of-mouth-chases down dead ends. Month after frustrating month, Jason remained terribly sick and we became increasingly isolated from our friends and family. And each other.

This went on for almost two years.

The breakthrough came when his mother – bless her – somehow tracked down a doctor in South Africa, Cecile Jadin, who had discovered that in some patients, CFS is triggered by a blood parasite called Rickettsia which can be killed quickly and effectively with a simple, strong, sustained course of antibiotics. Jason called her, sent over a blood sample and began treatment almost immediately. Within weeks he was noticeably better and a couple of months after starting treatment he returned to work.

Our house was badly shaken but still standing. At my urging, we got engaged. I desperately needed to resume the pace of forward momentum stalled by his illness for years. Jason, feeling guilty for capsizing our lives for so long, resisted his inclination to say slow down.

Then just as the wind died down, I was pregnant again. Unexpectedly. Again.

Delightedly, I leaned further into the momentum I'd created. Brought our wedding forward. Organised the wedding. Went on a pre-emptive honeymoon with Jason before I became too pregnant to travel. Got married. And then a few days afterwards, during a routine ultrasound, with my brand new husband by my side, we learned our baby had died inside me at five months.

Cue: tornado.

This time, our house did blow down, almost in

For many years I couldn't look at this photo because I was heavily pregnant when it was taken.

slow motion. Without the foundations most couples lay in those first few uncomplicated months and years of calm weather, our relationship collapsed around our ears.

We separated eight months after we got married. Our son was about to turn three. It was the worst of times.

The few years that followed, though painful and immensely challenging, were also a revelation.

Within weeks of separating, I called the therapist I'd seen for an emergency band-aid session seven months earlier when I'd lost our baby and 12 months before that when Jason's chronic fatigue syndrome was entering its second year and impacting our relationship.

I made an appointment to see her reluctantly, in the same way you arrange to have a pap smear or a mammogram. The reasons for our split were complex, as relationship breakdowns always are, and in many ways a mystery to us both but I knew a key component had been my innate need to sprint through my life. Always pushing towards the next stage, the next baby, the next house, the next milestone, the next announcement.

This sprint and the insatiable hunger that drove it had put incredible pressure on us as a couple. This stubborn refusal of mine to move more slowly and lay solid foundations had helped bring us undone. Because why would you do that? What's fun about foundations? Fast is exciting. Fast is sexy.

Fast is a motherfucking disaster. Whether it's drinking, losing weight or moving in together . . . fast is bad news. Even fast sex is problematic if you are prone to urinary tract infections.[18]

---

18 As well as using lubricant during sex and being sure to wipe front to back when you go to the toilet, the other thing to remember if you're prone to UTIs is to empty your bladder after sex. This is the single best piece of health advice I've ever been given. Get up and go to the loo. You won't regret it.

Everything good in life, everything solid and true and secure requires foundations, no matter how tedious going slow may feel.

Since always, I've been in mad rush. My mind works fast but harnessed properly, that can be a positive thing. The problems arrive when your *life* runs fast. When you make big decisions too quickly for reasons more to do with adrenaline hits and the thrill of the new than because they're sound decisions.

For the next two years after my marriage collapsed, I had a standing 'physiotherapy' appointment in the diary my PA could see and every Wednesday at lunchtime, I trudged across town to my therapist's couch where we talked for an hour.

Jason went to therapy too. That's an important part of this story even though it belongs to him. We went to the same therapist, in fact, although never together. When he'd been sick with CFS, we'd seen her as a couple a few times and he had a good rapport with her so we were all happy with the arrangement.

Both Jason and I had therapy to sort our shit out for ourselves not each other. We each had foundations of our own to build before a tentative reconciliation could even be contemplated, and during the first two years of our separation, it just wasn't.

Like me, Jason was emotionally aware enough to understand he had things he needed to process about our split and work he wanted to do on himself.

Today we are both big therapy advocates. He has encouraged many of his friends and colleagues to seek professional support during difficult times and it's one of the things I respect most about him, his willingness to challenge many of the stultifying conventions around masculinity somehow being entwined with not seeking help.

For anyone, it's not a sign of strength but of arrogance and naivety to think you have all the answers to anything, especially your own problems. During the years of our estrangement, sometimes we'd have angry phone conversations after one of us had been to therapy and needed to debrief. We came to learn the timing of each other's appointments and braced ourselves for those calls. Or screened them. There were extended periods where we stopped communicating altogether except about childcare arrangements because one of us felt too raw or pissed off. Dating other people threw up a whole new layer of complexity and pain.

Reconciliation was not why we were seeing a therapist.

There was too much work to do on ourselves before contemplating a serious relationship with anyone. Let alone each other.

For the next two years we worked hard to co-parent a son who had no memory of Mummy and Daddy ever living together. Luca thrived during this time. He had the undivided attention of both his parents, staying five days a week with me and two with Jason as well as extra visits. Our houses were only a suburb apart. Luca was happy and secure in our love along with the occasional presence of new partners that popped into our lives.

Early on in our separation we each consulted lawyers and the woman I saw gave me a piece of advice I took to heart: 'Fight about money and assets if you must but agree as much as you can about kids,' she told me. 'I see too many couples use their children to hurt one another and you don't want that for your kids, trust me, you don't.'

With this in mind, we split our assets amicably and organised Luca's custody without lawyers or mediation. While we were both always mindful to put his needs first, I can see how children can become collateral damage. When parents split, you have to decide – and keep deciding – to prioritise your kids' physical and emotional wellbeing above your own personal pain. It's not easy.

Things were often prickly between us and occasionally hostile but we kept a lid on it for the sake of our son. Mostly we were civil to one another and always in front of him. I'm proud of the job we did, shielding him from the worst of it.

Those two years of therapy became about building my own foundations. I learned some invaluable things about myself which have changed the way I live my life and interact with those closest to me, still to this day. With this new understanding, I gradually became more confident that next time the wind blew, I wouldn't fall down.

Not entirely, anyway.

Around my 30th birthday, several years after our split and with our divorce paperwork filled out but curiously, not yet filed by either of us, slowly, carefully, Jason and I began hanging out. At first with Luca and then sometimes just the two of us. Tentatively, after a few months of this, we went on our first date – again. Later, we would have our first kiss – again. And gradually, we began ticking off the milestones of a normal relationship in its early stages.

'I don't know if I'm ready to sleep with him yet,' I confided to my friend Paula, who had introduced us what felt like a lifetime ago. She laughed at me. 'You guys are still married. He's the father of your child. I think that horse has bolted.'

It had. In fact, it had cleared several fences and was currently galloping across the countryside.

And that was the problem. Last time around we'd done everything so fast, ticking off those relationship markers at a frantic, unsustainable pace. We didn't want to make the same mistake again.

Foundations.

In a way, the stakes were far higher this time. We couldn't drag our son through a half-arsed reconciliation only to have our marriage collapse again. We didn't want him to be emotionally damaged due to a rushed repair job.

So we lay down the groundwork of our New Life 2.0 with immense caution. We didn't sleep together for a long time. We deliberately chose to store – rather than discard – the divorce papers we'd each spent hours filling out and they sat benignly in the home office filing cabinet for the next few years to remind us this was not a done deal. We continued to go to therapy, individually and sometimes together.

In the process of repairing and reviving our marriage, we stopped taking each other and our future together for granted. I stopped rushing us forward.

We navigated the rebuilding of our marriage warily and with extreme tenderness, aware of the fragility of it. We shielded it from the wind, carefully protecting it from bad weather and external stresses. We took our time moving back in together. We continued renting for a long time because we knew there were no guarantees and we didn't want to add property ties to the weight of expectation that we could make this work. Slow and steady was our new motto. We were tortoises together, happily ambling along, side by side.

The decision we took longest over was the one to start trying for another baby. This was a giant.

A massive strain on our relationship had always been my insistence on more children.

More! Sooner! Now! Another! Yesterday! I'm not sure if

I was addicted to the big-news excitement of having more kids or whether I just wanted a big family. Both, I think.

Children bring a million different gifts and lessons and joys but they are wildly disruptive. The foundations of your house better be bloody secure before you introduce a new child into the mix.

And never make the mistake of thinking a baby will fix something that's already broken. I've observed the opposite to be true. A baby will amplify every structural weakness in your relationship. Make sure you're solid first.

They say every couple has only three fights – you just keep having slight variations of those same fights again and again. And again. This is certainly true of us. And working together has shone the light of a thousand suns on our differences. I won't pretend it hasn't been excruciating at times. Try sitting in a meeting with your husband and not pulling faces when he does something that pisses you off. That struggle is real.

And here's what I want to tell you about marriage: it's a choice. Not just when you say yes to a proposal or make your vows but every day thereafter. Well, not every day. Many, many days in your marriage just pass uneventfully without consequence. But there will be many times when you must actively make the decision to *stay* married. Times when you meet someone who isn't your spouse and feel the spark of attraction or the flicker of chemistry. Times when things are bleak between the two of you and you wonder if you can even climb back out of the hole. Times when the vicious cycle of your arguments feels like it can never be broken. Times when you can choose to go to counselling or not. Times when you can address the issues contributing to your relationship problems or . . . not. Times when one of you is going through a challenge with your mental or physical health. Sometimes the right choice is not to be together anymore. Just ensure you *are making* the choice. It's a mistake to be a passenger in your relationship.

Like dental work, servicing a car or having good hair, you're never finished fine-tuning and maintaining your relationship. We're all a work in progress. Jason and I still see a therapist occasionally when we need a tune-up, either as a couple or individually. I can't say I've ever gone skipping to a therapy appointment, but I've always walked away feeling like my head is clearer, my load is lighter and I understand myself even better.

Because self-awareness is the foundation of any healthy relationship. Cheesy and true.

THAT TIME I HAD A BREAKDOWN

I'M SITTING IN a psychiatrist's office. This is a first. I've seen numerous health professionals at various points in my life, including counsellors, therapists and psychologists, but I've never seen a psychiatrist. It feels suitably serious and I'm glad to be here.

Dr T seems like a kind man and I'm flooded with relief to be in the care of an expert after weeks of mental and emotional turmoil following a debilitating 11-day panic attack. I need help.

'A nervous breakdown' was how my regular therapist had described it and I was rather pleased when she did because it felt accurately dramatic, like the prickle of satisfaction you feel when you're really sick and you take your temperature and it's 40°C.

I'd eventually emerged from the rubble of my prolonged anxiety attack and stumbled back into my life, bleeding and in shock. I was no longer in panic's grip. But I was shaky and exhausted and terrified it would return.

So my therapist had referred me to a psychiatrist who specialised in anxiety disorders. She phoned me with the details. 'Now Mia, I can organise for you to go in via the back entrance,' she suggested. My appointment was at a private clinic where I was due to be assessed by Dr T who saw outpatients there too.

I didn't understand what she meant.

'Um, no, it's fine, I'm cool just going in the front . . . you know . . . um, why?'

'Well, the clinic specialises in eating disorders and most of the patients there are young women. Also lots of women are there as visitors. You will probably get recognised.'

I considered this for a moment before laughing. 'Yeah, me and Kylie Minogue.'

My therapist is extremely discreet, a characteristic with which I'm wildly unfamiliar. When I began seeing her a few years earlier, she'd said to me in our first session, 'So just to cover this off, if we ever bump into each other in the street and we're not alone, I will just say that I know you through work or . . . is there another story you'd prefer?'

'Oh no, it's fine,' I exclaimed, batting away her concern. 'I'll just say you're my therapist!'

After the hell I'd just experienced, it seemed I might need a greater level of assistance than just therapy. My therapist suspected – and I agreed – it might be time to try medication which is something I needed a psychiatrist (or GP) to prescribe.

*

Several weeks earlier, on Christmas Eve, I'd woken up, climbed out of bed and stretched a little. As I did, I noticed a tiny twinge on my lower left side and before I'd even focused my eyes, my brain was in fight-or-flight mode. Code Red. I had ovarian cancer.

This may seem like a bizarre leap to make without any evidence and it was. But the knowledge of my cancer diagnosis and impending death was as indisputably factual to me as my name or gravity.

I couldn't confide in anyone that I was dying. It was too gut-wrenchingly tragic. Dead before I was 40. My children, motherless. My husband, a widow. He would marry again, obviously, but my children. Oh God. It all felt so indescribably real in my head. I attended my own funeral. I watched my children and my husband grieve. I saw them grow up without me and I was crushed by the sorrow and the burden I'd left them with.

For 11 days, I felt physically like I was being chased around my house by a crazed maniac wielding a knife. That's how my adrenal system interpreted a panic attack, even though I was actually sitting with a friend on the beach watching my children build sandcastles, or queueing up at the supermarket to buy ice-cream, or sitting quietly on the couch sipping yet another cup of tea.

The feeling inside me was indescribable terror of imminent death. Of having to tell my children that I was going to die.

I lived with that feeling non-stop for 11 days while on our annual family holiday. Walking through my life like the ghost I would soon become when I succumbed to my terminal illness. I was in full-blown panic, the likes of which I had never experienced for such an interminable period of time.

Ironically, a few days into my panic attack, we had an attempted break-in while we slept. Nothing was taken. The dog barked and scared off the intruders and the next day the police came to take statements and brush for fingerprints as I took the kids to the beach so they wouldn't feel scared.

This situation would have triggered immense anxiety in most people but it didn't make me any worse than I already was. It barely touched the sides.

In fact, if anything, it was a welcome distraction. It provided a modicum of respite because my mind was temporarily occupied with a practical, knowable source of danger. Not like the one that sat inside my body like a toxic squatter and tortured my mind with its inescapable endgame.

Along with the high-intensity diversion of robbers, there were three other things which gave me some small relief during this hellish time:

1. *Alcohol*
2. *Sleep*
3. *Physical activity*

It was the holiday season so all three were readily available to me and I could fleetingly appreciate their benefits.

I've never been a big drinker or even a medium one. My nickname during high school was 'Cadbury' because I couldn't stomach more than a glass and a half. Today, I've stretched that to two glasses. It's taken me 30 years.

But during my breakdown, alcohol was something I soon began to crave earlier and earlier each day, until I began wondering if I could have a glass of wine at 10 am; anything to calm me.

I saw how easy it would be to self-medicate with alcohol and made one of the few sane decisions of that period: don't replace one problem with another. Drinking would not commence before 5 pm, I decided, even though I was dying.

Sleep was a surprising escape, although not to me. I've always been an elite-level sleeper. Anywhere at any time. Anxiety and panic attacks are often characterised by severe insomnia which can tip you even further into the abyss. My ability to sleep every night despite crippling anxiety baffled every health professional I told.

In truth I think the industrial quantities of adrenaline pumping through my system during every waking moment simply depleted me to the point where I passed out by the end of the day. I was frozen in fight-or-flight mode even though there was nothing real to fight or flee. Try telling that to my adrenal gland, which was behaving as if I was about to go over the wall at Gallipoli.

The respite I got from physical activity was less of a surprise because inadvertently, I have used exercise all my life to treat my anxiety. Or maybe it wasn't inadvertent. Exercising daily is something I've done for decades and I always assumed it was connected to body image and my history of having an eating disorder. Only recently have I learned that there's scientific proof that physical activity helps alleviate some of the symptoms of anxiety and depression.

During the 11 days of my holiday breakdown, I became Action Barbie. I went horse riding. I took surfing lessons. I went on long power walks and jogs through the hills and along the beach. I did yoga. And I struggled to eat. My stomach was churning, my appetite gone. I lost weight but not on purpose. I looked thin, drawn and strained, surely more proof I was seriously ill.

But for some welcome moments when I exercised, my elevated heart rate and the endorphin release that followed granted me brief absolution from the fear.

*

My thinking during this period was truly magical and not in a good way.

I would see a homeless man and envy him. *You are so lucky, homeless guy*, I'd marvel. *You don't have ovarian cancer. You have your whole life ahead of you.*

I had coffee with a girlfriend who was holidaying with her family nearby and imagined what she would say at my funeral, what she would wear. Would everyone wear black? That seemed a little boring and not characteristic of my OTT style but there's something deeply appropriate about your clothes reflecting the subdued state of your grieving heart. Black it would be.

I considered seeking medical help. If I'd been at home, I would probably have checked into some kind of mental hospital. I felt that unwell and unmoored.

But since I was in Byron Bay, the unvaccinated, un-fluoridated hometown of hippies and music festivals, I felt certain that any doctor would simply think I'd taken too many party drugs. I was paranoid.

I toyed with the idea of going to the local health-food store where they had a naturopath in residence who might be able to prescribe me some herbal remedy to calm me down, but again, I felt I wouldn't be able to persuade her I wasn't someone who'd had too much Molly, just a mother of three in her late thirties who was either dying or had seriously lost her shit and possibly, probably, both.

And still, nobody knew. I suffered in silence, going through the holiday motions with family and friends and sunshine and dolphins. Besides, I hid the extent of my problem pretty well.

My lowest point came around day eight: I was going for a walk one morning and contemplating the utter desperation of not being able to escape from my own terrified mind. As I

A photo taken during the depths of my breakdown.

Here's a selfie I took on the beach one day. Don't I look happy? An image doesn't always tell a thousand words. Sometimes it tells a thousand lies.

felt myself sliding into an unfamiliar state I recognised as depression, I finally understood how anxiety and depression can be conjoined. This was actually a nightmare and I couldn't wake up.

The only escape, I mused, would be suicide. Immediately, I giggled out loud.

Even in my tortured state, I recognised the absurdity of being so scared of death that you considered killing yourself.

I wasn't really considering it. I'd have to battle through. I knew that. Even though I had no idea what 'through' looked like. I was quite literally in survival mode, staying alive minute by minute and increasingly doubting my own sanity.

My husband knew something was up. I had become reclusive, despondent and withdrawn. I looked frail and anxious and I couldn't connect with him, our friends or my kids. I couldn't even relate to the dog. There was an invisible barrier between me and the world and I was trapped behind glass.

Jason had lived with me for almost 20 years and he'd witnessed my ups and downs so he wasn't unduly alarmed. Unlike me. I was alarmed.

*

So what does anxiety feel like?

Think about the butterflies you get in your stomach when you're nervously excited about something. Maybe giving a speech at a friend's wedding. Maybe the first day at a new job. Maybe thinking about giving birth during the final weeks of your pregnancy and meeting your baby.

Now give those butterflies the Ebola virus and attach machetes to their wings. How do you feel now?

Anxiety manifests in different ways for different people, but there are some common themes. Dread and fear are two of them. Sometimes it's dread of a particular thing like flying or exams or tunnels or spiders or cancer. Often, though, anxiety just attaches itself to those things and you start to mistakenly believe they are the cause.

At its root, anxiety is fear and whether it's an insect, a flight or a disease you don't have, some trip-wire in your brain believes you are under imminent threat.

Generalised anxiety disorder is different from panic attacks. It's more like a low-level hum that runs in the background of your life like a knot of dread sitting heavily in your stomach or chest. A sense of unease that you often can't attribute to anything in particular. I've lived with this on and off throughout my life.

Anxiety is not stress. Stress, I'm unruffled by. Going on live TV doesn't give me anxiety nor does giving a speech to 1000 people or doing a live radio interview or being under intense pressure at work. I get nervous, I get stressed and I get over-whelmed but I don't get anxiety. Lena Dunham, another anxiety sufferer, describes this paradox, in her book, *Not That Kind of Girl*: 'At the moments it should logically strike, I am fit as a fiddle. On a lazy afternoon, I am seized by a cold dread.'

While it often appears random, there can be certain triggers for developing anxiety if you are prone to it.

There's nothing like becoming a parent to confront you with the horror of your own mortality, and that of your child. Many women develop anxiety around flying only after they have a baby. It can be a crippling one to shake.

For others, large stretches of unoccupied time or a sudden disruption to your normal routine can spark a bout of anxiety.

HOW A HEALTH RETREAT PUSHED ME OVER THE EDGE

The basics were the same as every other hardcore health retreat: no sugar, tea, coffee, dairy, wheat, alcohol, media, wifi or fun.

Dedicated retreaters would dispute the fun part. They would say doing tai chi as the sun comes up each morning at 5 am with 60 strangers on a mountain is all sorts of fun. They would insist it's *so much fun* to get out of your comfort zone.

I would tell them to fuck off.

Wait, that's not fair. I was grumpy for the first few days due to sugar, tea and Internet withdrawal but I mainlined Panadol and by day three I had drunk the Kool Aid and was on board with the program. If I didn't quite experience anything I could describe as actual fun, I did have some blissful solitude and met some interesting people. One night after Quinoa and Broccoli Surprise (You're full! Surprise!) I was even invited to have a threesome with a very optimistic couple in their sixties. I politely declined while admiring their lust for life and hoping I would have the same at their age.

None of this made up for the fucking lack of tea or wifi.

People who attend deprivation-heavy health retreats tend to be either very wealthy, very desperate, or both. The wealthy use it as an opportunity for enforced weight loss. The desperate gravitate to retreats during times of crisis: physical, mental, emotional or existential. This makes for some very intense energy among your average group of retreaters. On the first day I noted on the map of the grounds that there was a private little hut away from the rest of the facilities. 'What's that for?' I asked one of the guides. 'Crying, mostly,' she replied.

It also tended to eliminate small talk.

'So what are you here for?' a fellow guest asked me one morning at a different retreat years earlier as we ate our five-grain porridge and sipped our warm water with lemon side by side at the communal tables.

'Oh, my marriage is falling apart,' I replied.

'I'm recovering from an eating disorder,' she said.

Health retreats are notorious for these kinds of conversations. A large majority of the guests are about to embark on a big life change or have had one unwittingly thrust upon them. New jobs, lost jobs, miscarriages, death of a loved one, divorce, eating disorders, disease diagnosis or recovery, breakups, breakdowns . . . it's all going on, all at once.

Everyone there is a little bit fucked up and looking for a reboot.

It's common to come across people weeping quietly in the bush after a group session of aromatherapy tribal dancing. Massage therapists tell you not to be surprised or embarrassed 'if this Ayurvedic chakra facial treatment stirs up a lot of suppressed emotional pain inside of you and releases it'.

Good times.

The theory is that you'll integrate some of these new habits into your regular life when you resume it while continuing to abstain from some of the bad ones.

More quinoa. Less Instagram. More meditation. Less caffeine.

That's what I wanted. A shake-up. A firm, encouraging prod towards change. Like most health retreaters, I was actively seeking to disrupt my own life which, with three kids and a demanding business that had been in the all-consuming start-up mode for several years, was draining my battery and grinding my mind.

I was hungry to recalibrate even if I was less hungry for raw kale and a shot of apple cider vinegar at 5 am.

For someone like me who is prone to extremes and is highly suggestible, however, the all-or-nothing approach of most health retreats (just like restrictive eating programs) is a dangerous one.

It wasn't the retreat's fault, it was mine. I was the one who chose to continue to try and maintain this austere kind of regime even after I returned to my regular life.

I think I tricked myself into believing this was possible because it was right before I went on holidays.

How easy would it be to continue this crunchy, clean life over summer! I would keep denying myself all the things I passionately love! Tea! Sugar! Carbs! Music! Media!

I would drive in silence! I would keep drinking herbal tea! I would continue to eschew all processed foods and only eat organic produce! I would refer to food as produce!

I was insufferable.

Worse than the piety I inflicted on everyone around me, though, was the fact that by trying to maintain a life with dramatically less stimulation than I was used to, away from the frantic timetable of massages and treatments and lectures and walking bush meditations . . . I was in fact laying the ideal conditions for my own nervous breakdown.

Elizabeth Gilbert has said of her mind: 'If it's not making something, it's breaking something.'

She's talking about her creativity and the way her brain, like a small child or yappy dog, needs a positive way to occupy itself or else it can become destructive.

Caitlin Moran has a similar formula for the way she manages anxiety: 'I basically treat myself like a nervy horse: lots of exercise, lots of sleep, lots of interesting work to keep the mind occupied, and generally avoiding being ridden hard by strangers.'

When I was interviewing Elizabeth I told her about Caitlin's quote, she laughed. 'I always say that my fear is a border collie: you know if you don't give it a job it will find a job and you will not love the job that it finds. So I try to make sure that it always has some stick to chase – otherwise it's going to eat my couch.'

Note the common thread for both these brilliant, prolific women: keep busy.

This is not the same as ignoring problems. It's about not giving your anxious mind too many open expanses of time to be idle.

To return briefly to the child analogy, imagine leaving a toddler alone in the lolly aisle of a supermarket. No good will come of that. And so it is with a certain type of person – of which I am one. I learned this when I left my mind alone with nothing to do and it *ripped open every packet of red frogs in the world and gobbled them down until it was so hyped up and over-wrought it just needed to run and run and run and oh my God I can taste the air can you taste it and why can I feel my skin and see my thoughts and I can't stop blinking and I hate everyone and why does nobody love me and I'm terrified because we're ALL GOING TO DIE BUT ESPECIALLY ME AND SOON.*

That.

So when I went from the fifth gear of stimulation I was used to all the way to neutral in one dislocating move, I broke the gearbox.

*

My first step towards emerging from my endless panic attack hell came after about 11 days when I decided I had to tell someone I was losing my mind and was most probably dying. I didn't choose Jason. It seemed like telling him I had cancer would make it even more real than it already felt. This is how crazy my thinking still was.

The person I felt safest to confide in was my friend Wendy. She and I had saved each other from emotionally abusive relationships at different times years earlier and we knew some deep truths about one another. Of my small circle of closest friends, she'd done therapy for an extended period of time and she'd always been open about her battles with depression. I knew she took medication for it. I felt safe telling her about the mess I was in.

By the time I called her, I'd been in a state of extreme panic for a week and a half and I could feel it starting to recede just a little. I was starting to comprehend that possibly I didn't have cancer although I probably did. As my adrenal levels cranked down a notch from Intolerable to Extreme, I began to realise how much I needed help.

If only I'd had the foresight or self-awareness to make that phone call 11 days earlier. Talking to Wendy was like balm. Not only did she listen with love and compassion, she was reassuring. Remarkably, she had a friend who had been through the same thing. For a time, he had become convinced he was dying of prostate cancer and had even admitted himself to hospital several times. She put me in touch with him and he generously gave me an hour on the phone and a name for what I was experiencing: somatism. It's where your mind becomes convinced you have a serious illness and your body helpfully creates symptoms to confirm your fears.

It's all in your head. And then your body. But actually just your head, even though you can feel real feelings in your body. But they're not real. It's a cycle and it's vicious. In your head.

For the first time in days, I felt tentative relief. My terror had a name and I wasn't alone. Maybe, just maybe, I wasn't dying.

This conversation gave me the courage to tell Jason and to call my therapist. Jason's reaction was exactly what I needed: he laughed.

There's an episode of *Seinfeld* where George Costanza goes to the doctor with a minor complaint, fully expecting a 'get-out-of-here'; that's when you are so wildly off base with your fear-based diagnosis that your doctor laughs in your face and says, 'Get out of here.'

On this occasion, George's doctor looks concerned and suggests running some tests. This is the opposite of a get-out-of-here and George spends the rest of the episode freaking the fuck out.

Jason laughing was the get-out-of-here I needed. His laughter was heavy with concern and empathy and I drank it in, dazed.

Clearly, though, I had a serious problem I needed to deal with. While I probably didn't have cancer, I appeared to be nuts.

Which brought me to the mental hospital for my appointment with the psychiatrist.

I told my story and the doctor listened, nodding every so often, his demeanour a mixture of empathy and kindness. I trusted him immediately. Before he even spoke, I felt understood.

When I finished, he said it sounded like I suffered from generalised anxiety disorder and I'd experienced a major episode while on holidays.

I slumped in my chair as I absorbed his diagnosis. Now that the adrenaline had stopped surging, I was utterly, utterly exhausted. I felt like a husk.

'Is this likely to happen again?' I asked worriedly.

It was, he admitted. Having a severe episode makes it highly likely you'll suffer another one; they often come in clusters. And the fear of that becomes, in itself, a source of extreme anxiety. A perfect circle of panic.

I sat up a little straighter, felt my stomach tighten and leaned in as we began to talk about medication.

It was time. I was ready.

He told me about a drug called Lexapro which is actually an antidepressant that's used in the treatment of anxiety. I asked about addiction.

I'd had a terrible experience with Xanax when I had to go to New York for a *Cosmo* conference six months after 9/11 and a doctor had prescribed it to me so I could board a plane despite my paralysing fear of flying. What she didn't warn me about was the rebound anxiety, meaning you feel great when you take a pill but as soon as the effects wear off in a matter of hours, you're hit with the accumulated terror the drug had parked while it worked.

So I was fine during the trip itself – so fine that I gaily spent $300 on lip gloss at LAX during a 25-minute stopover – but soon after we landed safely, my body reacted as though it was still on the plane, hurtling towards the ground at full speed. It didn't wear off for hours.

Lexapro was very different from Xanax, he reassured me. It wasn't addictive although I would have to be very careful when I started taking it or when I came off it if I decided to stop. Any problems you have with the drug are most likely to happen during those times.

We spoke about the dose and he suggested starting with half a pill. Still, I was nervous. 'I don't even drink caffeinated tea,' I told him anxiously. 'And I don't do any drugs, not even sleeping pills. My body is so sensitive, what if I have a bad reaction?'

He looked at me with kind eyes and patted my hand in a way I found immensely comforting.

'I can see you're anxious about the dosage of your anxiety medication.'

We both chuckled.

'Okay, let's make it a quarter to start with. If you can break it up that small.'

I left his office with a script and instructions to try and break the pill into four tiny pieces for the first week.

This proved almost impossible; the pill was small to begin with so I boldly graduated myself to a half by the third day. I had another appointment two weeks later and because I was still feeling very anxious, my doctor upped me to a full pill.

I'm not going to tell you my anxiety was cured overnight. I'm not even going to tell you I woke up one morning and it was gone. But one day it *was* gone, and I didn't even notice it leave. That's how imperceptibly it receded. It ghosted.

It was only in its absence that I came to see how pervasive anxiety has been throughout my life. Its tentacles reach back into my childhood when I would wait with fear knots in my stomach for my parents to come home from work each day, convinced they were dead. When they were home, the knots were still there, my fear transferring onto the idea that they'd get a divorce. I'd come to accept those knots, those toxic butterflies, as just the way life felt to me. Didn't everyone feel like that?

Waking up without inexplicable dread every morning after just a few weeks of medication felt like Christmas. It's hard to explain how the absence of something can feel so exhilarating, but it's like when a hangover or a headache lifts. When a fever breaks. A lack of wretchedness is a gift.

I still had breakthrough anxiety for the first year or so – and sometimes even today. Often it's just before my period and my doctor told me this is common for women. Some people increase their dosage for that week, he told me, but I decided not to. 'If I know it's hormone-related and temporary, I can cope,' I told him and myself. It's the feeling of drowning in it that's crushing.

So now, after being on the same medication for a decade

and understanding my triggers and coping mechanisms better than I ever have, I can push through any breakthrough anxiety, knowing it won't last. Like a sprained ankle or a sore back, I'm aware that it's there, I name it and I get on with my life.

During any period where my anxiety does break through, I take a quick inventory. Am I overtired? Have I been around people too much? Have I been triggered by a news story about cancer or some tragedy? Am I being weird about food? To self-soothe when I'm feeling anxious, I double down on routine but I never cancel work commitments or social arrangements because for me, distraction brings respite. What works for me might not work for another anxiety sufferer, though; everyone has different ways of coping. Some people aren't able to push through because their anxiety is too crippling. Listen to what you need to do to help yourself rather than what you feel like you should do.

Like pregnancy loss, anxiety and depression are clubs you don't ever want to join but once you do, you realise how enormous these clubs are and how many members you already know. There's a lot of support out there hiding in plain sight. And many of us use medication.

So what are the downsides of medication? You want to know. Good question. For the first year or so I had very vivid dreams. Not bad ones, just intense. A lower sex drive is probably the most common downside, and that's common with many anti-depressants. This is an individual consideration, to be sure, but for me, the alternative, Highly Anxious Me, is not someone anyone would want to have sex with. Fact.

*

It was years before I was ready to write about my breakdown, my anxiety diagnosis and my decision to take medication. As a writer, I process things by putting words around them, but when something life-changing happens and throws me so far from myself, I override my impulse to write about it immediately because it's just too raw.

Not that I mind being raw, but with distance comes perspective. It's impossible to have the full picture before the photo is developed. It's like eating a meal when it's still just a bunch of half-prepared ingredients on the counter. The same thing happened when I lost my baby halfway through my pregnancy. Years went by before I could write about it with any sense of coherence.

But with my anxiety there was a different layer. The layer of stigma. As someone in the public eye who attracts detractors, I didn't want to hand anyone the ammunition of my anxiety disorder. I was worried I'd be dismissed as crazy or unstable, unfit to run a business or to speak publicly about anything other than mental health. I was prepared to talk about it but I didn't wish to be defined by it. I have anxiety. But most days these days, I don't.

HOW I MANAGE MY ANXIETY

I think the biggest fear people have about taking medication for mental health problems like anxiety is that it will change their personality or their emotions. I was worried that medication would make me numb; someone who experienced no highs or lows.

That hasn't happened. I still feel joy, sorrow, rage and, yes, anxiety in normal, manageable amounts. I still experience the full emotional spectrum. What's gone is the constant beat of dread in my heart and my stomach. The toxic butterflies for no reason. The all-consuming fear. The spikes of panic, irrational terror and somatism.

But like all anxiety sufferers, there are certain aspects of my lifestyle I need to manage. Medication alone isn't enough.

Here's what I need:

1. **Exercise** – every day. Not negotiable.

2. **Minimal caffeine.** I don't drink coffee, soft drinks or caffeinated tea. I'm highly strung enough.

3. **No drugs.** It's been many years since I've touched non-prescription drugs. Messing with my headspace is a very bad idea.

4. **Routine.** From exercise to my breakfast to drinking a certain type of tea in a very large cup, I'm at my most settled on a goat track and I've learned to take the track with me when I travel (for example: cup and tea bags, staying at places with a treadmill) to minimise anxiety in new places, away from my usual routine.

5. **Time alone.** I have three children, a husband, a business and two dogs. I also have a close-knit group of girlfriends and Jason and I are both close to our families. But I barely socialise beyond that and I actively seek out time by myself to recharge. I sometimes do this by listening to podcasts when I'm at home as a way to be alone while not really being alone (see: parenting). My batteries are drained by being around people I don't know well and talking too much without a break. Conversely, seeing girlfriends at least once a week is like plugging my phone into a charger.

6. **Stuff to do.** I no longer chastise myself for wanting to be immersed in stimulation almost constantly. Podcasts and reading online, mostly. It's soothing for me. Like Elizabeth Gilbert, my mind is like a working dog that needs lots of jobs or else I'll start chewing up shoes and pissing on the rug. Of my mind.

THE HARDEST YEAR OF PARENTING

THE FIRST YEAR of your baby's life is hard.

When they're two it's hard. Also three.

Starting school can be hard.

The tween years.

Puberty.

Nah.

My hardest year as a parent was the one in which my son turned 18 and finished school.

By the time you become a parent and your kid leaves school, you may be surprised to discover that parents are far more involved in end-of-school rituals now. I was. This won't surprise your kids because this generation are used to having their parents involved in every aspect of their lives. You will hear about parents who attend schoolies with their teens and you will laugh publicly about this while secretly making discreet enquiries about booking a nice hotel room on the Gold Coast a block away from where your kid will be staying with 11 friends in a skanky one-bedroom apartment.

This does not make you an outlier. Partly due to the

mainstreaming of Helicopter Parenting, partly because of the collapsing of the boundaries between generations; it's just how everyone parents these days. You mostly enjoy this profound involvement in your kids' lives. It's all you know. And as your kid heads into those later teenage years, you realise their values are pretty much established, for better or worse. They're already drinking. They've probably tried drugs. They've definitely watched porn and probably had sex. In many ways and providing they haven't gone off the rails, this age can come as an unexpected relief, or at least it was for me.

So much of parenting is about standing in front of your kid and trying to delay the inevitable. As they head towards 18, you accept it's useless to try and police their activities with the urgency you felt when they were younger. This realisation allows you to relax your crack and explore how a friendship with your no-longer-a-child might look.

In the final months of your kid's final year of secondary education, there will likely be a series of events: dinners, breakfasts, speech days and other formal and informal gatherings that mark the end of the biggest chapter of their life so far.

You will be invited to many of them.

This is a good thing. Rituals are important in marking the transition from one life stage to another. What nobody warns you: this transition is not theirs alone to make. It's a shift you too must experience as a parent and your feelings may be more complex if you're female. (My husband spent the whole year watching me weep and shaking his head in bemusement.)

As they turn 18 and wrap up their schooling, you'll find yourself questioning what your role is as a mother. Where do you fit in?

The scaffolding of your relationship for the past 18 years – implementing rules; creating incentives; handing out money; providing transport, meals and snacks; imparting wisdom and teachable moments; monitoring study, data usage and academic progress; establishing discipline and consequences – it all begins to dismantle very quickly in this final year of school. They are exultant about this. You are bewildered.

What's the point of you now, you wonder: what is your role as a mother of an adult who can legally do almost everything other than have a beer in America?

The vulnerability knocks the wind out of you. You feel bereft for reasons you barely understand.

You dig deeper into yourself looking for answers but all you find there are small, anxious questions. If they don't have to spend time with you, will they want to? If you have no formal control over them, will they listen to you? Now that they're an adult with all the same rights as you, what even is your relationship to them?

Who is a mother when her child becomes an adult?

You feel disorientated. Why have you never read anything about this? Are you a freak to be upset for your own sense of loss while at the same time happy for your child at their impending freedom?

You will grapple with this for months. You will sob at final assemblies and share tissues with other mothers. Your husband will continue to be baffled by your emotional reaction to something he views as pretty uncomplicated: kid leaves school, kid turns 18, work as parent pretty much done, let's now celebrate together with a hug and a legal beer.

You will hate your husband for not understanding your swirl of conflicting emotions. You will shout at him. He will not shout back. He will try not to laugh at you and sometimes fail. This will make you angry as well as sad. You swing between shouting and crying for months and you don't know why.

Only the other mothers in your son's year will understand how you feel. You must talk to them. You notice some women sobbing even harder than you and discover they are the ones whose youngest children are finishing school. 'What are you so upset about,' they laugh-sob. 'You still have two more kids to go!'

This makes you cry harder at the thought that one day you will be them. One day, it will be even harder and how is that even possible because your heart hurts so much and you must surely be dehydrated from all the crying.

At the same time, your heart is full. Of love. Of pride. You look at your son standing in front of you and decide you've created the perfect man. You don't know how to feel about the idea that your job is done but you feel pure joy when you see how happy he is to have ascended the cliff of childhood and adolescence and be running towards the rest of his life.

*

I was ready for the firsts. Pumped. Especially with your first-born. With that first baby, you rush at every milestone cheering wildly, a ticker tape parade every time. First smile. First clap. First crawl. First sleep-through-the-night. First tooth. First solids. First word. First steps. First lost tooth. First Christmas. First birthday. First Mother's Day. First pair of underpants. First trip to the beach. First time on a bus, a train, a plane. First dry-night. First Wiggles concert. Then there are the emotional firsts – some bittersweet, some just sweet – marking each step they take away from you and towards independence. First time you leave them with a babysitter. First night you spend away from them. First playdate. First drop-off birthday party. First day at daycare. First friend. First day at kindy. First playdate without you. First day of school. First sleep-over. First day of high school. First crush. First period. First shave. First romance.

You note all these firsts vividly and celebrate many of them publicly or privately with your partner or someone else intimately involved in your child's life like a grandparent or godparent.

Wow, you think. *We got here.*

What you usually fail to notice are the lasts. These are the milestones that never announce themselves as they're leaving your life for the final time. The lasts aren't flashy like the firsts. Instead, they just slip silently past like smoke and you only realise they're gone much later with a pang of grief you never saw coming.

The last breastfeed. The last time you carried your child to bed. The last time she reached for your hand in the street. The last time you cradled him in your arms as he sobbed. The last time she called for you in the middle of the night. The last time you had a bath together. The last time you put a band-aid on a grazed knee. The last story you read out loud. The last time you snuggled together in bed. The last time she fell asleep in your arms. The last time he wanted to sleep in your bed. The last time you comforted him when he had a nightmare. The last time you made her breakfast. The last Christmas when he believed in Santa. The last time you go to buy school shoes. The last time you excitedly make lolly bags together for her birthday party. The last time the tooth fairy came. The last time you knew the names of all the kids in his class. The last time your opinion mattered more to her than anyone else's in the world.

Oh my heart.

Lately, I've found myself quickly flicking past the 'memories from this day 2/4/6 years ago' posts helpfully thrown up by Facebook or your photo library. I can't look at old photos or videos of my kids right now either. They make me feel too jolted by sadness, even when those same children are sitting right beside me. Because they're not the same children, they're not. Something I could never have predicted was how much I'd miss the people my children were at different ages.

Of course I love who they are now and that's a gift I get to keep on unwrapping, watching them grow and change and delight me with who they become. Two emotions can co-exist and the way I feel at the moment when I see old photos of my kids resembles a type of happy grief.

I miss those funny little people who are so similar and yet so different from the children I love and live with today. I miss them desperately.

Perhaps it's because I know I'm done. There will be no more little children of my own. No maddening, adorable little toddlers to cling onto me with sticky fingers. No inquisitive five-year-olds to ask me questions like, 'What does God wear?' or 'What's that?' while pointing to an errant tampon string.

The conversations I have with my kids now are infinitely more interesting albeit with far higher stakes. We talk about same-sex marriage and what it means to be transgender and racism and sexism and drugs and alcohol and terrorism. All the isms. So many isms. We also talk about less loaded things like Taylor Swift and whether sushi with chicken schnitzel can legitimately be called sushi.

And yet when I think about them at two and three and five and 12 . . . I discover all the aggravations large and small of those ages and stages have dissolved, leaving only the happy memories which are wrapped around my heart so tightly I sometimes feel like they're constricting it.

Can you love the children you have while simultaneously grieving the children they used to be?

Yeah apparently you can. I do it every day.

WHAT IT WAS LIKE GROWING UP WITH MIA FREEDMAN AS MY MOTHER (AKA HOW I LEARNED WHAT NOT TO DO) BY LUCA LAVIGNE

Note from Mia: There are plenty of books about parenting written by parents. But really, what do we know? Surely, our kids are the most important judges of our performance. So instead of banging my own drum or using the drumsticks to hit myself in the face, I took a deep breath and asked my eldest child, Luca, then 19, to write this chapter. Here goes nothing.

'Imagine if I wrote a book one day about what it's like having you as a mum' is a threat I've waved around a lot in my life. Every bizarre parenting decision she makes, every controversial or downright ridiculous thing she says. That's the response I whip out.

But it would never happen. Who in their right mind would give a kid the creative space to write about how unique (read: insane, immature, batshit crazy) his mum is? I assumed it was an empty threat; one that made the pair of us giggle on countless occasions.

And yet here we are.

Mum and I are close. I'd say far closer than the average mother and son. Pull a young adult off the street and ask them about their relationship with their mum: 'Yeah, all right I guess. Like, she's cool. We're pretty close.' Insecurity with a serious lack of enthusiasm to boot. Ain't none of that here.

Me and Mum (at age 5 and age 18)

My mum is my best friend. A woman I love and idolise and respect and cannot live without.

She is responsible for the person I am today in every aspect, good and bad. So when she asked if I was interested in writing a chapter for her book, I was floored. Stoked. You know when you're cutting wrapping paper and the scissors start to glide? That.

Between Mum and I exists a dynamic role reversal. It's fast and loose. Ever-changing. I am not the traditional son and she, by no means, the traditional mum. In fact, for the majority of my life we seem to have swapped roles entirely.

There was a brief period after I was born in which this wasn't the case. Mum changed my nappies and (usually) remembered to feed me just frequently enough to dupe me into thinking she had her shit together. Simply put, she fooled me into believing she was a respectable figure of authority. Not that I was a very naughty kid, but discipline was key: it's human nature to respect and listen to those who discipline us. If I didn't throw the ball for the dog, she'd punish me. Stole some Freddo Frogs from Nonna's house, she'd punish me. If I'm honest, punish is a harsh word for the consequences she imposed. It was more of a mild reprimand. Not grand enough for me to dwell on it for any length of time, but just enough for it to be annoying. She didn't smack me, shout at me, or make me do any physical labour. Rather, I wouldn't be allowed to use the PlayStation for two days. And usually those two days turned into one. Then six hours if I baked her some cookies, or gave her a cuddle.

But after almost two decades, I know the real Mia Freedman. And I want you to as well. I want the world to see the Mia that I see. The Mia that I live with. Not the one who writes books, edited magazines, appears on television, and built a media company with my dad. Rather the one that has the time management skills of a fish . . . the one who considers every parking fine she doesn't get as 'bonus' money she can spend . . . the one who is directly responsible for the young man I have become.

Infancy: Planting the seed

Little kids don't have to worry about a lot. They do not have to concern themselves with getting to school on time, making arrangements, or thinking ahead. Levels of responsibility are relatively low. Usually.

I've always liked looking forward to things. In primary school, I was always the kid that knew exactly whose birthday party was coming up two, three, even four weeks in advance. All I'd want to do was talk about it with everyone . . . what movie we were going to see, who was invited and how we would get there. For me, the excitement lay in the detail: the organisational tidbits that any other kid wouldn't even consider.

An invitation arrives via post (post is like a text but it comes to your house and it's on paper) for Ben's eighth birthday bowling party.

'Mum, who's gonna take me to Ben's party?'

'Who's Ben . . . ? Shit, is the party now?'

'No, it's six weeks from Sunday. And you know Ben. He comes over all the time.'

'Oh right, that Ben. Um . . . probably me. Or Dad?'

'Well, yeah, but which one, you or Dad?'

'Angel, I have no idea, it's six weeks away.'

Even her tone has me worried.

I bring up the party again three days later. Not only has she once again forgotten who Ben was but she has no recollection whatsoever of our previous conversation. Working from experience, I know what I have to do. I get my best mate Hugo on the phone in seconds, asking if I can get a lift with his mum to the party.

And this, routinely, is where I hit strife. Not only do my eight-year-old friends not know/care about how they're getting to the party . . . they don't even know the party exists. And when I tell them about it? They remain carefree. Because they can . . . because their experiences in life so far have seen them end up in the right place, at the right time.

Ben's party? If it wasn't for my eccentricity, Hugo wouldn't have found out about it until he was in the car on the way there. Wrapped present in lap with a thoughtful card attached. But how would he get home!? He didn't care . . . it would just happen. The party would finish and someone would just be there to pick him up. He wouldn't spend hours running over, and over, and over in his mind who would be there. He wouldn't call them 13 times to confirm when and where they had to be.

Growing up, none of my friends thought the same way as me. In fact I learned quite early on that the most efficient way of making these in-advance plans to get places was to confer with adults directly. Why call Hugo, who has no idea what his own schedule entails (fairly normal for an eight-year-old), when I can go straight to the boss? So I dial Hugo's mum's number, which I know by heart. Cut out the middleman. #efficiency.

'Hi Justine. Would it be okay if I got a lift with you to Ben's party on 20 August at 2 pm?'

'Luca! Of course that's fine [she's used to fielding my calls]. Umm, what's the date today . . . ?'

'I think it's 3 July.'

They say your character is a combination of two things: genes, and environment. Nature and nurture. In terms of my genes, I picked up

Dad's introverted personality and acute attention to detail. If I had just this to go on, I would've been a fairly normal kid. Like Hugo. But then there's the environmental front, which plays an equally significant role in shaping who we are. And my environment had something no kid (other than my siblings who were not yet born) did . . . Mia.

Believe it or not, there is in fact reasoning behind my eccentric organisational habits (read: moderate anxiety and pesky OCD). I'd tried and tested the whole 'be a kid' thing. Let it happen. Mum will sort it. I'm sure she has it under control. I tried this strategy for a year or two just after exiting the womb, but quickly found it to be an unreliable service, sort of like having a blind seeing-eye dog.

It was at this stage that our epic role reversal began. Instead of Mum apologising to Ben's parents for her misbehaving son, I apologise for my underperforming mother . . . I apologise for turning up late. Without a present.

This wasn't an isolated incident. There were a few parties where I arrived as the candles on the cake were being blown out. And a few cricket games where I was dropped at the grounds halfway through the first innings.

For a kid with extreme FOMO and deep-seated anxiety, this did an absolute number on me. Like the equivalent of waterboarding but for neurotic people.

The most frustrating part? Left to my own devices, I would've sorted it. Made my own little way to each and every event. With time to spare. I would have found a lift or caught a bus or hitchhiked or . . . something. I would've found some means of getting myself from point A to point B before people started looking around and asking, 'Where's Luca?'

But hindsight is a powerful thing. What I now know is that nobody cares where Luca is . . . nobody gives two shits if I'm five minutes late, or even if I don't come at all (because: Netflix). My logical type A brain tells me that over and over again. But feeling judged for walking in late has bred within me an urge to cohere to all arrangements. Meeting a friend for coffee? Gotta be there ten minutes early. Job interview? At least half an hour. It goes without saying that when I eventually get married I'll sleep at the venue for a couple of weeks prior.

I'm still figuring out if this is for better or worse.

On the negative front? I become disproportionately flustered when it comes to being on time and I'm equally intolerant of others who don't make the effort to do so. In fact, on my wedding day (after I wake up and tidy the makeshift living space I've created under table six), anyone who arrives less than 10 minutes before the service won't be let in. And upon considering the logistics of this system, that means Mum missing my wedding. Without a doubt.

And on the positive front? I arrive at parties before the bar tab runs out.

Everyone has their rituals. Some people wake up at 6:14 am every morning, drink a bucket of tea with skim milk, then run three kilometres on a treadmill (read: jog 300 metres then stop and check Facebook until the odometer says three kilometres). #MIA. Others might go for a surf on Fridays after work. #NOTMIA

I've always been a creature of habit . . . I like it because I always know what's coming. No surprises. You know when you drive the same route to work every day, and eventually know where all the red light cameras are, and the best spots to do sneaky drop-ins? Like that, but with life.

Up until I was 10, bedtime was my favourite part of the daily routine (my daily routine has evolved since I was 10 and now includes less education, more alcohol, but the same number of girlfriends. #zero). Bedtime was the best part of the day because it meant cuddles.

When I was a little kid, Dad would usually be the one to put me to bed, turn my light off, and give me a kiss goodnight. As he walked out of the room, I would say the same thing to him. Every night.

'Can you ask Mum to come and give me a cuddle?'

I'm not sure why I always asked. 'Night-time cuddles' was so ingrained into our daily routines that neither of us needed the nightly reminder . . . but me asking almost became a part of the ritual.

I think it allowed us both to breathe a sigh of relief: I could be the traditional little boy . . . not trying to organise his mum's life or reminding her that she needs to pay for the parking fine she got. It was a reprieve for both of us – from the role reversal that we had become so used to. For those 10 minutes every night, I could release my profound urge to control her, to help her, and to do whatever I could to make her proud. I could stop worrying. I could take comfort in the fact that my mum has her arms around me . . . that my mum is protecting me from everything bad. And, simply from the look she's giving me, I'd know that she loves me more than anything else in the world.

We cuddled, and we talked. About our days, about our worries, and just about funny shit in general. After 10 minutes, she kissed me goodnight, told me she loved me, and went off to do whatever it is mums do after their kids go to sleep. Some do washing, some drink wine. Some watch *Sex and the City* with the volume turned up loud enough for me to hear Carrie talking about periods.

My favourite nights were those when she'd accidentally fall asleep, wrapped around me. Every night I could fall asleep knowing that I was safe and that I was loved. And with the power of hindsight? That's far more important than getting to a party before the candles are blown out.

Teenager: Making a man

The sexual awakening of the teenage male is an important time. The guidance received and the decisions made at this critical point in any boy's life directly shape not only his attitude towards women (or men), but the man he will ultimately become.

Fortunately for me, I had one of the best guides in the business.

Puberty was the only occasion where Mum's lack of verbal filter served me well. Most mothers would select their words with extreme care and intense thought. They'd mull over how to explain a blow job to their son for 12 days before getting self-conscious and convincing themselves it was a talk they may never need to have. Which is normal. Nooormal. How could any mum not be embarrassed at the thought of talking to their son about orgasms and sex and sperm . . . ?

Enter Mia. Vaginas? Excellent. Periods? Let's sing about them.

No sexual stone was left unturned.

This was by no means intentional. It's traditional to mull a thought over before converting it into speech, but every thought Mum has is out of her mouth and into the ether without any form of consideration. Her speech is an infinite procession of baseball players heading out to the pitch without warming up properly. Some players head on out without their helmets. Some have never played baseball before. Others are both blind and deaf. But they all come out swinging just as confidently as one another. She treats the household as most people do their personal minds . . . lots of unrelated, fleeting thoughts popping about. Sometimes just noises.

As a result, by the age of 12 I was completely desensitised to what most of my friends would find horrific. Mum always told me that her goal was for me to be unashamed to walk into a chemist and buy her tampons. At the age of eight? I would cringe at the thought of a tampon and where it goes and why is there blood and what's a uterus (no, but seriously, what's a uterus?).

By the time I hit 14?

'Mum, I'm going out, you want anything?'

'Tampons.'

'Sweet, what size?'

Her methods were unconventional. If all the mothers out there are a standard military unit, she's the rogue general with a li'l glimmer of crazy in her eyes, feared on the basis of unpredictability and possible insanity. But what she was doing was exposing me at a young age to concepts that are critical in developing a respectful attitude towards both women and sex. And when the time finally came – when I hit that fork in the road around age 13 and became interested in girls – the path I needed to take could not have been clearer. I needed to be 'the good guy'. Not *a* good guy. *The* good guy.

In high school, mixed-gender gatherings became a thing. And it was just great. Girls were cool and I liked them and they liked me and when we connected mouths it felt kinda good. Everyone brought their own plastic Mount Franklin bottle that had been emptied out and refilled with equal parts Kahlua and Absolut from the family liquor cabinet. And this is where the opportunity to be 'the good guy' really presented itself for the first time.

Alcohol gives voice to your moral compass. Not only does it amplify words and actions that might otherwise remain hidden, it also presents situations (and opportunities) that wouldn't otherwise arise: the drunk girl lying on a beanbag in the corner of the room; the beautiful girl too drunk to say no when you follow her into the bathroom.

Mum made her message crystal clear: 'Be the guy who holds her hair back, not the one who tries to get in her pants.'

That girl on the beanbag? Sit with her. Make sure she has a way to get home. If she doesn't? Call her a taxi. Give the driver enough cash to make sure she gets home safely. If she's really in a bad way? Ride in the cab with her. Walk her to the door. Hell, CARRY HER to the door. In short: #alwaysbethegoodguy.

My group of friends started drinking around age 15. Both the guys and the girls. And with drinking came the need for somewhere to drink. Parks are great, don't get me wrong . . . but I was fortunate enough to have a mum who accepted the fact that I was going to drink, regardless of what she said. She decided it was better that I drink at home, in a safe environment. She never explicitly condoned it, she never bought or provided me with alcohol and I didn't drink in front of her until I was closer to 18, but she knew what was going on.

Mum facilitated a situation in which she guided me while simultaneously allowing me to make my own decisions. A situation in which I could learn to understand alcohol, and respect it. Most young teens are forced to drink behind their parents' backs. They skol whisky from the cabinet while nobody's looking, sneak out, and walk the streets in large groups yelling insults at pedestrians. They inevitably come home, parents smell their breath, and ground them for drinking. And so the cycle repeats . . .

But Mum was different. I had no reason to sneak out. No reason to walk the streets shouting, 'Fuck the Po-leeeece' and stealing the numbers 'six' and 'nine' from houses. No reason to rebel. Because there was nothing to rebel against.

Pres (pre-drinks for you non-millennials) is always the best part of any evening. At pres you walk a fantastic line: a line where you're tipsy enough to have a dance and open up about your fears, but not so drunk that you're up on the table, twerking. And because Mum wanted us to be somewhere safe, my group of friends would often come to our house for pres.

At some point during pres, Mum would inevitably make an appearance: she'd poke her head around the corner, initially under the guise of saying hello to everyone. In retrospect, I realise this was a ploy to make her way into the room without raising eyebrows. Small talk over, and now somehow sitting in the circle, Mum would begin a pre-match huddle of sorts.

Have you seen footage of those sports matches where the teams huddle up before the games, with the captain in the middle, leading a cheesy call-and-response chant? Think that but feminism:

'WHAAAAT ARE WE GONNA DO?!'

'HOLD HER HAIR BACK!'

'WOOOOOO, DAMN RIGHT!'

screams and cheers

It wasn't good enough just raising me to be 'the good guy'. Whenever a friend came over, she utilised the short window she had to talk to them about being good guys too. She did the same with kids who weren't my friends. And with strangers.

She hurled women's rights and pro-choice values at me faster than I had the ability to process. But she figured that if I could manage to retain even a third of the propaganda she flung my way, I'd absorb feminism by osmosis. Have you seen that video where the little kitten is raised by dogs and adopts all their canine mannerisms? That.

In this sense she was mature: A leader by example. One who I strived to impress. A forward-thinking, upstanding example of morality for young men everywhere . . . who at the same time would leave spat-out mouthfuls of discarded chicken on a napkin in the middle of the dinner table because 'that tasted funny'.

Something she still struggles with is picking the right time for a feminist teaching or a life lesson. She thinks ALL the times are right. Sleeping? Let's talk about how ovaries work. Mid-meal? Here's a pre-prepared diagram of a baby crowning.

However. The success of her feminist teachings can be solely attributed to the way she delivered them.

It didn't take long before I was terrified of the car. Once that passenger door shut behind me, Mum had AT LEAST 15 minutes of one-on-one time. And during that time? No. Possible. Escape. In those 15 minutes, it was either listen to what she had to say or open the door of the moving car and roll into oncoming traffic. Often, I found myself considering the latter.

Her issue is that she likes words. Regardless of what the words are, she likes to be speaking. Always. At all times. Her favourite thing to do? Employ all the oxygen in a certain space, and convert it to non-sensical verbal excrement.

I made the error once of accepting an early morning lift to my Year 9 French exam and was madly trying to conjugate verbs in my head.

MUM: How much do you know about abortion?

ME: Mia. Seriously. It's not the damn time.

I redirected my attention away from the feminist mosquito next to me, and back to my French book.

MUM: Oh. Sure ... But there's an election in the US at the moment and there are lots of people trying to take away women's rights and this is important, not just for women but for men too because there's every chance you'll get a girl acci-dentally pregnant one day and you do know women should have the option to have an abortion, right, because it's their bodies and pro-choice is so important like you actually have to be pro-choice because it's not up to you it's actually up to the woman you might get pregnant one day like what if you get a girl pregnant and she has to have the baby and you're a dad at 14 like you do think that's crazy right? Right. RIGHT?

ME: Mia, I love you ... But. Shut. The fuck. UP.

MUM: Sure, sorry ... But you do understand, right, like, you know what pro-choice is and you agree with it?

ME: I hate you.

And so another teaching was imparted. You better believe I was pro-choice. Mum knew that I was. Because she'd raised me to be.

She knew that. But it didn't matter in that moment because she'd read something about abortion and wanted to talk about it. And there was brief silence in the car. And when there's silence we fill it with FEMINISM.

It didn't take long for me to jump aboard the feminist train. Mum had bred the concept of 'the good guy' into my very essence. I was 'the good guy'. Instead of finding myself in tough situations and asking, 'What would 'the good guy' do?' I simply did what I did. So when that fork in the road arose . . . there was no internal doubt whatsoever surrounding which path to take. Because she'd been guiding me down the right one before I was even old enough to know she was doing it.

She may not have been a well-prepared guide: by no means did she strive for quality over quantity. She rather walked blindly in circles blurting out things about labias. But hey. In retrospect? It got the job done. She raised a 'good guy'. And I'm forever in her debt for that.

*

The unbreakable nature of the relationship Mum and I have means that we sledge each other. All. The. Time.

'Mia. I . . . I can't even . . . you ACTUALLY have the organisational skills of a frog.'

'Shut up, you're a bum.'

And yes, that's an actual comeback she uses. Regularly.

I poke fun at her for being a child. She lays into me for being uptight. It's how we roll.

I'm allowed to make fun of her because I'm her son. And because the stones I throw come from a good place: one of undying love and respect. But when it's not me doing the throwing? It's hard to sit back and let it happen.

Growing older, I adapted to the perks and pitfalls that come with having a mother in the public eye: hearing from my 12-year-old friends that 'your mum said penis on TV'; the elevated stress that accompanies book deadlines; the tickling fear that any conversation we have might find its way onto something she writes for Mamamia.

But the online abuse is another story.

It only really started as Mamamia took off, circa 2008. It wasn't an issue when she edited *Cleo* or *Cosmo* or had her weekly article in the paper. But suddenly for every word she put out, one thousand threatening ones came back her way via comments or social media. Twitter was the worst.

I'm not pretending she's some hard-done-by feminist martyr. This is par for the social media course. I understand that public backlash is a central facet of journalism in 2016. I really do. But that doesn't make it any easier to accept when the journalist in question is your mum.

People believe that because she expresses her voice in the public domain that she's their property: theirs to insult. Theirs to tear down. Theirs to ridicule and slam. And I'm not one to say if that belief is right or wrong. Sure, it hurts when people diss her opinion and slander her writing style.

But what truly breaks my heart is when people overlook the opinion, and abuse the woman behind it. People see themselves hurling abuse at a name. At 'Mia Freedman the journalist'. A static headshot. Not at the beautiful mother-of-three with real-life emotions and insecurities.

'Mia Freedman's voice is annoying. And she looks like a French Bulldog.'

That was my personal favourite. Mum and I had a laugh over it. If only all the abuse was that benign. But the hurtful reality is that most trolls employ vile expletives and threats of violence. And I simply can't bring myself to read them anymore.

'Mia Freedman is a whore she should die.'

'Mia's a disgrace of a mother. She should have her children taken off her.'

Watching trolls attack Mum is distressing. It's a primal instinct for mothers to defend their kids but for me it's the other way round. I swell with this confusing mix of heartbreak and fury. All I want to do is jump to her defence. To absolutely rip the trolls to shreds. I would honestly take a bullet for her. And watching people destroy her with such glee destroys me too.

I can't jump to her defence, for a few reasons. Primarily? Tearing down the trolls takes away the one thing I have over them: dignity. It puts us on a level playing field. Which we most certainly are not. I use every ounce of strength and willpower I have to go high. Because I can't sink to their level. And secondly? There's always the chance it might turn into a headline: 'Mia Freedman can't hold her own against Facebook trolls'.

I'd be deceiving myself if I didn't admit some of the criticism she receives is completely justified. Not the personal attacks – they're unforgivable. But occasionally (not that occasionally) she sends an unfiltered, poorly assembled thought out into the universe. And people hit back hard. Such is life when you have no filter.

She really does have no filter. It's not a ditzy persona she creates to sell more books or peddle her podcast (actually called *No Filter*). She doesn't present herself as 'Mia Freedman, the journalist and mother who has no filter'. She is that. And that can be a problem for her family.

I remember talking with Mum about a girl I had a crush on. I was in primary school, extremely self-conscious, and only willing to divulge information under duress. I explained that the girl was two years older than me.

'You say you like her. What does that mean?'

'Umm . . . I dunno.'

'What do you feel about her?'

'Umm . . . I guess I . . . just like her, y'know.'

'But, like, do you find her pretty, do you like her personality, do you think she's funny . . . ?'

'Yeah, I guess . . . she's kind of . . . pretty. I can't really put it into words, I just . . . like her.'

We moved on and started talking about other things. Probably tampons. Or periods.

In retrospect I didn't tell her much. But at the time? The fact I had a crush was a huge deal. Especially given I'm such a secretive person.

So you can imagine my face when, three days later, I came across a transcript of our entire conversation on her computer. I was appalled. Traumatised. And deeply, deeply betrayed. It was clearly intended to be the focus of an article, which, thankfully, never made it much further than its inception. I confronted her about it, in an outraged flurry of embarrassment and shame. If I hadn't, I may not have found out until my friends asked who my crush was that Mum had written about it.

I don't have an answer. Only a question. It's one I asked myself back on that day in primary school, and have asked myself every day since . . . Can you trust someone with no filter?

The thing that terrifies me is that . . . she just doesn't get it. It would be different if she transcribed that conversation we had with knowledge that she was overstepping a boundary. It would be sneaky. And conniving. But at least it would be predictable. At least then I'd be able to understand where she sits, and think twice about confiding in her.

But it's not like that. She isn't cruel. She's just clueless. There's no red flag when she oversteps a confidentiality boundary . . . and no sense of whether information is hers to share or not. So every time I tell her something in private, I run the risk of it popping up in public conversation. Or in a book. Maybe this book.

It's not something she's aware of. Or has any control over. It's not a problem I can solve – trust me, I've tried. All I can do, really, is proceed with caution. And accept that, by no intention – but some fault – of her own . . . I have a mum with no filter.

I never thought I'd be spending more time with my mum at 19 than I did at nine. But here we are. Not only do I still live at home with my parents and two siblings, I'm now with Mum and Dad every day as well.

I work at Mamamia. That's the latest stage of our relationship. And, in terms of my job as a content producer, I absolutely love it.

The funniest part is seeing her through the eyes of my co-workers.

'Mia's just like, got her shit together all the time, you know? Like she comes up with this brilliant idea, and then works through it in logical steps.'

At work, sure.

But it's tough to see the slightly feared figure of authority they do. Instead, I see a woman who eats dry cereal for dinner. And forgets to put the lid on the blender when she turns it on. Every. Day. I see a woman who bangs her car up twice a week; who doesn't always remember to pick her kids up from school; who genuinely thought Argentina was in Europe. I see a woman who's deeply imperfect . . . just like the rest of us.

I also see a woman who loves her kids more than anything else in the world; who puts us before herself, and has done since the day we were born; who held me in her arms until I fell asleep every night; who acts as a role model for young women all over the world; who, every day, shatters glass ceilings. And redefines what it means to be a woman. And a feminist.

But that's all meaningless. Because really I see none of that. I mean, sure, it's there . . . Mia Freedman is all of those things. And so many more. But really? When I look at her? I just see my mum. My best friend. A woman I love, and idolise, and respect. And simply cannot live without. And who thankfully, now that I can drive and order an Uber, I no longer have to rely on to drop me anywhere on time.

BALANCE

A LONG OVERDUE – AND
WELCOME – CORRECTION

The first thing people say to me when I tell them I have ADHD is, 'How did you know you had it?'. The answer is gradually and then all at once. The slow bit was my whole life and the fast bit was the three months before my diagnosis.

In this regard, I am a very basic bitch because lately it seems like you can't open Instagram without a woman in her 30s, 40s or 50s announcing she has ADHD.

Today I'm adding my name to that list.

To be honest, I didn't want to write this essay. I'm acutely aware that ADHD is having a social media moment and I know some people believe it has become somehow trendy to say you have it. This is why for months I've felt paralyzed by all the noise on top of my own raw feelings, wondering what, if anything, I have to add to the conversation.

I was diagnosed with ADHD – Attention Deficit Hyperactivity Disorder – a year ago and I'm still processing what it means. Until now, I've not been ready to talk about it because I've needed time and privacy to percolate something that feels confusing, destabilising and embarrassing.

What has finally prompted me to share my experience is my realisation that what appears to be a trend is, in fact, a long overdue – and welcome – correction for many women, including me.

Let's start at the beginning.

*

I was in my mid forties when I began to suspect what might be wrong with me.

The thing is, you're not meant to describe a neurodiverse brain as 'wrong' or 'broken' or 'abnormal'. The more positive spin is that it's just . . . wired differently. But I reject the policing of how people talk about themselves because a few years ago, I did notice something was wrong. There's no other way to describe it.

Behavioural quirks I'd had all my life were growing into obstacles and then liabilities.

I was finding it harder and harder to organise my time. I kept missing meetings at work and when I did remember to turn up, it was impossible to concentrate, my thoughts flicking around incessantly, unable to land on any one thread for more than a few seconds.

It felt like my brain was frantically searching for something it could never find. An internal restlessness that felt deeply uncomfortable and pervasive.

I began to have more minor car accidents. I've never been a great driver but I reversed into my son's car in my driveway twice within a few months. Then I did the same to my husband's car. I was losing more things. Dropping more things. Spilling more things. Breaking more things. I was constantly late no matter how hard I tried not to be. I felt constantly impatient in a way that was disconcerting and impractical. What was I impatient *for*? I couldn't say. I was shopping too much, spending too much. My senses felt hungry all the time, like I couldn't see enough, hear enough, know enough. I desperately needed to absorb all of the information all of the time and I was exhausting everyone around me.

Daily life had begun to feel like an obstacle course for reasons I couldn't understand, much less articulate.

None of these things were entirely new but they were becoming noticeably worse. For decades, my inability to manage basic tasks has taken a toll on those closest to me. For example, it was a relief when each of my kids got their own phones so they could call me when I forgot to pick them up from school or sport. Again. The mortification was intense even when we all tried to laugh it off.

How does anyone forget their own child?

From the start of our relationship, my husband has managed most aspects of our lives – the bills, the house, car registration, our money, holidays – because the disruption caused by me invariably fucking it up causes twice as much work for everyone but mostly him.

The fact my husband runs our home life in addition to our business certainly doesn't align with the way I think of myself; as an independent and capable woman. It makes me sound like a child. Or a spoiled princess. To share this makes me feel deeply embarrassed and ashamed even though the more potent emotions are relief that Jason is so capable of taking up my slack plus gratitude that I've found a partner who understands my limited capacity to function in so many shared aspects of our lives.

In the last few years though, that limited capacity began

to shrink even further. To my great distress, I found myself becoming less and less capable, putting all sorts of strain on my family to the point where they started referring to me as 'human chaos'. They said it jokingly but I cringed every time because we all quietly knew it wasn't a joke; it was true and getting truer. I felt anguished by the constant mini-dramas I kept causing with my carelessness, but I just couldn't seem to get my shit together no matter how hard I tried.

My word of the year in 2019 was 'impact' and I spoke endlessly with my therapist about how I wanted to impact less negatively on those around me. By 2021, life had become harder and harder for me to navigate; I was constantly getting in my own way, even when lockdowns meant I barely left my house.

At the time, I put it down to working in the high speed world of digital media, the pressure of running a large business with Jason and then to the epic disruption of COVID. Also perimenopause.

I wasn't wrong. All these things were factors, especially peri. It was my job, my hormones and the pandemic, I reasoned. Plus, of course, my personality, which has always been . . . a lot. Big feelings and a tiny tolerance for boredom have been defining qualities since I was small.

Other ways I was described as a kid: *bossy, precocious, a chatterbox, speedy and a show-off.*

Ways I would describe myself both then and now: *impatient, obsessive, anxious, impulsive, restless, fidgety and with a pathological fear of stillness.*

The most vivid memory of my childhood is the distress of being bored. It made me panic. It still does.

As a result, I unconsciously seek out a lot of sensory stimulation. My need for it often feels insatiable. Bright colours, intense experiences, strong sensations but most crucially, huge amounts of mental activity – my brain always needs to be consumed with a job, preferably several at once. And by 'job' I don't mean my actual job although work is almost always front and centre in my mind. But it could also mean making six Spotify playlists simultaneously or re-organising everything in my bathroom or making seven fashion videos for Instagram or baking three cakes at a time or doing a deep dive on the author of a book I just inhaled in one sitting.

It's impossible for me to be overstimulated; I'm at my happiest when I am consumed, immersed way past the point where most people would feel overwhelmed. In fact, a high volume of sensory noise brings me a deep feeling of calm I cannot replicate any other way. The louder and faster information is coming at me – especially visually and mentally – the more peaceful I feel.

The way all this manifests day-to-day is in a bunch of personality quirks which are wide-ranging and well known to anyone close to me.

- When invited to any social occasion, the first thing I ask is, 'what time does it finish?' and I am always the first to ghost.

- I'm either obsessed with something or utterly disinterested in it.

- I've come home early from every holiday I've ever been on, including my honeymoon.

- I've never booked a flight I haven't changed or cancelled.

- I own a ridiculous number of sequined clothes. I would eat sequins if I could.

- I'm always the designated driver because I need to be able to leave in an instant. Waiting for an Uber or relying on anyone for a lift home feels intolerable.

- I regularly buy bright coloured throw cushions that go with nothing in my house and enormous random teacups that are garish and mismatched.

- I eat the same thing for breakfast and lunch every day for months or years. It feels easier than having to decide each time.

- Every few weeks I rearrange the furniture in my office. In the earliest days of Mamamia, I made everyone switch desks all the time to 'keep things fresh'.

- I can't go to any type of performance with an interval. I've bailed early from every concert I've ever been to, including Beyonce, Kylie and Gaga even though I loved them. The thought of staying until the end makes me claustrophobic.

- Tea is my favourite thing in the world but I'm incapable of making myself a decent cup because I can't wait for the teabag to steep.

- My food is always cold and my toast is essentially warm bread because I have to press 'cancel' on the microwave and toaster before they're finished.

- The thought of any kind of road trip or meditation makes my skin crawl.

- My fingers are often bleeding because I pick at them.

- 10 minutes is the amount of time I think it takes to get anywhere no matter the distance, traffic or time of day.

- Several times every day, I get changed into different outfits, even at work. I've been doing this since I was three years old.

- I interrupt people incessantly. I become so excited by my next thought or next question that I have to vomit it out immediately before I forget. This is a disaster when you host an interview podcast.

- Similarly, I blurt out inappropriate things. My family says it's like my thoughts fall directly out of my mouth before I have time to process them. This is why I no longer do live TV.

- In a restaurant, I cannot relax or focus until I've ordered. It only ever takes me 10 seconds to decide what I want but if my dinner companions are not ready when the waiter comes, I bark, 'Hurry up!' which isn't appreciated by anyone except the waiter.

- When I have to go to a big meeting at work that requires me to listen to other people talking, I will bring a colouring book or playdough. It helps me concentrate.

- If a meeting lasts longer than 20 minutes, I'll sometimes need to quietly get up and leave the room.

- I love Mondays. My work brain has no off button, ever.

The people in my close orbit are very familiar with these quirks and either find them amusing or infuriating depending on the day. Their reaction also depends on how badly my behaviour impacts them and how long they've had to endure it.

Jason sits at the top of that leaderboard after 26 years of living with me and 15 years of working together. He's a very tolerant person but it takes a toll on him and on us. It can also be hugely challenging for our son.

In the past year it's been revelatory to learn how all of these 'quirks' are actually ADHD related and that I've spent my whole life trying to compensate for the way my brain works. It's helped the people around me feel a little less exasperated with me too, I hope.

*

Two women I've never met led me to my diagnosis.

The first wrote an article for Mamamia about discovering she had ADHD as an adult that felt powerfully familiar. And the second was Caroline Hirons, a skincare expert who mentioned her own recent ADHD diagnosis on an Instagram live about eye creams that I happened to be watching.

It was the start of the long winter lockdown in 2021 and after procrastinating for months, I finally decided to seek out some answers about myself.

An ADHD diagnosis is not something the Internet or even your GP can provide, only a psychologist or psychiatrist. So I reached out to a clinical psychologist and adult ADHD expert who'd been interviewed on a podcast I listened to.

A week prior to our first Zoom appointment, she'd sent me an extensive diagnostic questionnaire that asked about my behaviour, my childhood and my experiences navigating the world.

Now it was finally time to find out . . . did I have ADHD or did I just have a short attention span? Did I have ADHD or was it just my anxiety? Did I have ADHD or was it just the pandemic making my head feel so scrambled? Did I have ADHD or was I just disorganised and forgetful? Did I have ADHD or was it just peri? Did I have ADHD or was I just a lot?

All of the above.

But also, I had ADHD.

*

Here's what ADHD is not: a behavioral disorder or a mental illness. Nor is it a mental health condition. ADHD is not a specific learning disability and it has no bearing on your IQ. Like other types of neurodiversity, ADHD is about how your brain is wired, from birth. You can't cure it, catch it or develop it later in life. You don't grow out of it. But you can manage it with varying degrees of success.

Simply put, ADHD is a neurodevelopmental impairment meaning the brain has developed differently. This particularly affects the brain's self-management system which is known as your 'executive function'; a bit like having a badly organised CEO in charge of your brain. I've also heard it described as having a car engine with bicycle brakes.

Common ADHD symptoms include inattention, distractibility, poor time management (known as time blindness), inconsistent impulse control, emotional intensity, interrupting, hyperfocus, difficulty with emotional regulation (a capacity to go from 0 to 100 very quickly), blurting, hyperactivity and an impaired ability to judge risks or consequences.

Hyperactivity can manifest physically or as thoughts that jump or race around. The inside of my brain sometimes feels like I'm accidentally sitting on a TV remote control that's rapidly flicking through channels while I try to focus on a single show. It can feel frantic and uncomfortable and it is always unwanted. For me and most people with ADHD, there is no aspect of this that feels like a superpower. Or fun. It can feel like my brain is incessantly looking for something it can't ever find.

Having some of the symptoms I've mentioned doesn't necessarily mean you have ADHD; most people are disorganised or late or impulsive or distracted sometimes. Many people have periods where their thoughts race or they can't concentrate. But a clinical diagnosis of ADHD means you have a lot of these symptoms a lot of the time, you have had them across your life, and they are significantly interfering with your functioning or development. It's the severity of the symptoms and the impact of them on your ability to function that makes it ADHD.

For people with ADHD, symptom presentation can be inconsistent; there may be times when you can focus easily but other times when it's hopeless. There is a super wide variability of your ability to concentrate – far wider than a neurotypical brain – and you're more likely to go to extremes, even within the same day.

It's a myth that people with ADHD can never concentrate; it's actually that we have trouble regulating our concentration. If we're interested in something, we can go into a state of hyperfocus to the point where we can forget to eat or go to the bathroom. Or pick up our children from school.

When you think of ADHD, you probably imagine a hyperactive little boy who can't sit still in class. Until recently, me too. And there's a good reason for this; historically, most research into ADHD was done on boys which led to a gaping hole in our scientific and social understanding of what this condition can look like in girls let alone women.

Girls with ADHD often present very differently to boys. At school, these girls are often dreamers, more likely to be staring out the window during class rather than bouncing off the walls. They may be overly talkative or 'chatty', more interested in their friends than listening to the teacher . Or they may just be disorganised, which can be misread as lazy or stupid.

Some of these behaviours are quite feminised though so until recently, being a little girl who was chatty or dreamy in class wasn't understood to be a possible flag for ADHD.

The physical hyperactivity that most parents, teachers and doctors have come to associate with ADHD is far less present in girls which means that multiple generations of girls were never diagnosed.

Those girls are now women, many of whom have struggled in different aspects of our lives due to our ADHD without ever knowing why. Nor did we realise that so many of our quirks, struggles, failures, problems or inadequacies – also some of our strengths – may be due to the way our brains are wired. And not just because we're fuck ups as we often secretly believe.

There are three types of ADHD: inattentive, hyperactive and combined type which means you have both. People with inattentive ADHD are more likely to be easily distracted and disorganised while hyperactive ADHD-ers may be more intense and speedy.

I have combined type which is a sort of double whammy. When I was diagnosed, the clinical psychologist said I was an even split between inattentive and hyperactive.

'Is there any doubt about the overall diagnosis?' I asked.

'No,' she replied evenly. 'It's one of the more definitive results I've seen.'

In a way, this was a relief because it meant there was no grey area of *maybe-I-don't-have-it-really*.

I definitely and officially had ADHD.

*

What happened next was Big Feelings. That's the only way to describe it. The most intense ones were shame, relief, anger, grief, curiosity, frustration and overwhelm.

Is shock a feeling? That too. It's hard to explain how you can be shocked by something but not surprised by it.

Like everyone else, by mid 2021 I was already feeling depleted and unmoored by the pandemic; like the foundations beneath my feet were wobbly. And then my ADHD diagnosis arrived at the start of a three-month lockdown and said, 'Hey COVID, hold my beer'.

Metabolising my diagnosis, cautiously confiding in people around me and then seeking treatment . . . it all felt insurmountable.

Within days, I began telling my family and close friends about my diagnosis which turned out to be unexpectedly painful. And fraught. Mostly, I think, because I wanted them to be shocked. *'What? You? No way! I would never have picked it! You seem so together!'*

Nobody was shocked. Just me.

Learning something about myself that felt so epic and foundational was largely met with mild interest at best by every single person I told. Or occasionally, benign amusement. A couple even burst out laughing. They may have been my children. Some conversations went very badly and ended in tears (mine), rage (mine) or hurt feelings (also mine).

Disconcertingly, a couple of people challenged my diagnosis. Here's something not to do when someone tells you they have ADHD: try to convince them they don't. That, in fact . . . *'you're probably just a bit busy and maybe overwhelmed, who wouldn't be and of course you're going to find it hard to focus sometimes because we all do, you know, it's mobile phones and we're all a bit ADHD these days, aren't we?'*

No.

Some of us are busy and distracted. And some of us have been diagnosed with ADHD. Some of us are neurodiverse and most of us are not and life is a fair bit harder when you are and it's unsettling and bizarre to discover that a lot of your struggles are because of the way your brain works. Not because you are a useless twit.

And shame has joined the chat.

In the weeks after my diagnosis, the feelings breaking over my head felt like trying to swim in rough surf. Shame was the most pervasive and more than a year later, it's still something I grapple with every day, the deep shame of feeling like I'm useless and incapable. It's a shame rooted in the internalised belief there's something wrong with me because basic tasks that are easy for others, are hard for me and sometimes impossible.

There are so many aspects of my personality that I might describe as quirky if I'm feeling charitable towards myself but more often manifest as an intrinsic belief that I'm hopeless at life. The lateness. The interrupting. The blurting. The bad tea. The big feelings. The obsessions. The inability to prepare meals for my family or remember to get petrol or charge my phone. The disorganisation. The talking too much. The being too much.

There's a particular loneliness that comes from knowing that those around you think you're too much. Too intense. It's a shame you lug around like a carry-on suitcase you're never permitted to put down because you can't help talking non-stop or feeling too much or being too . . . much.

Spending time with me can sometimes feel like being attacked by a woodpecker as I rapidly peck, peck, peck at you for more information, asking question after question which can be terrific in an interview but less relaxing when it's your mother or friend or the person sitting next to you at a dinner party.

*

Grief was the next wave to hit me. Along with regret and anger. And I toggled between all these big feelings faster and faster as the shock wore off sometimes in the space of a day or even a minute.

The anger came from not being diagnosed until I was 49. *How had all the many therapists and health professionals I'd seen over my life missed it? How had my family missed it? How had I missed it?*

My resentment that I'd had to work it out myself after decades of struggle was irrational because it's only recently that people knew what to look for. And I'm a grown woman. But that didn't make me any less furious or bitter for the years I'd lost and the damage it caused.

I grieved for the girl and the woman who flailed about, constantly getting in her own way and impacting on others in ways that cause me profound regret. I grieved for the time and energy I've spent trying to do things that should have been effortless but felt like trying to run with my shoelaces tied together. And this is why I waited a year to write about it. There was a lot of emotion to process. Plus, the way I feel about it has changed.

For a while, I saw everything I did through the lens of having ADHD. 'Oh, that's my ADHD,' I would announce to others and myself each time I did something strange or annoying, part explanation, part identification, part excuse. Metabolising my diagnosis into my identity felt a bit like when you're falling in love with someone and you want to shoehorn their name into every conversation. By saying it outloud and connecting different aspects of my dysfunctional behaviour to having ADHD, I was trying to help other people understand me while at the same time seeking to understand myself.

Lately though, I'm trying to do this less because I don't want ADHD to be my identity. And I don't want to feel like I'm making excuses. Just because you are neurodiverse doesn't mean you get to behave like a jerk or impact negatively on others without consequence.

It's not a get out of jail free card, despite the temptation to use it as one. For me, having ADHD and being accountable for my actions are not mutually exclusive.

*

So, why the flood of diagnoses among adult women lately? Has something triggered this stampede towards neurodiversity?

No and yes. No, because we've always had it. It's not a pandemic.

But yes because there has undoubtedly been a sharp increase in women being diagnosed and I believe it's for three reasons . . .

1. **More kids are being diagnosed.**
    ADHD is as inheritable as height. For women in their 30s and 40s, their kids are likely to be in primary school which is often when it's picked up in children. Going through the diagnosis process with their son or daughter causes some parents to think, 'ohhhhhhhh, same'. They mention it to the psychologist treating their child, get tested themselves and discover they too have ADHD. This has been the recent experience of several women I know but it's not what happened to me. In my family, I was patient zero. Since my diagnosis, one of my children has been diagnosed and I have extremely strong suspicions about one of my parents.

2. **Perimenopause.**
    This is a big one. For women in their early to mid 40s, lowering estrogen causes many symptoms which are similar to ADHD like brain fog, forgetfulness and mood swings. If you have ADHD, you may have been able to

work around those symptoms your whole life; that's called masking and you might not even realise you're doing it. Then peri comes along and tips your life over the edge into chaos, prompting you to seek help. That was me.

3. **Other women.**
   I'll say it again ... the effect of disclosure is exponential. The more people read about it and hear from friends and strangers who have it, the more women recognise themselves in those stories. It turns out there are a lot more of us than anyone realised.

Here's something interesting I learned from my therapist: 70 percent of adults with ADHD have one comorbidity (another condition) and 50 percent of adults with ADHD have two comorbidities.

What this means is that often when someone sorts out treatment for their mental health, the clinician would commonly pick up and treat that condition (substance use, eating disorder, autism, depression, anxiety) but potentially not realise they were treating this condition in an individual with ADHD and thus miss the need to treat the ADHD.

I had an eating disorder in my late teens and was diagnosed with anxiety in my late 30s after a crippling 11-day panic attack. Nobody was thinking about ADHD back then.

*

So, where am I at with it now? A year on, I'm still trying to understand what it means to have a brain that works differently to most people's and how to manage it. Well, that's not entirely true; I've been managing it for 50 years, albeit with mixed results.

Coming to terms with it however, continues to be profound and intense. It's been a crisis and a revelation all at once.

Also exhausting.

The flourishing of ADHD TikTok with lots of funny videos and the positive public spin some sufferers try to put on their neurodiversity can be a way to own your diagnosis but I want to be really clear about something: for the vast majority of people, ADHD is not a superpower or a special way of thinking or a magical gift. It is a functional impairment that impacts your life in a detrimental way. If it doesn't, it's not ADHD.

Parts of neurodiversity are interesting sure, in the same way it would be boring if everyone looked the same way. It's no coincidence that people with ADHD are three times more likely to own their own businesses. We have a high appetite for risk because we struggle to perceive it while also being drawn to it; that's a quality that's fundamental to being an entrepreneur. On the down side, this inability to judge risk is why so many untreated or undiagnosed people with ADHD (especially men) die young, in accidents.

Hyperfocus can also be helpful in some situations if the thing that interests you is beneficial to your career or helps you achieve a goal. For me, I've always been obsessed with women's media and making content and I've used that to my advantage. The fast-paced nature of digital media is tailor made for my jumpy brain and because it's so stimulating for me, I have an enormous capacity for work. So much so, that it can become a liability for our business and family if I'm left unchecked.

I can be hugely punishing to work with because I have no off switch and I want to start all the podcasts, do all the projects, have all the events, write all the stories, post all the things, all the time. This sounds like a humble brag but it's the opposite.

Growing a business requires careful prioritising; shiny object syndrome is a well-known liability for entrepreneurs and it's one of the reasons why I could never be the CEO of Mamamia. If I'd tried, the business would have quickly failed. Jason and I are not just partners at home but co-founders at work; I'm the content and he runs the company. In the past year we have come to see how we've shaped our work and home lives around my ADHD, years before we even knew I had it.

Being diagnosed with ADHD and treating it with medication as I've been doing for around nine months now (it took four adjustments to land on the best type and dosage) has benefited every aspect of my life, from my marriage to my work to my relationship with my children and even my friendships. That's not to say I'm cured or that I don't experience difficult symptoms every day. I do. I always will. But now I understand why certain things happen and so do the people around me. That understanding alone has removed a huge amount of friction from my relationships and my daily life.

The self-loathing, the frustration and the shame, I'm still working on. Some days are better than others and it's a work in progress.

I'm just glad I know.

DON'T COMPARE YOUR REAL LIFE TO OTHER PEOPLE'S HIGHLIGHT REELS

IT'S NOT JUST our bodies we judge harshly against other women; we also judge our lives. The carefully curated shots posted on social media. The sycophantic interviews accompanied by heavily styled photos of female celebrities in their photogenic kitchens or shoe cupboards.

Sweet Jesus, my life is a garbage fire, we think sadly.

Stop. The comparison is a crooked one. In most cases, we're placing our authentic lives beside the inauthentic ones silver-served to us by the media or other women themselves.

After 25 years working in women's media and social media, I have an excellent eye for this kind of fakery. And the more I see women do it, the more I feel compelled to post shots like these:

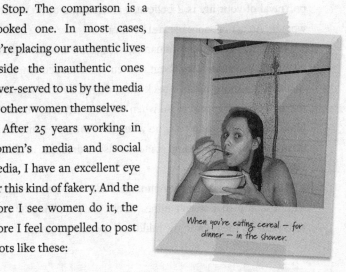

When you're eating cereal — for dinner — in the shower.

When you spill your soup on the carpet and you're too sick to make more so you just get a spoon.

When you forget to pack your sports bra.

Seeing another women editing out reality compels me to shine an even brighter light on my flaws and my fuck-ups because to deliberately peddle falsehoods in order to create a perfect portrayal of your life is, I believe, a shitty thing to do to other women. An act of sabotage and betrayal.

About two years into Mamamia, a magazine wanted to interview me for a career story about women who were self-employed.

I was far more passive back then, driven by that signature female need for approval. So when they arrived at my house to photograph me, I didn't say no when they brought someone to do my hair and makeup and someone else to dress me in clothes I didn't own.

I didn't say no when they photogenically arranged me sitting with a laptop that wasn't mine (Look! She's working! On the Internet!) on the floor in the middle of my family room.

And I didn't say no when they asked me to change outfits three times so they could make the pictures more interesting. After they'd left, I didn't have the opportunity to say no when they used Photoshopped to make my skin poreless, my hair longer, thicker and glossier, my face thinner and my age 10 years younger. Even my house looked spotless. It wasn't. There was a pile of unfolded washing, kids' toys and used tea cups strewn just out of frame. Probably also a dog. My nanny had taken the kids to the park, I'd just had an argument with Jason, I had my period (sure I'll wear these white pants you brought!) and I was in a foul mood.

This is the shot they took of me, working:

Walk into my house in those first couple of years, at any time of the night or day and you would have found me looking more like this:

Fake news

Reality

Still do. A bucket of tea with the bag still in it. Distractedly attempting to eat hands-free while I work. I look like that right now as I type this.

And yet the image where my life and appearance were airbrushed would have been passively absorbed without any conscious thought, just a small 'oh' of comparative inadequacy humming quietly in the background.

Several years later, *Women's Weekly* did a story on me. By then, I was firmer and insisted on no Photoshop. The editor reluctantly agreed.[19]

A crew of more than 20 people turned up at my house for the shoot. If it takes a village to raise a child, it takes the entire population of a small country to take a magazine photo of a privileged white woman. Photographers, assistants, assistants for the assistants, hairdressers, makeup artists, stylists, fashion interns, people to lay out muffins . . . for the best part of a day, my house was overflowing with people whose job it was to make me and my life look perfect and enviable.

Two hours of hair and makeup. Racks of clothes. An abundance of fat-sucking undies. Three hours of actual shooting. Dozens of lights. Hundreds and hundreds of images to obtain a tiny handful deemed acceptable. The end result was four awkward photos that were used to illustrate the story in one of which I was inexplicably lying at the top of a hill in my garden wearing a ballgown and bare feet.

Between shots, I kept rolling down the hill. I can't even say it was surreal because in my 15 years in women's magazines, I'd presided over dozens of similar shoots from the other side of the camera. It's just how it's always worked.

After the issue came out, the editor admitted to me her staff

---

19 Not everyone feels the same about Photoshop as me. Tina Fey says, in her book *Bossypants*, that she feels similarly about Photoshop as some people do about abortion: 'It is appalling and a tragic reflection on the moral decay of our society . . . unless I need it, in which case, everybody be cool.'

had battled to overturn my Photoshop ban. 'Please let us airbrush Mia,' they'd begged. *'We just want to make her look better.'*

Wheeee!

And they could have with just a few clicks. But who would that have helped? Me? Not really. I know what I look like, stomach rolls, wrinkles and all. The readers? Pah. How can it help anyone to be deceived by imagery? We know the opposite to be true.

Who really in their hearts believe this is how we want to see other women portrayed? Is all the artifice involved in a professional photoshoot involving 23 people not escapist and glamorous enough for you? Must we go from glamorous to pure bullshit? And how did we as women become co-opted into being our own oppressors by altering our images on social media which has now taken the mantle from magazines and the fashion industry as the arbiter of beauty standards?

Caitlin Moran says she was no fan of *Sex and the City* because it caused women to compare themselves unfairly and unfavourably to Carrie and co. She told me, 'Every Christmas, I used to get a jigsaw, and one year my sister walked past me and she said, "Why are you doing a jigsaw? You've just bought yourself a problem." And that's what *Sex and the City* seemed to be for me; it was women buying themselves a problem. You watched it to the end and you went, "Shit, I didn't previously know that my life needed to be fabulous and revolve around racketing around bars, experimenting with my anus, and coming up with fifty new kinds of hair." It seems that any woman that wanted to live the *Sex and the City* lifestyle bought themselves a massive fucking problem.'

As much as I have spent this book exhorting you not to compare yourself to supermodel mothers, fitspo bloggers and anyone else whose life appears suspiciously perfect, I am not immune. I still do it. That shit gets in.

One day when my daughter was about 20 months old, she was sitting in her highchair eating a can of baked beans with a spoon.[20]

So there I am, looking at my daughter, with the words of everyone from Miranda (agave juice!) to Gwyneth Paltrow (her kids are only allowed to watch TV in Spanish) seared onto my internal definition of 'good mother'. I feel the familiar sense of guilt, inadequacy, hopelessness and failure kick me in the shins.

Reaching for my phone, I revert to my default response in such moments of self-doubt. I take a photo and text it to someone, thirsty for reassurance. In this case, my mum. I caption the image 'Mother Of The Year' because I am fishing. Kathy bites immediately. This is what she texts back:

> Darling, there's SO much protein in baked beans and doesn't she look happy!

I'm flooded with relief. I exhale. I smile.

---

20 At some point, my children got the idea that eating any food directly out of the can was a special treat. Not sure how this happened but I have been careful to avoid disavowing them of this belief. Less washing up.

I receive another text:

> Also darling I just noticed they're salt-reduced! Aren't you a wonderful mother!

In the decade since, I've thought again and again about this exchange. When I'd looked at the scene in front of me, all I could see was everything wrong with it. The home-cooked meal that wasn't there. The basic lack of crockery. The missing fruit and vegetables and possible resulting scurvy. The store-bought birthday cake. The missed soccer game. The forgotten lunch-order. The failure.

But when someone who loved me looked at the same scene, all she saw was everything that was right. My mum saw a good mother, a happy, safe child who was fiercely loved. A meal packed with protein. Reduced salt!

In every aspect of women's lives this inner critic is our default dialogue and it harms us badly. Too often we see the hole instead of the iced doughnut with the rainbow sprinkles. We compare our achievements, our wardrobes, our weight, our wrinkles, our homes, our relationships, our pregnancies, our jobs, our ages, our followers, our diets, our bums, our likes, the contents of our kids' lunchboxes and even our pets to glossily curated stories and depictions of other women's lives which are fed to us for vanity and marketing purposes.

Is it any wonder we deflate when we find ourselves lacking?

We must stop doing this, really we must. Instead, we should try looking at ourselves through the eyes of someone who loves us. Our children. Our parents. Our partners. Our friends. Our dogs. We must look at ourselves the way literally everyone except Donald Trump looks at Meryl Streep.

We must try to see what's right with the picture. We must defiantly turn away from the images, publications, people or brands that make us feel like shit. We must observe our reactions as we scroll through our social media feeds and determinedly prune anyone whose posts trigger feelings of inadequacy.

At the same time, we must actively seek out content that makes us feel confident, uplifted, powerful, inspired and self-assured. We must reward the brands, media and people who promote authenticity, honesty, diversity and acceptance because by following them, buying their products or liking and sharing their posts, we cast our vote for a more realistic and female-friendly portrayal of women. And by doing this, we can truly help make the world a better place for ourselves and all the women and girls in our lives.

FUCK YOUR DREAMS

FUCK YOUR DREAMS. That's the title of the self-help book for millennials my 27-year-old friend Kate wants to write and I think it would be a bestseller.

My suggestions to her for chapters include:

1. Stop Reaching for the Stars
2. You're Not as Good a Singer as You Think
3. Even If You Can Sing, That Doesn't Mean You Should Be A Singer
4. Take a TAFE Course Instead of Making a Vision Board
5. Believing in Yourself Won't Pay Your Bills
6. Just Because You Really Want Something, Doesn't Mean You'll Get It
7. You're Not as Special as Your Mum Says You Are
8. Nobody Cares About Your Journey
9. Dreams Are Not The Same As Jobs

This helpful guide to dream-crushing will be a much-needed antidote to the modern industry of empty motivational gurus, inspirational memes and tedious TV talent shows that all insist the only thing standing between you and your dream is *wanting it badly enough*.

This is patently untrue. There are plenty of people, more and less talented than you, more and less deserving, who want things really badly. There are plenty of people who wish upon a star and try exceptionally hard and still don't achieve their dream to be . . . a successful fashion blogger. A working actor. A Grammy Award–winning singer. A pilot. Cured of cancer. Free from domestic abuse. A travel writer. A doctor. Ruby Rose's girlfriend. A yoga instructor who earns enough to pay her rent.

Here is where helicopter parenting and the modern self-help movement collide in a steaming pile of unrealistic expectations that can cause real damage: *Wanting something badly is not nearly enough.* Neither is believing in yourself. Not everyone can land their dream job. Most people never will. And no amount of empty rhetoric and calligraphy quotes on Instagram will change that, no matter how many times you share them.

That's not to say you shouldn't have dreams or passions or that you shouldn't seek work that makes you feel happy and fulfilled. *Of course you should do all those things.* Just don't automatically expect money to flow from them. Your passion and your job may never converge and you need to be okay with that. If this is a new and shocking concept for you, chances are, you've been thinking about your work and maybe even your life in the wrong way.

One of the best pieces of writing on this subject I've ever

read was Elizabeth Gilbert's Facebook post called 'What Are
You Doing with Your Life?'.[21]

With breathtaking clarity, Liz explains how crucial it is
to distinguish between these four things: hobby, job, career,
vocation.

She points out that while these words are often interconnec-
ted, they're not interchangeable. So much of the pain, confusion
and frustration people feel when mapping out their lives comes
from not understanding that *these four things are distinct.*

A HOBBY
Is something you do for fun with low-stakes. Like yoga, baking,
blogging, making funny Snapchat stories or listening to crime
podcasts. You don't earn money from a hobby except maybe a few
bucks from selling your hand-knitted pink pussy hats on Etsy.

A JOB
Is how you look after yourself in the world. It's how you earn money.
You don't have to love it but it's better if you don't hate it. Unless you
are independently wealthy, everyone needs a job, especially women.

A CAREER
Is built over a period of years and with different jobs or roles that
add up to a bigger, themed picture. Not everyone needs a career! A
career is something you should love and be committed to if you want
one – because it takes a lot of time.

A VOCATION
Is something you feel driven to do, regardless of income. It might
be writing. Acting. Feminism. Advocating for the rights of animals
or children. It's something you feel in your bones and you can't not
do it because it's wrapped up with your identity. Not everyone has
a vocation and they can develop as you get older. Don't stress if
you don't.

I have a lot of overlap here but not everyone does. My *job* is
working in the media which also happens to be my *career*. My

---

21 Google it immediately.

vocation is making the world a better place for women and girls which is the core purpose of Mamamia. I fulfil my vocation via the content I create and my public advocacy for things I believe in like vaccination, reproductive rights, pregnancy loss awareness, domestic violence prevention. Also via the company I've built with Jason who has shared this same vocation ever since we began working together.

Hobbies? I like doing puzzles.

DREAM

I would expand on the categories above to include dreams. The dream shared by most of the boys and men in my family is to be a Formula 1 driver. My dreams include working with Sheryl Sandberg, being friends with Tina Fey and being able to dance like Beyoncé.

A dream is part hope, part fantasy. Dreams are lovely things . . . to *dream* about. Don't let them get in the way of your real life.

While hobbies, careers, vocations and dreams are optional, jobs are vital for everyone, especially women so we can support ourselves and our children if we have to.

WAIT A MINUTE: please don't feel defensive if you currently don't have a job because you're home caring for small children or someone else who needs you, battling a health problem or facing any of the other issues that routinely pull women out of the workforce. There are times when this is inevitable.

I'm talking about long-term. Many years out of the workforce. That's when it can become problematic because you lose your financial independence. Life can become extremely difficult and compromising for a woman who has no income when she needs to change her circumstances.

I've never been in a physically abusive relationship but I've been in an emotionally abusive one and even though I held all the cards – he lived in my apartment, drove my car, took my money to buy dope . . . I still felt utterly trapped.

On paper, it made no sense. I had a job I loved, a reliable income and a supportive circle of family and friends. We had no shared bank accounts, no children, no pets and no financial entanglements.

And yet. Despite there being no reason for him to have any power over me whatsoever, I stayed with someone who treated me appallingly. Even when I finally decided to end it after two years, I found the process quite gruelling. After we broke up the only thing in my life that changed was him not being in it. I stayed in my house, continued thriving in my career, kept my car and was held tightly in the aftermath of our split by my relieved friends and family.

Think about how arduous it must be for women to extricate themselves from destructive relationships if they can't support themselves financially.

You don't ever want to be that woman. And making sure you aren't starts with a job. Get a job. Even if you're blissfully happy right now.

Because what happens if your partner leaves? Gets sacked? Or goes broke? Commits suicide? Or dies? Or cheats? What happens if your partner gambles away everything in your joint account? Or hits you or your kids? Or abuses you emotionally?

How the hell do you leave if you don't have your own bank account or any future means of financial support that doesn't rely on your partner?

If you've sidelined yourself from the workforce for a large chunk of your adult life, you will find it tough to get back in. What will happen to you when being supported by a partner is no longer a positive lifestyle choice or even a choice?

This isn't about feminism in a theoretical sense. It's lived feminism. It's practical. It's survival. Because at its heart, feminism is about women having choices over our lives. And no matter whether you choose to identify as a feminist or not, I can't imagine you saying, 'No, thanks. I don't want to bother myself with those big decisions about what happens to my body or my life. I'll just let men decide for me.'[22]

I know we haven't met yet but if you're holding this book right now, I can't imagine you saying that.

So. A job. Get one.

A job is often a means to an end. It need not define you or be your passion or your dream or your career, it just needs to pay you a living wage. You know what else your job doesn't need to do? Feed your soul. You don't even need to love it. Sometimes, a job is about going to work, doing a thing – to the best of your ability – and collecting your pay cheque. It can be as uncomplicated as that.

So many people confide in me that despite being a lawyer or an admin assistant, what they really want to do is be a Pilates instructor or start a blog. Go for it, I always say. Record your own podcast, open an eBay store or launch a dumpling catering page on Facebook.

Start a side hustle. See what happens. Just don't give up your day job. Not yet and maybe not ever.

You can earn your money in one way and feed your soul or your creativity in another *at the same time.*

There are very, very few people who are able to overlay their hobby, job, career and vocation. For most of us, they are separate if overlapping entities because not everything of value will earn you money, and that doesn't make it any less valuable.

---

22 Hint: if you can't imagine yourself saying this, it means you're a feminist.

SO WHAT ABOUT WORKING FOR FREE?

There are a lot of Very Cross People, mostly on Twitter, designated gathering place of the Very Cross, who insist nobody should ever work for free. They are particularly cross about interns. They believe all interns are being exploited and perhaps some are. Somewhere. In some cases. But the only people who can really decide this are the interns, not controlling strangers ranting angrily on social media. I started my career by working for free as did most of the people I know who are currently working in the media. Unpaid experience can be quite literally invaluable.

To short-circuit this tired debate, I've drawn up a handy flow-chart to help you work out if interning is a good idea for you:

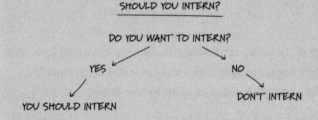

SHOULD YOU INTERN?

DO YOU WANT TO INTERN?

YES

YOU SHOULD INTERN

NO

DON'T INTERN

Working for free doesn't just apply to interns. Throughout your life as a working person, particularly if you have a career, you will be asked to work for free. Happens to me every week. Can you come and give this speech? Do this interview? Write this story? Host this function? Appear in this video? MC this charity gig? Sit on this panel? Talk at this writers' festival? Speak at this conference?

Each time, I apply the mutual benefit test.

Is there something in this for me? Will it benefit my career? Or does it support my vocation? Maybe it will just be fun. There's value in that sometimes.

I then ask myself, what will I have to sacrifice to say yes? I weigh up the time and attention it will take from my business and my family because time and attention are finite.

Sometimes free wins and sometimes it doesn't. But the idea that doing something for free is always inherently exploitative is a myth. Don't believe it.

AT SOME POINT YOU WILL HAVE TO CHOOSE BETWEEN YOUR FACE AND YOUR ARSE (UNLESS YOU CHOOSE TO PUT YOUR ARSE IN YOUR FACE)

I'M SITTING IN a restaurant drinking wine and eating tapas with three friends in their forties and one friend in her twenties.

Guess which one of us wants to have Botox.

Me: Shut up, I'm going to tell your mother.

Millennial: Stop it, she'll disown me.

Gen X #1: What are you talking about, you idiot, you don't need Botox.

Millennial: Listen, you guys, I went to a hens' weekend and all the women were in their thirties and –

Me: WHAT? THEY ALL LOOKED SCARY AND OLD?

Millennial: No! None of them had a single wrinkle because they'd all had Botox!

Gen X #2: Oh for fuck's sake.

Gen X #1: Don't do it. You have no lines!

Millennial [frowning and pointing to forehead]: I do!

Me: That's called A FACIAL EXPRESSION.

Gen X #3 [pointing to her own face]: Look, these are what actual lines look like.

Millennial: Shut up, you all look great.

Me: You're 20 years younger than us. If you start now, what will you be doing in your forties?

Millennial: Is now a bad time to mention I also want to get a boob job? Stop shaming me.

Old ladies [in unison]: I need another drink.

We demand women stay young and beautiful and we insist it appear effortlessly so. We shame them if they look old (or even their age) and we shame them if they look like they've had work. We command them to walk an impossible tightrope of expectations and we laugh cruelly when they fall.

I know more women in their twenties who have Botox than women in their forties. For us, it feels like a big decision. Crossing an invisible line to erase the visible lines on your face. We feel conflicted. Particularly if we have daughters. What message am I sending to my girl if I erase my facial expressions? That Stepford wives win and a blank face is the ultimate goal?

I ask these questions a lot and not just inside my head. Over the past few years I've embarked on my own personal Botox research project, quizzing all manner of women, particularly those in the public eye whose appearance is brutally scrutinised and who feel the klieg light of attention on how young – or old – they look. 'Have you had it?' I ask. 'And should I? But what would I tell my daughter?'

I'm looking for guidance but really permission. Absolution. Responses vary. Ita Buttrose told me to just shut up and do what I want. 'It doesn't matter what anybody else thinks. If you're not happy about something and there is a surgical procedure that might help you . . . you don't have to tell your daughter anyway. I do feel, with great respect, that a lot of young women do overshare. You don't need to share with your children or your partner. There are things you do just because it makes you feel better about yourself.'

I particularly liked that she called me a young woman. It's all relative, I guess.

In talking to women I learned that very few tell their partners they've had Botox. Men generally are horrified by the idea.

But that doesn't mean we're doing it 'just for ourselves' or that it's 'an empowering choice'.

Choices are never made in a vacuum, especially women's choices about our appearance. When so many women are making the same choice to 'empower' ourselves in the same way, some gendered shit is going on.

Women aren't deciding to, say, chop off one of our earlobes as an empowered choice. That's because society doesn't deem earlobe-less women to be more desirable. So we get to keep them, yay.

The choices we make to conform to a societal standard of beauty are not about being 'empowered' as women at all but about subjugating ourselves to an external arbiter of what's 'hot'.

So while an individual woman may exercise her choice to have Botox or plump up her lips or have a boob job, she is making this choice in the context of a much bigger picture, one that tells women how we should look.

I conform to this bigger picture every day, willingly. I dye my grey roots. I shave my legs and underarms. I wear makeup and I enjoy all of these rituals. Not having Botox or a boob job does not for a moment make me a better feminist or a more authentic woman than anyone who does. This isn't about natural beauty points or a spectrum of smug.

But whatever you choose to do to your face or body, it's worth understanding what's motivating your 'choice', even if you don't consciously realise it.

Consider this: what if the universally accepted sign of masculinity, power, success and virility was a big nose. Big noses were male currency. Men with big noses earned more, got better jobs. There were big noses on billboards, in ads, on magazine covers and all over social media. The bigger your nose? The more likes you got. Every actor and rock star had a big nose, every reality star. Male newsreaders and every man on TV had a big nose. So did every CEO.

There were virtually no images of men with small or medium noses anywhere in society. All the noses you ever saw in public were Photoshopped to look bigger, regardless of their true size. Men were pretty pissed about this because in the general population, only five per cent of men had naturally big noses. And men's noses got smaller as they aged. Older men were fighting a losing battle to keep their noses looking big. Occasionally, a famous man would wait a while between nose injections and proudly display his natural nose in an arty black and white photo shoot. These images would go viral with the hashtag #bravenose.

All the other men in the Western world, if they wanted to be considered masculine, successful, virile and powerful, had to have fat injected into their nose. This was painful and expensive and the fat was absorbed back into their body quite quickly so they were forced to have the procedure redone every few months. The other option was a permanent nose implant. This was really expensive and invasive. But it's what all the male celebrities and CEOs were doing. Many men felt like they had no choice if they wished to stay relevant in a society that valued big male noses above all others.

Women said, 'But we don't care about the size of your nose!' and many truly didn't. Yet somehow every rich and powerful woman, every successful woman, every career woman, every beautiful woman had a big-nosed man by her side.

Insecure teenage boys began begging their parents for nose-fat injections or nose surgery while still at school.

Some men wrote essays and books about the tyranny of societal oppression that was leading men to have these invasive procedures. They questioned how a big nose became the ideal facial feature for men and called for more facial diversity in bedrooms, boardrooms and in the media. Other men made documentaries, exploring why only one type of nose was considered masculine and desirable. What about all the other different shapes and sizes of nose? What about nose diversity? What about nasal hair?

Defiant and dismissive, most young men rejected the idea that they were conforming to an unrealistic nasal standard as they queued up for appointments with plastic surgeons. They insisted they were having their noses enlarged because it made them feel empowered. They claimed it had nothing to do with wanting to be seen as powerful or virile or masculine. 'It's our choice,' they insisted. 'We choose our choice!'

Over time, things escalated. Even men who had naturally big noses began having nose injections and getting implants to make them even bigger. Alarmed and responding to a growing sense of anger among men, the government quickly launched an urgent Royal Commission Into The Portrayal Of Men's Noses which resulted in a raft of measures that were quickly voted through both houses of parliament. Nose injections were banned and so were all forms of cosmetic nose enlargement surgery. Media organisations and advertisers were no longer allowed to use

Photoshop to increase the size of men's noses. There were heavy penalties imposed. Community service campaigns were funded and broadcast to help men feel good about their noses and to recalibrate societal expectations of how big a man's nose 'should' be. #Freethenose went viral. The nasal revolution was upon us.

Funny how society doesn't mandate physical expectations for men. Imagine if they did. Turn on your TV and you'll see men of all shapes, sizes, skin colours and ages in advertising, hosting shows, reading and reporting the news. The men who have won Gold Logies – considered the ultimate industry accolade for the most popular person on Australian television – are the definition of physical, religious and racial diversity. Female Gold Logie winners are uniformly blonde, white, slim and young, almost without exception.

If you're a woman in the public eye whose income is determined by her appearance, you'd better be hot or pay a team of people to help you look hotter.

This is not about sex. Being desired, for women, is about power, not over a particular man but over her own life. Power gives a woman agency and influence. A woman who is considered attractive has a higher worth. She is more popular. She can command a bigger salary, elicit more likes and followers on social media and then reap the financial rewards that come with that.

But feeling good or sexy or young is not the same as having real power. It's transitory and personal. Feeling empowered is not the same as having power.

So can we debate and judge the idea of Botox without judging the women who choose to have it? I think we can. Some of my best friends and many women I love and admire use Botox and it changes how I feel about them not a jot.

As for me, this is it. I'm finally here, at the point in my life where I have to choose between my face and my arse if I want to be considered an attractive woman.

Because I can only choose one. Either I can look young in my face, or have a hot arse.

This has always been the choice for women at a certain age, usually around 40 because that's when fat starts to fall out of your face. Losing face fat ages you. You need it to plump out the wrinkles. And since you can't selectively put weight on in your wrinkles, you must put it on everywhere, which means your arse – and everything else – will also be larger.

You okay with that? Because society isn't. Society demands you have filled-out wrinkles and a slim body all at once. This becomes increasingly physiologically impossible after your late thirties. I know for sure that I'm at the arse/face inflection point because my weight has been stable (according to my doctor who weighs me every couple of years; we deliberately don't have scales in our house) for a long time and yet people keep asking me if I'm tired. Which I often am, but not for an entire year, which is about how long I've noticed my face looking drawn.

Shut up. Never ask a woman if she's tired. That's a passive-aggressive act right there.

There's no escaping the fact that . . . I look my age. Which has, perversely, become an insult when it's applied to women because we've been taught to fear looking our age above most other things.

Exclaiming, 'Wow! You don't look it!' when a woman tells you how old she is, is part of the unspoken female code. It's how women suck up to each other, just like asking, 'Have you lost weight?' or complimenting someone's necklace/lipstick/shoes/hair. It's girl-girl shorthand for 'I want you to like me'.

Since we can't keep our arses small without our faces looking old, whatever are we to do about this vexing, complexing issue?

Until recently, generations of women have had to choose between their face and their arse, but happily, ladies, there's now a third choice: put your arse IN your face. With a needle! Simply pay a plastic surgeon thousands of dollars to extract fat from your arse, shove it into a syringe and then shoot it into your saggy baggy face to make it less so.

This is such an excellent development for women everywhere and it's also feminism because that's what feminism is about, right? Choice! Gah.

*

There is no question the female face (and body, but you knew that) has been politicised. Think about the term 'Resting Bitch Face' to describe a woman who looks grumpy even when she's not. There is no similar term to describe a man's face. He just has one.

The author of *Botox Nation*, Dana Berkowitz, points out that the rise of Botox use in young women is of particular concern. She told me: 'The way that Botox works is when it's injected into these facial muscles that allow us to pull our eyebrows together and push them down, it paralyses this motion. And this is the expression we use to project to the world that we are pissed off. For women who from early childhood are taught to look happy and pleasant, this can be quite appealing since we are penalised when we look judgmental or angry or bitchy. This unapologetically sexist pop cultural idiom refers to a woman's face at rest that somehow looks bitchy simply because she isn't smiling. And of course there is no name for men's serious, pensive and reserved expressions because we allow men these feelings. We allow men the space to display these feelings. But women are always expected to be smiling.'

How many times has a man told you to smile?

I'm sorry, I think you have me confused with a nature strip or something else designed to make the street more visually appealing. I'm a human, like you, and I'm not here for your visual pleasure.

Back in the restaurant, there's a good reason why the women at the table in their forties are imploring the woman in her twenties not to get Botox or a boob job. We are not just being altruistic. We are sad and scared and angry all at once. Because if a woman nearly half our age is worried about looking old, how must we look to her? To the world?

Elizabeth Gilbert told me she'd had Botox and urged me to stop angsting about it. She says it's disingenuous when women say they're 'sad' about another woman having cosmetic surgery. We're not sad really, she chides. We're just judgey, elevating ourselves to a morally superior platform from which we can condescend to our sisters who've had work.

When I first read her take on this, I was startled. Because that's often how I feel when I see a woman who's noticeably altered her face; sad. I thought this was an improvement on how I used to feel – angry – but according to Elizabeth, not so. I could never understand my anger and I gave myself stern lectures about it. *That poor woman looked in the mirror and felt so bad about what she saw, she paid someone to shove God knows what in her face*, I'd remind myself. By doing this, I morphed my angry into sad.

And now Elizabeth Gilbert was telling me the sadness was also a bullshit act of passive-aggression? Oh no. I listened to her and thought about it some more. Eventually, I realised this:

I was never angry with the women or sad for them. I'm angry at society and sad for myself. Being vain and competitive, it makes me furious to know that if I want to be considered attractive, I must play by the rules being forced upon me by a culture that fetishises youth and Anglo flawlessness. Women older than 22, darker than a spray tan or larger than a size 8 have a heavily reduced currency.

Face injections are the new hair removal. Boob jobs are the new Brazilian bikini wax. The baseline for being considered an attractive female is getting higher, more painful, more invasive and more prohibitively expensive. And for what? So we can all look the same?

The goalposts are shifting faster than we can sprint towards them. We have skin in this game. Skin etched with laugh lines and frown lines and the lines of our lives. If everyone erases their faces and inflates their lips, cheeks and breasts, what happens to those of us who don't? Do we become marginalised inside our own faces and bodies? Cosmetic surgery is a feminist issue because it's an issue that affects only women. Only one gender is having injections in their faces and putting implants in their bodies (notwithstanding the outlier men who are doing the same; they are only the exception that proves the rule).

This is not an attack on any individual woman who has had her face or body temporarily or permanently altered with a cosmetic procedure. If you're reading this and you've had work, and you're feeling unfairly maligned, please stand down.

I'm casting no aspersions on your choices. I promise this is not about you. In fact, by the time you read this there is every chance I will have crossed the line myself. I reserve the right to be a hypocrite. Not having had Botox yet doesn't make me feel smug or superior in the same way drinking a green smoothie doesn't make me feel better than someone who eats a Cronut. These are choices that exist outside the moral sphere.

But the choice to have cosmetic surgery is a political one in a way drinking a smoothie is not.

Just because you do something, doesn't mean you can't also question it and consider the context in which you made your choice. That doesn't mean you have to regret or reverse your decision. It doesn't cost you anything to think.

As Ita Buttrose put it, 'There is nothing you can do about getting older. You either get older or you drop dead.'

And as Lisa Wilkinson says, 'Any woman who complains about getting older needs to go visit a cancer ward.'

YES, IT'S POSSIBLE TO MAKE
PEACE WITH YOUR BODY

IT'S SATURDAY MORNING and I've just finished exercising. I collapse happily on a yoga mat and, looking down, I catch sight of my stomach. Not ripped, not shredded, not flat. Despite regular exercise, including sit-ups, I still have rolls when I sit down. I'm 45 years old and I've grown three children in there. Why wouldn't I?

What's remarkable to me in that moment is less how my body looks and more the way I feel about it: nothing.

I check myself. Nothing? No shame or frustration or insecurity? Nope. No vulnerability? No envy of the fitspo bodies I see on Instagram? No. Not today.

This is a big deal. Just a few weeks earlier I'd been on holidays at the beach and had felt uncomfortable about wearing a bikini. I'd bought one of those high-waisted granny-knicker two-piece swimsuits in an attempt to strike a balance between confidence and concealment and then taken it back because it looked ridiculous. 'Just don't wear a bikini if you're worried,' my husband had said. Wrong answer. 'Just get your guts out,' my friend and podcast co-host Monique had said. I wasn't sure.

I did get my guts out in the end, protruding over the top of a normal bikini, but I felt self-conscious. My stomach is soft and it wobbles gently when I walk. The rational part of my brain rejects this pervasive idea that a female stomach must be hard and flat. But the lifetime of images I've been subjected to all point to only one type of female form being desirable or even acceptable.

Society tells me that my size 10 body is a 'before' shot because it's not toned enough or thin enough or tall enough or young enough. Society does not tell me that my body is okay.

I fight against this conditioning as fiercely and as often as I can but sometimes, if I'm feeling vulnerable, I'm swept backwards onto my ass by the force of the current.

Which is why on this day, looking down at my stomach and feeling utterly comfortable with it, is something to marvel at. I decide to take a quick stomach selfie and post it to Instagram:

miafreedman   Follow

5,716 likes   1w

miafreedman No matter how much you
exercise, no matter what size, sometimes -
espesh after you've had kids - your body
looks like this and it's FIIIIIIINE.
I exercise for so many reasons, not just the
pursuit of a particular type of body. I hate
that exercise has been hijacked by this idea
of posting photos of ripped abs and perky
bums. For me, it's about how it makes me
feel not how it makes me look.
My stomach will never be flat or ripped and
why should it be? I'm a 45 year old mother
of three.
I am not my body. ❤️❤️❤️❤️

view all 337 comments

judysinclair AMEN @miafreedman

v4vigilante 45? You are not trying hard
enough lazy. I can make you look how u
should at 45 if u motors afra

184080 Right on sister

Log in to like or comment.   ⚫⚫⚫

I immediately forget about it until the following day when a girl-friend texts me a link – with some laughing emoji – to a *Daily Mail* story that appears under the headline 'Mia Freedman posts confronting image of her stomach'.

Confronting. I burst out laughing.

ISIS. Syria. Donald Trump as President. My stomach. CONFRONTING.

My kids are with me and want to know what's so funny, so I show them.

I'm genuinely amused because it says less about me and everything about the messed-up world in which we live; where the body of a healthy 45-year-old woman is considered *confronting*. My daughter is shocked by the story but also by my indifference. 'Mum, any other normal person would be freaking out and crying right now.'

That's when I realise something: she's watching to see how I react to being body-shamed. 'There's nothing to freak out about,' I reply. 'It's just so ridiculous that the media would say that about a woman's body. I'm fine with it!'

And I am fine with it.[23]

Self-acceptance is a constant process of talking back to the endless meteor shower of unrealistic images hurling through space, dictating how you should look as a woman. It's an active effort to repel these rubbish expectations that are based so far from reality and refuse to reflect the diverse way women actually appear.

Women's bodies have long been viewed as public property, there for the visual pleasure of men. Smile! Show us your tits! And somehow we've taken this objectification and internalised it, offering ourselves up for scrutiny on social media with bikini-body selfies and post-workout ab-flashes, thirsty for external validation. 'We're proud of our bodies,' insist many of these women when they're challenged to explain why they do it.

---

23 In fact I've turned it into a running joke on Instagram. #confronting stomach

And so they may be. But why is there only one type of body considered worthy of pride? How come women only feel confident and 'empowered' enough to show their bodies when they conform to the very narrow ideal deemed 'hot' in our culture? What about all the other women with all the other bodies? Why are we branded 'confronting' and defiant and brave instead of empowered?

When I see an image of Lena Dunham's body, naked in *Girls* or wearing her undies on Instagram, I feel very differently compared to seeing a Victoria's Secret model portrayed in a similar state. By displaying her body, Dunham is being subversive and doing her bit to widen the definition of what a sexually desirable – or even just normal – female body looks like.

The price for doing this is high.

As forcefully as society and social media pushes this unrealistic image of women's bodies onto us, we have to push back twice as hard, and that starts by being aware of what we're being fed. If you feel bad about yourself when you flick through a magazine at the nail salon, put it down. If scrolling through Instagram makes you feel fat (fat is not a feeling, remember, it's just an avatar for inadequacy, insecurity and self-loathing), change who you follow.

Sometimes, our bodies can physically hamper us in the world and we do need to make changes. Like having enormous breasts that give you chronic back pain. Or being overweight to the point of discomfort or illness.

I was warned early by a therapist that whenever my relationship with food went haywire, it was a red flag that something else was wrong in my life.

Being aware of this was invaluable. In the years after I'd recovered, whenever I started restricting my food intake or occasionally throwing up after eating too much, it was a warning sign that there was something deeper I needed to address, something unrelated to food.

Another way of putting it: Know your tell. Learn the behaviour you display when you're stressed. Some people eat their feelings. I buy clothes for mine. My feelings have an extensive wardrobe.

This is now my tell.

When something unsettling is going on for me under the surface, I shop.

*

So how did I escape the cycle of bulimia back when I was 20?

Oddly enough, it began with getting dumped.

I'd had a short, passionate, disastrous love affair with a guy who ditched me after a couple of months to reconcile with his ex-girlfriend. The shock of it killed my appetite and for a few days, as I sat wrapped in a blanket on the couch, I lost the desire to eat, let alone binge.

And the cycle was broken. Before then, I'd felt unable to stop. The only two states my body recognised were starving or painfully full; both feelings were unpleasant and dominant, allowing me to focus on little else.

Heartbreak crashed through everything. The emotional turmoil effectively flicked off the switch to my stomach, giving it some time to recalibrate.

The breakup was like a reset button and I used it to apply the work I'd done with my counsellor; something that had been impossible when my life was overwhelmed by the compulsion to binge and purge.

Years later, I learned that some kind of big emotional

upheaval can be a common trigger for recovery. The jolt of it. For my part, I highly recommend getting your heart broken by a jerk who never deserved you in the first place.

So am I cured? Is anyone ever cured of an addiction? For a long time my eating was disordered. For years, I had strict internal rules about 'good' food and 'bad' food. These days it would be called 'clean eating'.

Although the chronic binging and purging stopped quite abruptly when I was 20, clawing my way back to normal eating – is there such a thing? – was a long process.

For a time, I ate in strange ways and I was very ritualistic with food; eating the same things at the same times and being very restrictive and weird in the way I ate. I'm sure people noticed. Like in the office kitchen at *Cleo* when I'd pour myself a bowl of Sultana Bran and then surreptitiously pick out all the sultanas and add a splash of water instead of milk. I knew it was messed up and it was certainly an exhausting way to live but it was better than vomiting.

There were many things it took years to integrate back into my diet, foods I hadn't allowed myself to digest during my bulimia. They all came back eventually and it was crucial they did.

It also took years to slowly mute the continuous food conversation in my head, which tallied up everything I ate against weight and kilojoules and overlaid it with a perniciously moral judgement of myself.

Pregnancy really helped banish my demons. Conceiving, carrying, birthing and feeding my babies gave me incredible respect for what my body can do, as opposed to how it looks. When my pregnant body wanted to eat ice-cream with Coco Pops, that's what I gave it, without any bargaining or angst.

By the time I hit my thirties I could eat whatever I felt like and these days I deny myself nothing, especially dessert. That's very important.

Also important: there are certain behaviours I know I must avoid, even today.

Dieting is one of them.

I do understand that for some, abstinence is easier than moderation. I have friends who apply the same principle to alcohol. For them, removing the constant struggle of choice is easier than having to summon willpower again and again. These people need externally imposed rules to absolve them of the burden of negotiating with . . . themselves.

I apply the abstinence approach to exercise but in reverse; it's easier for me to do it every day. Same time, same exercise. Non-negotiable, like brushing my teeth. It frees my brain and gives my willpower a rest.

The way you eat and exercise is an entirely individual thing; work out what's best for your body and your head.

But for someone who has a vulnerability to disordered eating – and there are a lot of us – strict, prescriptive eating programs like quitting sugar or going paleo come with hidden dangers that are rarely acknowledged by their marketers.

Know your vulnerabilities and do what works for you. And remember, like religion and politics, your food choices are not something you should ever shove down others' throats.

CONFESSIONS OF A THERAPY BULLY

MY PARENTS WERE never the kind who fought behind closed doors. As a blended family, we had extra issues on top of the standard, nuclear variety and Mum and Dad went to counselling together on and off when I was a kid, sometimes with my brother. My mother was a psychologist who attended various self-development workshops in the '70s and at one point, my father was on the board of the Marriage Guidance Council.

This is undoubtedly why therapy-stigma has never rated a mention on my long list of neuroses. Growing up in a family where getting counselling was as unremarkable as getting petrol obliterated any possible embarrassment associated with seeking professional help.

My earliest memories of it are traumatic, however. It was the '70s and my parents were having counselling in some inner-city terrace because that's where therapists always practise. I was in the waiting area, playing with some decrepit old toys, the kind of sad relics that limp into doctors' waiting rooms to die.

I was perhaps six or seven years old and if I peeked down the dim corridor, I could see the unlocked screen door at the front of the house.

I was convinced I would be kidnapped and nobody would hear my screams because my parents would be too busy talking to the counsellor about the then parlous state of their marriage (they're good now, FYI, great actually).

Decades later, I would learn that this thinking is a classic symptom of the generalised anxiety that wouldn't be diagnosed until I had a breakdown.

*

When I was in primary school, Mum became a counsellor for Marriage Guidance – the organisation now known as Relationships Australia. This required some intensive training and a wardrobe change.

Kathy had always dressed a bit bohemian, a bit hippy. A bit sexy. It was the '70s, after all. I recall lots of singlet tops with no bra. Hairy armpits. When she became a marriage counsellor, however, she suddenly began wearing very boring, frumpy clothes in earthy colours. She wore bras. She covered up.

'I became so conscious of my body when I was working with couples,' she told me when I asked her about it years later. 'The idea was to make myself utterly sexless and almost invisible.'

I guess it worked. My memories of her counselling years aren't great.

Whenever she returned from work, she would lock herself in her room and listen to music made up of the sounds of whales calling to each other. That's the only way she could decompress. Given these unpleasant memories, I could easily have rebelled against the idea of counselling but because it was such an unremarkable thing throughout my childhood, it seemed natural to reach for it when my ship capsized.

I first saw a counsellor at age 19 to help treat my bulimia and I applied that same quick-fix approach of emergency counselling throughout my early twenties: get in, talk it through, find my bearings, get out. Just a band-aid, thanks, and I'll be on my way. I never had the appetite for corrective surgery to address the root cause of a problem.

The band-aid method worked for me until it couldn't. The loss of a child halfway through my second pregnancy and the subsequent collapse of my marriage less than a year after our wedding suggested I had deeper issues to address. Surgery it had to be.

Probably, if I hadn't had a young child at the time of our separation, I would have just seen a counsellor, addressed the drama of the moment and then fled, as usual.

But as a mother, I realised I could no longer use spak filler to treat my issues, and unless I wanted to drag my son along behind me to the next doomed relationship, and the one after that, I had some shit to sort out.

It's one of the things I've loved most about becoming a parent; abdicating your throne in the centre of the universe and making room for your children to sit there in your place. Don't read that as martyrdom. I mean, it can actually be a relief to have someone else's wellbeing as your northern star. It doesn't always have to involve self-sacrifice, although parenting invariably does if you want to do it well or even adequately.

For me, becoming a mother nudged me to make better choices for myself, choices I might not otherwise have made if I hadn't decided to place someone else's welfare above my own.

So to therapy I went. A gift to my child, my future children and most of all, to myself. An investment. Two long years of it, once a week.

My friend Wendy – who has also done the hard yards of therapy – describes it as 'doing time in the hall of mirrors'.

In therapy you will see ugly versions of yourself and you will recoil. If you don't, you should find a new therapist. Therapy done properly should be uncomfortable at times.

You will want to run away from it. To the moon and not back again. You will find reasons to cancel sessions. You will turn up late. You will pretend to be sick or away at a conference. You will be prepared to pay for an appointment you don't attend just so you can cancel with less than 24 hours' notice and the relief that floods through you will be like an orgasm mixed with a sneeze.

You will spend many moments from the end of your last session thinking about how you can cancel your next one. Don't. *Don't.*

None of these feelings is a sign you should stop; they're a sign you must continue.

The more deeply entrenched our destructive behaviour, the more we resist the idea of disrupting it because the psyche does not like to change. It will throw all manner of excuses and obstacles in the way of us shifting patterns and habits, even if they're causing us pain and messing up our lives. Your mind hates being told what to do and if you've ever tried to meditate you will know this.

Today, I am a terrible therapy bully. I think everyone should go at some point and I'm genuinely baffled by the idea that anyone could navigate their life without ever seeking help when they encounter a serious roadblock. (If the cost of therapy is prohibitive, there are some government subsidies and group situations which can be cheaper and are worth investigating.) A death. A divorce. A heartbreak. Addiction. Eating disorders and mental health challenges. The loss of a parent. Miscarriage or infertility. Being sacked. Feeling lost. Falling out of love. Infidelity. Being diagnosed with a serious illness. Loving someone who is sick.

The stuff of life can be difficult to process. It's easy to become stuck in a destructive pattern or a loop of despair. Therapy is like GPS for your head.

And yet still so many people resist it.

I also spoke about therapy with Magda Szubanski because she's always been honest about it in every interview she ever did during the period that she was the face and body of a diet company. She didn't want anyone to think it was just about signing up for some meals and waiting for the kilos to fall off. Therapy was an integral part of losing weight for her and she wanted the world to know it. 'I was really conscientious about that and certainly, I've done a ton of therapy in my life,' she said. 'You know, I think everyone should do it. I don't see why you wouldn't avail yourself of the skills and the tools if there's a smarter way to do something. There are really complex emotional psychological things that go on with weight.'

Would you try to cut your own hair? Fix your broken iPhone? How about administering your own epidural?

It would be considered naive, arrogant and foolish to DIY in any of those circumstances so stop thinking you can sort out your mental shit. You really can't. Not in any long-lasting, deeply impacting, life-benefiting way. And neither can your friends or family. They have skin in this game because they love you and because they bring baggage.

So, think about seeing someone neutral, someone not emotionally invested who isn't just going to tell you what you want to hear. It won't always be easy but believe me, it will be easier than living a life where you don't understand or even like yourself.

YOU CAN CHOOSE YOUR
FRIENDS. CHOOSE WISELY

I'M SITTING IN the Mamamia podcast studio, harassing one of my co-hosts about therapy.

'You need to go,' I say while the tape rolls. That's the kind of podcast it is and this is the kind of person I am: insufferably bossy. A therapist once called it 'control through overconcern' and it's something that has temporarily derailed several friend-ships. I'm working on it, just not today.

'I think I'm okay,' she says uncertainly.

'No, you're not. You've had huge changes in your life recently. Getting married, having a baby, moving to a new city, leaving your job; it's a lot.'

'But I've been going on these long walks with my friend Ashley and it feels a lot like therapy.'

'Stop it.'

'No, it does! I feel really calm afterwards.'

'That's called friendship, you goose, not therapy.'

'But I don't feel calm after I see my other friends. This doesn't feel the same.'

'Different friends elicit different emotions. Ashley is just your calm friend. Not your therapist.'

Afterwards, I can't stop thinking about how I feel after seeing particular friends. It's one of those gear-shifting revelations that suddenly teaches me an unspeakable amount about my friendships and it's not all good news.

THE ONE-MINUTE FRIENDSHIP HEALTH-CHECK:

Think about the word that MOST OFTEN describes how you feel after spending time with a particular friend. The most-often part is key. Everyone has periods when they're needier, more distracted or more fun to be around. All friendships endure turbulence.

The secret is to look for patterns because they're always there.

Here are some thought-starter words:

Invigorated	Guilty	Motivated
Anxious	Mentally stimulated	Calm
Frustrated	Jealous	Energised
Reassured	Drained	Joyful
Insecure	Warm	Negative
Uplifted	Pissed off	Euphoric
Diminished	Entertained	Resentful
Contented	Bored	Peaceful
Exultant	Envious	Depressed

You'll notice that about half of those words are negative. If you regularly feel bad – about life or yourself – after seeing a friend, it may be time to work out why and consider whether you're pushing shit uphill. A healthy friendship should be mutually beneficial, not a community service. It might be time to let that friendship go or at least reduce the resources you allocate to it.

I was eight years old when I learned the term 'fairweather friend'. A girl from school who lived up the road suddenly became interested in hanging out with me. She was a year older so this was thrilling.

It took my mum to call it. We had a swimming pool and Mum noticed this girl only came around during summer to use it. 'Darling, I'm afraid she's a fairweather friend,' Mum explained to me gently.

'You mean she's pretending to like me just so she can swim in our pool?' I asked incredulously.

'Think about it,' Mum said, and I did and I realised it was true.

She was quite literally only my friend when the weather was fair. As soon as autumn came, she no longer did.

It was mildly devastating and very instructive. One of my earliest memories of a Life Lesson.

Throughout my childhood my friendship style was monogamous. For two decades I had a series of best friends, perhaps because I craved a sister or perhaps just because I was a girl. When it was good it was glorious.

The friendships that girls have as kids and through our teens are invaluable practice for adult romantic relationships, equal in intensity and with the same propensity for heartbreak.

For this reason, at my daughter's school, the practice of best friendery is actively discouraged. 'Have a wide group of friends!' the girls are urged by their teachers. In some grades they even have weekly 'play away' days when they are matched with girls they'd never otherwise hang out with. I love this initiative even while I accept it's probably doomed to fail. Girls like who they like. There's chemistry in friendships too and social engineering will usually struggle to create that kismet.

As with romantic relationships, the real trouble with child-hood friends is when those passionate levels of devotion are not reciprocated. I think we've all been there. 'She's just not that into you,' can be a brutal realisation when you're 11. Less brutal, more burdensome is the knowledge that you're the one holding the balance of power. Nobody likes a clinger.

Male friendships seem infinitely simpler to me. My son met his best friend, Hugo, at pre-school aged four and they're still best friends decades later. I've never heard a single bad word about their friendship. To my knowledge, they've never had an argument and have always been as close as brothers despite attending different schools for several years and now living in different states.

Simple is not a word I would use to describe any of my friendships. They are many wonderful things but they are rarely simple.

And yet – or perhaps this is why – my female friendships form the bedrock of my emotional life. They love and challenge me in a way my husband cannot. They support me and nurture me and see me in a way my family cannot. They reassure me and push me and tease me and know me in a way that fills my cup with tea and wine and love and raucous laughter.

It's said for optimal emotional health, every woman needs a tribal council of five friends. That sounds about right. Five in your inner tribe and wider circles extending outwards towards the horizon of Facebook friends.

We have a fantasy, a handful of my girlfriends and I. For a few years now we keep trying to plan a weekend away without part-ners or children. Even though life keeps getting in the way and it hasn't yet happened, we take enormous pleasure just from talking about how lovely it would be. We have one rule:

Nobody who has been into or come out of our vaginas is invited.

It's a noble pursuit, just for a weekend.

This is our dream.

THE SEVEN TYPES OF FRIEND I HAVE IN MY LIFE

1. *Sleeper Friends*

Geography can rupture a friendship or at the very least change its patina. Some of my oldest and dearest friends live overseas and we don't speak for months or even years at a time. This is probably generational.

Between social media, Facetime and WhatsApp, proximity is no longer a requirement of friendship. When I was in my twenties and my friends moved overseas, there was an inevitability to losing touch.

Still, if we find ourselves in the same city we can easily pick up where we left off, even if it was three children and two decades ago.

Sleeper friendships can lie dormant for years with social media updates keeping you vaguely across each other's lives without either of you having to actively be involved in maintenance.

2. *Work Friends*

Everyone needs a work wife. This is Your Person on the job. The one to whom you can detail every petty grievance, piece of gossip, impulse you have to quit or steal a yoghurt out of the communal fridge because it's 3:30 pm and you're starving. These friendships can be intense but they're usually temporary. When one of you leaves and the daily structure of your friendship is dismantled, you inevitably discover you had less in common than you thought.

3. Mother Friends

When I had my first child I knew nobody who had kids. I eagerly bounced along to my first mothers' group meeting, organised by my local baby health centre, which grouped together a dozen new mums who had given birth in the same month. *We'd have so much in common!* We had nothing in common. Except the age of our babies. This became glaringly apparent during an earnest discussion with another mother within 15 minutes of our first get-together at a local park. 'I didn't know how to find a babysitter so I consulted my psychic,' she told the group.

I don't remember what she said after that. I was out.

Occasionally, though, your kid can choose you a brilliant friend. This happened to me when Luca chose Hugo whose mother Justine has turned out to be a beloved friend with the added benefit of being a doctor. I love doctors so much. They make me feel safe to be around. For years I was forever shoving Justine onto various sporting fields from the sidelines where we stood so she could tend to an injured child. I found it baffling that she was always reluctant to do this.

'Doctors prefer to mind their own business if they're off duty when it comes to non-life-threatening situations,' she hissed at me for 11 years, pointing out half a dozen doctors she knew who were pretending they weren't doctors each time someone else's kid sprained an ankle. If I were a doctor I would not take this approach. I would wear a sparkly cape with a red cross on it at all times and I would rush to the aid of anyone who looked even mildly unwell just to show off and be a hero.

Anyway, mother friends can be awesome but it's a type of friendship that can also be fraught if you have disparate parenting styles or lifestyles. See above re: psychic.

4. School Friends

As a rule, I find men are far more likely to have strong ties to their school mates who often form the majority of their adult friend group. Women less so. But there is nothing quite like your school friends to time-travel you back decades. Childhood nicknames, warm references to each other's parents ... there's a depth of knowledge there that adult-made friends can't possibly share. School friends cut through everything. They know who you were before you took on the mantle of adult with all its associated need to have your shit together.

5. Adult Friends

The friends you make as a fully formed adult are unique because they're self-selecting friendships of choice. They're not born of circumstance; a shared workstation or decisions your parents made about which school to send you to. While there is, of course, the opportunity to click with people even in pre-selected groups like work and school, adult friendships are forged from an infinitely wider pool. These are the friends whose parents you will probably never meet and whose children and parents may be of little interest to you. History is not a factor here. You're not friends just because you *were* friends. These are people you've chosen and who've chosen you because of who you've become.

6. Couple Friends

These are the friends you meet through a partner and some-times these friendships outlast the romantic relationship from which they grew.

One of my closest friends is someone I met through an ex-boyfriend, so ex that I refuse to acknowledge him on Facebook. That ex. Our partners at the time were best friends and interestingly, every one of those relationships has dissolved. Me and the jerk broke up. She and her partner got married and had kids but then divorced. The two guys no longer speak. But the shining light of the worst relationship of my life is this beautiful friendship, the gardenia that grew out of a steaming pile of manure.

7. Family Friends

My eldest son is one of my closest friends. You're not meant to say this about your kids, I know, shut up. It's less controversial now that he's an adult but it was true even when he was a kid. He's always been adult-like, a state greatly enhanced by being an only child for the first eight years.

Being friends with your kids gets an awfully bad rap, associated as it is with the likes of Lindsay Lohan partying with her mother Dina Lohan.

I understand. Blurred lines can be problematic for parents.

To me, though, friendship is defined by who I like to hang out with. Whose values I share. Whose opinions about the world and life I'm most interested to hear. Around whom I feel my best, most authentic self.

By those measures, all my kids tick every box, especially my eldest because I can swear in front of him and I no longer have to shield him from the vulnerable parts of me.

My husband ticks those boxes too – as any partner should. I don't know if he's my best friend though. I'm wary of that. I think it's risky to put all your emotional and intimate eggs in a single basket and expect that basket to meet all your needs 24/7. Who would want that JD?

I like to spread my need for intimacy across a variety of people, including but not limited to my husband. He's the only one that gets the sex because he's lucky, but his capacity for fulfilling everything I need emotionally is limited. Not because he is faulty, but because he's human.

Still, we are extremely good friends. Now. Friendship is a crucial basis for a marriage or any long-term relationship and I learned that the hard way.

Then there are my parents and my brother. I'd include them all on my friend list. You can't choose your family but you can choose to be friends with them or not. That's the bonus part.

We accept that romantic relationships often have an expiry date. So do jobs. Flowers. Milk. And so do many friendships. Sometimes they end, sometimes they *should* end and it doesn't mean you've failed or that the friendship has necessarily failed.

The aphorism: 'People come into your life for a reason, a season or a lifetime' applies most coherently to friends.

Reason and season friends are brilliant. It means you were both travelling on the same path for a period – months, years or even just the time it took you to reach the front of the Portaloo queue at Bluesfest – but now your paths have diverged and that's okay. You haven't failed. You have grown.

Here are some of the friends that fall into the reason-or-season basket . . .

Friends with whom you have nothing in common anymore – except history. School and uni friends are often in this category and so are work friends, friends from mothers' group or parents of kids your child is no longer friends with. Also, parents from the school your kid no longer attends. Sometimes the connection transcends the circumstance and the friendship sticks. Often it doesn't. Don't force it.

Friends whose lives or world views are just so different from yours that it becomes difficult to remain close or even attend dinner parties without wanting to throw your cutlery at their heads. People who don't support marriage equality. People who think Trump is a terrific president. Put your fork down. Just let them go.

Friends who move countries, who get busy, who make other friends. Let them go too. Or at least loosen the connection. Let your friendship settle at a different level. Allow the perimeter around you both to become looser, porous. Let the friendship ripple outwards. Don't force it.

Friendships born from an intense experience. You might have met while travelling. Or at a bereavement group. Or birth classes. What held you together was real but once the experience recedes, there isn't enough left to maintain a solid bond. That's okay. You'll always have Oktoberfest.

Friendships that are one-sided. Several years ago, I had to break up with a friend who I realised had no interest in me as anything other than a narcissistic mirror in which to admire their own reflection. It became obvious to me that the friendship was one-sided when I went through a very public crisis and there was no acknowledgement from him – not even a text. When he finally got back in contact it was to talk more about himself. Friends who drain you over long periods of time are destructive. Cut them loose.

THE TWO WAYS TO EUTHENISE A FRIENDSHIP: A HANDY GUIDE

1. *Blow it up*

This is the method most often applied to romantic relationship breakups. It involves one or more heated conversations in person, on the phone or by text where you angrily list all the reasons why you're ending the friendship and the myriad ways in which they've been a dick.

Benefits: it's fast – in theory. You'll feel vindicated by venting all your pent-up frustration, leaving your former friend under no illusions as to What Went Wrong.

Downside: it's dramatic, tedious and draining. This is a plus for some people who enjoy drama but nobody enjoys feeling drained. Things will be (and will probably remain) ugly, of that you can be sure. And you will have to listen to all manner of claims about your own shitty behaviour as a friend which will be unpleasant and uncomfortable regardless of their veracity.

2. Death by neglect

This approach is the one I've inadvertently taken with every plant I've ever owned and it works for friendships too, except you do it on purpose. Starve it of water, time, attention and love. Ignore the friendship, basically, until it curls up and dies. Or drifts slowly away off into space like George Clooney's character in that movie with Sandra Bullock which Tina Fey accurately described as 'the story of how George Clooney would rather float away into space and die than spend one more minute with a woman his own age'.

Benefits: it's slower and less dramatic than a detonation. Less hurtful. Less confrontational. Requires minimum effort.

Downside: you won't have the cathartic experience of detailing all the reasons you're walking away, which can be disappointing to miss if you're feeling the need for vindication. It takes longer. Is less definitive. More passive. Friend may be confused or fail to notice. That's annoying.

From experience, I find that the second way, although less satisfying in the short-term, is ultimately the most efficient.

Because if you confront your soon-to-be ex-friend and make your case for a breakup, they will inevitably defend themselves. People tend to do that even though in your fantasy, they listen to you with their eyes lowered and pause to let your cutting words absorb before saying, 'You're completely right. I'm responsible for the terminal decline in our friendship. I'm just lucky to have had you in my life for this long. I hope you can forgive me and I wish you well for the future. I will cherish the memory of our friendship for all eternity. I didn't deserve you. I'm deeply sorry. Goodbye.'

More likely is that they will accuse you of doing all sorts of things that have contributed to the negative dynamic between you and they may well be right. Probably they will be right. Who cares, you're out of there.

If you go the confrontation route, there will most certainly be argy bargy over text. It will be painful and emotional and at the end of it, if your friendship truly is as broken and irretriev-able as it feels, nothing much will have changed.

That's why I've come to favour the death-by-neglect approach. Scale back communication. Take longer to answer texts. Be unavailable for social arrangements. Eventually, they'll get it.

And you'll be free.

THE GOOD MOTHER MYTH

TIME SPENT WITH Child = Good Mother Points Earned

Work outside the home? *Lose points.* Have a nanny or send your child to daycare? *Lose points.* Need to travel for work? *Lose points.* Work long hours? *Lose points.* Miss an open day, swimming carnival, concert, dance recital, parent-teacher meeting or sports game? *Lose points.* Send your kids to before-care or after-care? *Lose points.* Put your kid in front of a screen so you can have five minutes of peace? *Lose points.* Close the door when you go to the toilet? *Lose points.* Send them to tennis camp, art camp or any type of holiday care during the 234 weeks of school holidays because you have to work?

Bad news: you have as many points left as you do annual leave days, which is none.

Bonus Good Mother Points can, of course, be earned in the following ways:

1. Doing tuckshop duty.

2. Being a class parent.

3. Breastfeeding your child for at least six months but not longer than 12 months because then you will lose points for being weird.

4. Taking lunchbox 'inspiration' from Pinterest, e.g.: making a lunch that includes depictions of all the main characters in *Finding Dory* made from raw, organic vegetables.

5. Staying at the birthday party despite the invitation clearly stating 'drop-off' (be aware this will piss off the birthday child's parents who really do not want you there and they may deduct points).

6. Pushing your kid on the swing at the park for as long as they want.

7. Doing every drop-off and pick-up yourself instead of after-care.

8. Ferrying your child to multiple after-school activities.

9. Hand-sewing your child's clothes.

10. Doing craft. Any type.

11. Teaching your kid to read and write before they start school.

12. Knowing the names of all the other kids – and parents – in your kid's class.

13. Leaving loving notes in your child's lunchbox, in words if they can read or hand-drawn illustrations if they can't.

14. Home-schooling – bahahahahahhaha!

Needless to say, I'm in a constant deficit of Mother Points and so are most mothers I know. That's the thing. The system is rigged. Unless you devote your every waking and sleeping moment exclusively to the care of your child and only have one child and literally do nothing but spend time with that one child and focus your entire being on anticipating and then meeting that child's every whim, you cannot win at mothering. And if you did, imagine what an arsehole your kid would be.

There's a quote I read in a glossy magazine interview with supermodel Miranda Kerr a few years ago. She was talking about a birthday cake she made for her son Flynn, who was a toddler at the time. It was gluten free, organic, sugar free and packed with agave juice. Oh and she made every part of it from scratch.

Look. I may have been having a particularly bad day but when I read about Flynn's beautiful little birthday cake I wanted to curl up in a tiny ball and cry hot, angry tears of defiance.

Perhaps this is because the birthday cake I serve at my kids' parties year after year looks like this:

Happy Birthday!

It was under $10 from Woolworths and I am quite certain it is neither sugar-free nor gluten-free. It's definitely not organic and contains no agave juice, whatever that even is. But do you know what my supermarket birthday cake *is*? Delicious. It also fancies up a treat with some Smarties and candles chucked on top and most importantly: it does the job.

It's not like I don't own the *Women's Weekly Children's Birthday Cake* cookbooks. I do. They are heavily annotated with post-it notes stuck hopefully on dozens of pages by all three of my children over the years as they've carefully studied each cake and chosen their favourites. In the interests of trying to see my parenting fails in a more positive light, I'm going to take those post-its as incontrovertible proof that I have raised optimistic children. Good job me.

Birthday cake cookbooks (also all cookbooks) in my house are a bit like porn for middle-aged men: it all looks marvellous but nah, it's never gonna happen for you in real life.

It's taken years but my kids understand this now. They know I'm not That Mother. I don't use this term in a passive-aggressive way because I realise there are many women who take great joy in creating fancy kids' birthday cakes and who am I to suggest it's not a worthwhile pursuit. I also understand some women like to cook delicious food for their friends and families as an expression of love and nurturing. Gwyneth Paltrow appears to be one of those women, as are all the other glossy-haired, beautiful celebrities beaming wholesomely at me from the covers of their cookbooks. I'm simply not.

Comparing my birthday cake or my dinner table to Miranda or Gwyneth is as helpful as comparing my body to that of a Victoria's Secret Angel, whose income is directly indexed to what she weighs.

Again, no slight on those Angels. *Good for them! But not for me.* We all make different choices about every aspect of our lives based on our beliefs, our priorities, our abilities and how pre-menstrual we're feeling on any given day.

This is why it's so self-defeating to compare ourselves to other women in any sense. Of course, every choice we make precipitates other choices by default. Pulling one thing from the queue and dragging it to the front automatically pushes everything else back a bit further. Wait your turn. I'll be with you in a minute, maybe tomorrow or possibly never.

That is that triage women do. All day every day. In our heads. Failing and succeeding. *Prioritising*. It's like an app constantly running in the background, refreshing in real time, draining our battery.

The incessant application of triage to our lives is a level on which most women continually exist that men wouldn't even be aware of.

So each time one of my kids has a birthday, I must decide if baking and decorating a cake takes priority over everything else that needs me. In my life as a full time working mother of three with no cooking skills? The cake does not make it to the front of the queue, not yesterday, not today, and not for the foreseeable future, and I'm okay with that. I've taught myself to be okay even when I'm judged harshly by strangers because nobody judges a good mother more brutally than she does herself. Truly bad mothers? And yes they exist. They're not the ones worrying if they're bad mothers.

After posting pictures of my store-bought birthday cakes, social media commenters have slammed me for not baking them myself and I give no fucks because birthday-cake-making is not a unit of measurement I use to judge parenting quality and nor should it be one of yours. The impact of a birthday cake on your child's life is less than negligible. Even if it has agave juice in it or Jimmy Giggle popping out of it.

Let me take you through my thought process: baking an elaborate *Women's Weekly* cake in the shape of a swimming pool with tiny edible pool toys in it or working out how you even make a cake without gluten or sugar would have taken me several hours – more if you include the time required to go buy the ingredients. Instead, I chose to use that time to work my way through the long list of things that have a greater impact on my life and my family. Like my job. Sleeping. Spending time with my children.

See what I did there? I implied that I was a better mother than someone who makes a fancy cake because I opt to spend quality time with my kids instead of faffing about in the kitchen with gelatine sheets and blue food colouring, trying to make a pool fence with tiny chocolate biscuits shaped like wooden palings.

That's bullshit. I'm no better than the mother who does that and she's no better than me. We just made different triage choices based on our lives at that time. Because that's what women do.

HOW I KNEW I WAS DONE

Disclaimer: if you are currently undergoing fertility treatment, grieving after a miscarriage or stillbirth or are childless and wish you weren't, this chapter is highly likely to piss you off.

I know. The greed of a woman with three children – with any children! – kvetching about wanting more when there are some women who have none? Screw you, Mia Freedman, and the insensitivity train you rode in on. You are lucky and blessed and STFU.

I know this, I see you. I acknowledge your pain. Genuinely. Telling my story is in no way meant to undermine yours. But my story is true for me and, I think, for many other women. Maybe skip this chapter if you're in that place. I was there myself for a long time. I completely understand.

IT'S A SUNNY Sunday morning in December and I'm standing in the middle of a three-year-old's birthday party with my phone pressed hard against my ear, trying to organise an abortion. Or, at least, an appointment at an abortion clinic to talk about the possibility of having an abortion. The phone call isn't going well due to the fact that (a) I don't think I want one and (b) I'm in someone's backyard with my youngest son and 34 other pre-schoolers, all of whom are bouncing on an inflatable jumpy castle in the shape of Thomas the Tank Engine while shrieking loudly. I'm finding it hard to concentrate on the task at hand.

'Hello, Marie Stopes Women's Health Services, how can I help you?'

'Oh hi, um, just one second – *Darling, no, I can't come and watch you jumping right now, Mummy's just on the phone* – I wanted to enquire about making an appointment for, um, well, to find out about RU486.'

[Sounds of children laughing and squealing in the background.]

'Yes, of course, I can help you with that. When is it convenient for you to come in?'

'*STOP IT! I'm on the PHONE, go play on the jumpy castle, I'll be there in a minute!* Oh look, sorry about that, ah, yeah early next week would be great if you have an appointment then?'

'Okay, I just need to get some personal details. What's your name?'

[In background: *'Come on kids, it's time to sing happy birthday! Who wants some ice-cream cake? MEEEEEEEEEEEEE!'.*]

'It's Mia, M-I-A . . . '

*

'Whatever you do, do not get pregnant,' my friend Caroline had implored me six months earlier, as if we were teenagers fooling around with boys at a party.

There was a party coming up – my 40th – and as one of my wisest friends who, at 41, was just that bit further down the hormone road, she was telling me to keep my legs crossed. According to her, this desperate need I felt to have another baby would pass. I just had to sit it out.

I didn't want to cross my legs though. I wanted to have

enormous amounts of unprotected sex and then elevate my hips on several pillows while lifting my feet to the ceiling so I could enlist gravity to help all those sperm in their heroic quest to swim to my egg.

My poor remaining eggs would need all the help they could get as they were growing more elderly by the day. They were definitely wearing Comfs and would soon graduate to orthotics and then a walker before quietly lying down to die inside my ovaries, leaving me a husk of a woman for whom the prospect of becoming a mother again was a sad joke that wasn't funny and made me weep.

So who wants a root?

Tick tock.

It was a happy, sexy time for me and my marriage.

'I promise this ache for another baby will pass as soon as you turn 40,' Caroline assured me from the other side of the mile-stone and the ache.

She wasn't finished with the wisdom.

'That need for a baby, do you know what it really is?'

I nodded dolefully. 'Yes, it's that I desperately want another one. It's the feeling of not being finished.'

'No, it's not,' she shook her head wisely. 'It's actually your body getting ready to become a grandmother. Historically, this is the age when we used to become grandparents. That's why you think you want a baby but you don't. It's a grandchild your body wants. Don't let it trick you into getting knocked up.'

So my body thinks it's Nana o'clock? This just gets better.

Whatever biology was causing this, it felt far beyond my control. It was a different feeling to when I'd been trying to conceive after my late term miscarriage more than a decade earlier. Back then I'd been demented by grief so fierce it devoured my marriage and nearly my sanity. Or the crazed desperation I'd felt years later after we'd reconciled and we were trying to get pregnant and it wasn't working.

This felt deeper, sadder, more profoundly . . . inevitable.

It's not that I felt my body couldn't conceive although I was well aware of the statistics and the risks of pregnancy at this age. The obstacle this time was different.

'If you want to have another baby, that's fine,' my husband would joke in front of our friends whenever the subject came up – and it came up a lot because I was incessantly raising it in the hope that I could enlist the popular vote to boost my campaign. 'You just have to find another husband!' Bada-boom. Hilarious punchline. Cue laughter.

Punched is how I felt, although not in the sense of humour. I felt punched in the heart.

Tick tock.

Jason was implacable. And yet I wouldn't give up.

I was used to getting my way when it came to babies. Two of our three children had been happy surprises, if by surprises you mean me wanting to be pregnant and Jason not wanting me to be and us both being irresponsible about contraception. SURPRISE.

Despite the surprised part, on both occasions he quickly overcame any reticence and got with the program wholeheartedly; literally with the whole of his heart. He is a terrific father to each of our children in a unique way. He's the consistent one, the one with the discipline and the boundaries; the one who teaches them things.

I figured I'd just have to give the surprise approach another go. 'Nobody regrets a swim or a baby,' I reminded him repeatedly because I'd heard that saying somewhere and as someone who views swims as unenthusiastically as my husband views babies, I thought it might be persuasive.

It wasn't.

Simultaneously, I waged stealth campaigns, shamelessly trying to conscript our children to my cause. Results were mixed depending on how much they hated their existing siblings at the time.

'Wouldn't it be great to have a sister so we could even up the number of girls in this house?' I'd say conspiratorially to my daughter each time she fought with one of her brothers which was most days.

'Imagine having a little brother you could boss around and play Nerf wars with!' I whispered to my youngest son as we snuggled before bed when he was at his most sleepy and suggestible.

I didn't bother trying to convince my teenager. He still hadn't forgiven me for robbing him of his only child status years earlier. 'Mum, you can't even manage the children you've got,' he pointed out with genuine confusion. 'Why would you want to add more?'

Ouch.

Et tu, Brute.

Onwards.

For years I grappled to deconstruct this longing, in conversations with therapists, girlfriends and people I'd just met. I thought about it and talked about it and angsted over it constantly after my third child was born. What was this obsession about?

What emerged was something like this:

1. *I actually enjoy being pregnant.* It's the most comfortable I ever feel in my body. Nature does a stellar job of erasing all the bad memories of physical and emotional ailments from my hard drive so I

only remember the good stuff. I feel powerful when I'm pregnant. Like I have a secret. And superpowers.

2. *The rush of giving birth and having a newborn, of MAKING A NEW PERSON, is the ultimate drug for me.* I love everything about it. Being the centre of attention, the miraculous power of being able to create a human and then push it out of my body, the way a newborn makes the outside world recede and your perspective and priorities realign in a way nothing else can.

3. *The sense that you're in the literal peak of your life.* You are creating life, nurturing it. For a long time, I felt that being pregnant and a new mother and the mother of small children was the pinnacle of my life as a woman. I wasn't ready to give that up and enter the next chapter marked 'menopause and decay'.

4. *I love having kids* – my children are my favourite people in the world so why wouldn't I want to make more of them?

5. *The smell of a newborn.* The End.

On the day of my 40th birthday, I had a lunch for the 40 most important and beloved women in my life. On that day, both my sisters-in-law were pregnant, one with twins. Three of my other girlfriends were pregnant. It felt like everyone was pregnant but me. Had Helen Mirren, Julia Gillard, Queen Elizabeth or Hilary Clinton announced their pregnancies at this time, I would not have been surprised. But I would have flinched because the news of every new pregnancy – regular or celebrity – was making me flinch in the painful way it does when you want to be pregnant but aren't.

I was unpregnant, I was unlikely to ever be pregnant again and it felt like a death, the death of a part of my life and the symbolic trudge further towards my actual death.

Tick Bloody Tock.

I gave myself many stern lectures.

Mia. You have three healthy children and for that you are unspeakably grateful. No hashtag. You have friends whose babies have died when they were just a few months old; friends whose babies have been stillborn, died soon after birth or died from SIDS before their first birthday. You have friends who have had countless miscarriages or who've never been able to fall pregnant at all. You have friends whose children are profoundly disabled. Bitch, please.

I know. I know.

But the longing inside me for another baby knew nothing of gratitude or perspective. It knew only that the prospect of never being pregnant again, never feeling that first kick, never pulling a baby from my body or holding it to my breast, never . . . never . . . I just couldn't make peace with the never.

So my question is: *How do you know when you're done?*

For years I asked this question of other mothers incessantly. So much is written about the best time to start a family and the agony of not being able to conceive but we rarely talk about when to stop.

Should you let nature decide for you? Your finances? The time you have available to give to each child? Because it's finite, you know. Love can stretch but time cannot.

Are you done?

I ramped up my unscientific survey as I headed towards 40 and I learned there were two types of answers. Neither of them were 'no'.

The first was unequivocal. 'HELL YES!'

It was usually accompanied by a perceptible wince at the thought of having more children. Sometimes it was a cringe or a widening of the eyes, in shock. Very occasionally, a dry retch or the pantomime of one.

I once greeted a friend who answered the door soon after having her third child with a cheery, 'Having any more?' and she reacted as though I'd suggested she grab Donald Trump by the testicles.

The women who categorically knew they were done made me envious; they answered my question with a certainty that blew away any prospect of regret.

'Kitchen's closed,' they exclaimed emphatically. 'The gas has been disconnected, power turned off.'

The second type of answer told me everything in the pause before it came. '*Welllllll* . . . ' or '*Ummmmm* . . . '

It would often be paired with a head tilt, a raised eyebrow or a simple shrug.

I've never met a woman who definitively declared, 'No, I'm not done.'

Perhaps being overt about wanting more kids is seen as tempting fate? Too greedy? Too vulnerable? Or maybe it's just our reluctance, as women, to say what we want in no uncertain terms.

A bit of all those things, probably.

It was for me. I never said, 'No, I'm not done' even when I knew I wasn't.

Fill in the blank, just like the future of my uterus.

For me, this blank grew into an elephant who quietly moved into our house and my heart after our first child was born. I thought he might move out after my daughter was born.

Nope. Then surely after we had our third child. Three children and a traumatic miscarriage? Time to go, elephant! You'd think.

Still there.

I began to fear I would never feel finished. My poor husband. He adored our children, his heart and life was full and he was really done now. And yet I persisted, pleading my case to go again. One. More. Time.

He point-blank refused.

By the time our youngest was three, we'd fallen back into our hilarious-but-not, 'Fine, but only with a different husband' routine but it masked a hairline fracture between us that was widening.

I know very few couples who are in complete agreement over when to stop having kids. Sometimes she wants to keep going, sometimes it's him. I know same-sex couples who have the same divide. So who wins? More importantly, who loses? Because someone always loses. I've seen resentment simmer on both sides and I've seen marriages break from the strain of one too many children, as well as one too few.

*

My friend Bec called to say she's pregnant. She's shocked. It's her fourth pregnancy in six years. Her second child, Georgie, was stillborn and from the ashes of her grief, she'd fallen pregnant with her son Finn who had only just turned one. Her eldest, Ava, was four.

In just a few months, though, Bec was going to have three children under five at home and we spoke for a long time about what that meant for her and how it made me feel. She knows better than anyone the turmoil I've felt about calling time on having more babies.

I surprised us both.

'You know? I think I might actually be done,' I told her. 'The kids need so much of me. We've been doing this for 16 years and Jason just wants to move on to the next phase of our life. I'm starting to agree. We're done with nappies and prams and cots and bottles and wipes and Remy is almost at school. We can travel now, go to restaurants with the kids, have rational conversations . . . we can sleep! Everyone can operate an iPad, shower themselves and make a snack. Two of them can even make me a cup of tea. We have a huge chunk of our lives back and we're in a good place.'

Bec made agreeing noises down the phone. 'Sounds like you're done.'

'So that probably means I'm pregnant,' I laughed.

And I was.

*

I'd like to say I was 100 per cent on board with this pregnancy and I should have been but there was definitely an element of Be Careful What You Wish For. It was daunting. I was 40. The risks of a bad medical outcome for this baby were high. My kids were less physically demanding but their emotional needs were cranking up which nobody tells you about.

They needed more of my time and I wanted to give that to them freely. Mamamia continued to grow and it needed more of me. The demands on my time were escalating and I was having to travel more.

I was already so stretched, it was true. There's no such thing as maternity leave when you own your own business. How would we manage?

And that's assuming the pregnancy was fine and the baby and I were healthy. What if something went wrong? I wasn't just rolling the dice for myself and this child but for my whole family for the rest of all our lives.

And what about my anxiety? Would I be able to continue my medication?

I was anguished and exultant.

Jason and I had some incredibly difficult conversations. In my head and then online, I explored the idea of ending the pregnancy. Googling to find out about RU486 I was shocked to discover it couldn't be prescribed by my GP. Only certain clinics could supply it and the process – while far simpler and preferable to a surgical abortion – was more involved than just picking up a script

And that's how I found myself at a three-year-old's birthday party on the phone to an abortion clinic trying to make an appointment over the sing-song strains of *Happy Birthday to You*.

*

Caitlin Moran argues that society views abortion on a spectrum of 'wrongness' and we divide abortions into two types: good and bad. 'Good' abortions are those required by victims of rape or incest or when a mother's life is in mortal danger. These abortions remain pretty free of stigma. 'Bad' abortions sit at the other end of the spectrum and include repeated abortions (any more than one, really), late-term abortions, abortions after IVF and mothers who have abortions. She writes: 'Our view of motherhood is still so idealised and misty – Mother, gentle giver of life – that the thought of a mother subsequently setting limits on her capacity to nurture, and refusing to give further life, seems obscene.'

Soon after she had her second daughter, Moran found herself pregnant and decided immediately to have an abortion.

'Motherhood is a game you must enter with as much energy, willingness and happiness as possible,' she said and while some women find the idea of abortion less palatable after they become mothers, Moran was the opposite. It was only then, she said, that she knew what was truly involved in bringing a baby into the world.

Having a third child would, for her, she knew with complete certainty, change the very essence of who she was and very probably stretch her way beyond her capabilities as a mother. And who would that serve? Not her, not her children or their father and not a baby who would potentially push the whole family to breaking point.

Would having a fourth child do the same to me? I knew I could survive it but could my marriage? And what impact would it have on the three children I already had? Was it a good idea to risk blowing up my family for another baby? Having grieved for the baby I'd lost and then tried so desperately to get pregnant again with my daughter, how on earth could I willingly end a pregnancy? I'd been banging on for years about how I wanted a fourth child and now here one was. What was wrong with me?

*

Two days later I sat in the clinic valiantly trying not to make eye contact with any of the other women in the waiting room. We'd all made a silent agreement that none of us were here. This is abortion clinic etiquette and it's unspoken. No chatting.

No matter how much of a feminist you are, no matter how pro-choice, there is something tremendously vulnerable and exposing about sitting in the waiting room of an abortion clinic. I was fairly sure I didn't want an abortion but I did want some more information about my options.

To be honest, my research had informed me that they had to give me an ultrasound before they could prescribe RU486 and

I wanted to see what was in there. Maybe it would be unviable or there would be no heartbeat and that would be my answer. Saved! No decision necessary! Or perhaps it would be twins and that would be a sign. I always thought I'd have twins some day.

The receptionist checked her notes and called across the waiting room, 'Mia Freedman? Are you still at –' and then she read out my address.

Still? What did she mean *still?* I'd never been there before! I'd just given the clinic my details over the phone! She made it sound like I was a regular.

If only I'd known how much more excruciating it was about to get.

Two days earlier at the birthday party after I'd made the clinic appointment, I'd been chatting with one of the dads from pre-school. Our boys were mates. His son had two dads and I knew them quite well from playdates, drop-offs and parties. The dad I was talking to at the party did something in the theatre, a producer I think, and the other dad was possibly a doctor.

The other dad was a doctor.

The other dad was a doctor at an abortion clinic.

The other dad was a doctor at this abortion clinic and I was about to be seated across from him for a consultation after my ultrasound.

I tried very hard not to take this as a sign.

What are the chances of your kid's mate's dad being your abortion doctor? This wasn't weird at all.

Having sat there conspicuously for a while waiting to be called in, I'd sussed out the drill. Your name was called and you went into the ultrasound room with a nurse before going into another room for a debrief.

The doctor then came in for a consultation before giving you the drug that would trigger the end of your pregnancy. You took one pill at the clinic in front of the doctor and the other pill at home.

I looked down, burying my face in my phone each time the pre-school dad walked past and I waited to be called for my ultrasound. It was a bit anticlimactic really.

The nurse couldn't see much although she confirmed that I was pregnant and there was one foetus. It's early, she assured me, which I found disappointing. The more progressed the pregnancy, the more likely I would be to go through with it.

Still, I knew I didn't want to end this pregnancy. I wanted another baby. I told the nurse I wanted to think about it and left the clinic, managing to avoid the world's most awkward encounter.

Out on the street I took some breaths. I'd decided.

A week or two later, I went to see the obstetrician who had delivered my last two children. He was surprised to see me and we laughed about how my eldest son would be able to drive me to mother's group because he just got his licence and wasn't that hilarious and then I hopped up on the table for an ultrasound and he couldn't find a heartbeat and the tone of our conversation abruptly changed.

Here I was again.

More than a decade earlier I'd lain on a table just like this with my top hiked up just like this and gel on my stomach and peered desperately at the grainy ultrasound screen, uncomprehendingly, searching wildly for the flickering light of a heartbeat that wasn't there. Just like this.

This time, I wasn't desperate and certainly not uncomprehending. Just disappointed. Like being refused entry to a nightclub you're not sure you want to go into because it's 2 am and maybe you should just go home.

Apparently my entry into this club had been considered for about five or six weeks before being summarily refused. Perhaps my ambivalence had been taken into account?

The whole experience was very different to the 19 weeks I'd spent desperately wanting to be pregnant 12 years earlier and the way my world had imploded during another routine ultrasound.

I don't remember crying this time. I doubt that I did. It wasn't a tragedy so much as a pity, both my doctor and I were in silent agreement about that.

We switched almost seamlessly from jokes about me having four children to a business-like discussion about what to do next.

'We can do a D&C,' he said, referring to the dilation and curettage procedure that's common in failed pregnancies. Failed. Yes, here I was again. Having failed at something I wasn't even properly trying to do. I felt the sting of shame. Of being too old, too incompetent to sustain a pregnancy. I felt embarrassed for ever assuming I could.

'What are you doing tomorrow?' he asked me.

We were back at his desk, the ultrasound gel wiped off my stomach, my pants back on, the banter extinguished.

'Going on holidays for three weeks, our flight's in the morning,' I replied, marvelling at how mundane a conversation I was having after just learning my future, the future of my family and its shape, was going to be so different to the way it had looked just five minutes earlier.

'Okay then,' he said neutrally. 'You can just wait. The pregnancy should eliminate naturally. It's actually better to avoid a procedure and an anaesthetic.'

I nodded. 'Oh. Okay. How long should it take to . . . eliminate?'

Failure. Elimination. The language of pregnancy loss is part gut-wrenching part prosaic.

'It could be anytime from now or as long as a few weeks. If it hasn't happened by the time you're back from holidays, call and make an appointment and we'll make a time to do an ultrasound, okay? Either way we should do one to make sure it's all gone.'

All gone.

All. Gone.

He was lovely about it, not unkind, but doctors aren't therapists. They don't have time to counsel you through the emotional whiplash of crushed expectations.

I was all business too. I thanked him, we had a little hug – the man had helped me pull two babies from my body and I loved him for that – and I found myself back out in the waiting room.

'Need to make another appointment, Mia?' the receptionist asked me brightly.

'Um, no . . . ' My answer drifted off and she understood immediately.

'Ah . . . Okay. Well, listen, you take care.'

Dazed, I took the stairs down to the street, trying to anchor myself in reality. Eleven flights I walked, carefully, in heels, emerging out into daylight and blinking hard as I made my way back to my car.

My body had made the decision I couldn't, wouldn't. Or my old eggs had. Or nature had. Or the universe had. Or the little soul who'd been thinking about coming through had simply decided not to.

It was done.

I felt a million things. Relief, devastation, deep sadness, disappointment. I didn't feel bereaved so much as bereft. I felt a bit shocked but I wasn't reeling. I knew this had been my last shot at another baby. My husband would never agree to try again and I would never willingly push us back onto this ledge.

My kitchen had been closed for me.

I watched the prospect of that fourth child float away, it was almost like I could see it.

I drove to a cafe near my house and ordered a large slice of banana bread and a hot chocolate.

Comfort food in which I found no comfort.

The cramps didn't come for another two weeks. When they did, I was shocked at how strong they were. I thought a miscarriage would be more like period pain but it felt like early labour and that made me terribly sad. As my body cramped and began to bleed, my mind was tricked by the familiar contractions into believing I was about to give birth.

But there was no baby this time. The pain of this pregnancy leaving my body cut through the dull malaise that had enveloped me since the ultrasound in a way that was almost a relief. It jolted me back into the world.

Naturally, I became angry because that feels less painful than heartbroken. I was struck by the full force of my fury at Jason for not wanting more kids; for standing between me and the fulfilment of my life as a mother of four. This was his fault.

We went out to dinner, just the two of us, and I picked a fight before our meals arrived. Scrambling to my feet, I huffed out of the restaurant, marching angrily through town and ignoring his pleas as he came after me to let him drive me home. I arrived back at the house half an hour later and miscarried in the toilet. It's quite a primal thing, having a miscarriage. The last time it had happened to me I'd been 19 weeks and had the choice of either enduring labour and giving birth or having the baby removed while under general anaesthetic. I chose the latter and woke up empty and sobbing.

This was far less emotionally awful while being far more visceral. It was more private. Just me. The heaviest of periods. No doctors, no clinic or hospital.

Somehow, the physicality of it helped move me through my anger which slowly shifted to sadness and then settled into an uncomfortable, resigned acceptance.

I tried to ride the waves of my hormones and just hold on as they battered me around.

A few months later, I wrote:

> I'm envious of women who say with complete certainty that they're done. I wonder if I'll ever feel that, ever have that sense of completion. Or whether the hole is just something you learn to live with, something that closes up over time.
>
> ∧ | ∨ · Reply · Share ›

A few years later, here's what I have to tell you.

It does close up, the hole. Imperceptibly at first. Caroline was right about shifting from looking at babies with anguished yearning to looking at them with . . . well, horror. Or at least relief they aren't yours.

It took me a bit longer than age 40 to feel that shift. For me it kicked in at about 42.

That's when I was able to declare with complete certainty, '*Hell yeah*, I'm done.'

Finally, I was ready to close the 15-year chapter of our life called 'Baby Making And The Rearing Of Small Children' and I was excited to see what came next.

Finally, I stopped viewing that chapter as the single climax of the book but simply just one of many.

Finally, I was ready to stop harassing my husband for something I could no longer have, even if he'd been willing. My eggs were most likely cooked and even if they weren't, I was no longer interested in finding out.

The thought of going back to that age and stage made me flinch in that same primal way as I'd seen in other women who were done.

Finally. Babies? Ugh.

Jason and I were on the same page for the first time in our relationship and this was the making of it, of us.

Something in our marriage imperceptibly shifted and we both relaxed as he stopped having to pull away from a place I was straining so hard towards.

My friend Wendy never had children, partly by choice and partly by circumstance. She has not always been at peace with her situation but soon after turning 40, she too felt something lift. When I told her how relieved I was to feel done, she cried, 'Hallelujah! Now can you understand how I feel when people ask me if I regret not having had children? I've passed that point, not just physically but mentally and emotionally. I'm delighted with my life. I love other people's kids but I don't envy my friends who are mothers.'

If only people could stop trying to 'save' her from her child-free life. 'Now that people like Sonia Kruger and Janet Jackson are having babies with donor eggs at 50, people keep saying to me, "Oh, but it's not too late" and I'm like, it is because I don't want to have a baby! Stop trying to fix me! I'm happy!'

SELF-DEFENCE AGAINST TROLLS

'Mia Freedman is the load her mother should have
swallowed.'
Some idiot on Twitter

I'VE TALKED A lot in this book about quieting the trolls inside
our heads that tell us we're not pretty enough, not thin enough,
not young enough, not maternal enough, not capable enough,
not sexy enough, not flawless enough, not balanced enough.
Not . . . enough.

Don't believe everything you think.

Women have always had a lot of experience dealing with
trolls long before the word even existed other than to describe
that creepy dude under the bridge with the goats. We're introduced to our inner trolls at an age that would shock the men in
our lives, as would the frequency with which we battle them.

Annoying little fuckers.

By comparison, the external criticism we all risk on the
Internet every time we tweet or Instagram a selfie or leave a
comment on a Facebook story about Trump or post our opinion

about Australia Day or share a meme ridiculing anti-vaxxers is relatively mild. Still, what makes it pernicious is the way that criticism plays out in front of an audience and the fact that the person delivering it is usually a stranger.

This is weird.

It's disconcerting to be attacked online, often personally, sometimes brutally, by someone you've never met.

The growing popularity of Mamamia meant more readers, more comments and more decisions about deleting them. It hadn't occurred to me to pre-moderate comments, so they were all published automatically. Even if it was vile or defamatory to me, another commenter or a public figure named in the post.

There were often hundreds of comments per post per day and I was drowning. I had to quickly glance at them all and make a fast call on what to delete while at the same time writing all the new content that would (hopefully) generate more traffic – and more comments.

In 2008, before social media had taken off, the comments section of blogs and websites enabled everyone to be part of the conversation for the first time and this was a steep learning curve for publishers and journalists who weren't used to this kind of instant, unfiltered feedback. After writing and publishing six posts a day, I felt added pressure to participate in the comments sections myself, replying to as many comments as I could, trying to encourage engagement and defuse aggression. Many readers would address me directly in their comments and expect a reply. Promptly.

Most days felt like sprinting on a treadmill wearing flippers as I scrambled to climb out from under the vast pile of comments pouring onto the site, all requiring my attention in real time.

Early on, I established commenting rules. I hadn't yet heard the word 'troll', but I understood what one was; someone who wanted to make trouble. An arsehat[24].

Sometimes, though, this was difficult to articulate or even identify. Whenever I deleted a comment, the commenter would usually leave an aggressive follow-up comment demanding an explanation and threatening to 'quit' the site. I barely had time to breastfeed my child let alone engage in a debate with every abusive commenter who was demanding I reply to them about how and why exactly they'd crossed my line. For a while I used humour as a defence. 'If you want to quit visiting this free website, you need to submit your resignation in writing with three months' notice.' It helped me to highlight the absurdity of these nameless trolls threatening to withhold their clicks.

Resolutely, I wrote my first commenting policy and added it to the bottom of each post, which at least spared me from having to justify every action I took on my own site which I paid for:

> Think of the comments section of
> Mamamia as a dinner party. Differences
> of opinion are most welcome but if you
> are deliberately rude, insult the host or
> start throwing food, you'll get kicked out.
>
> ∧ | ∨ · Reply · Share ›

---

24 It was hectic to be on the receiving end of this all day every day and I had it good compared to journalists I knew who worked at websites with a male-dominated audience, where the levels of aggression and abuse were sickening.

This made some people indignant. They insisted it was their right to say whatever they wanted, even if it was calling me a stupid whore. They cried 'censorship' if their comments were deleted and accused me of being 'too precious to handle criticism'. For a long time, this manipulation worked a treat on me. In hindsight, I can see it was a tactic called 'gaslighting' widely used by emotionally abusive men where the abuser twists the truth of a situation to make you feel like it's your fault. For example, my abusive ex-boyfriend used to insist I was being 'slutty' whenever I wore a bright colour. 'You're just trying to get attention from other guys,' he'd sneer. *He* wasn't jealous, controlling or unreasonable. *I* was a slut. Was I? I changed my clothes. See how gaslighting works?

This small but vocal group of commenters would try to shift focus from their reprehensible behaviour onto mine for calling it out, duping me into believing that anything less than approving all their comments was censorship. For a long time I complied, fearful that deleting anything would piss off individual commenters, compromise the independence of the site and most worryingly, decrease traffic.

It's not that I wanted all the comments to be positive let alone sycophantic; Mamamia was meant to spark conversation, after all.

At Mamamia, I only had to delete around one per cent of the comments on any given day, although this increased as the site became more popular and my poppy grew taller. More abuse, more of it personal. I was less concerned about myself than I was about commenters abusing each other. That's not what I wanted at my dinner party. For Mamamia to be successful, I needed everyone to keep coming back, and creating a safe environment was an integral part of that.

There's nothing in our evolution that's prepared us for the sudden unfiltered feedback the Internet allows. What other people think of you should be none of your business but now it's everyone's business because social media has provided a megaphone, a spotlight and an audience to everyone with an Internet connection. If you're in the public eye, it's also given anyone the ability to put their words into your ears and your eyes.

If you let them.

For a long time, I let them. There's something perversely intoxicating about knowing what other people think of you. It's the sirens luring you onto the rocks. You know there's looming danger and you should probably navigate away quite urgently but you just can't.

Because for a long time – until very recently and even sometimes still – I believed that if I just explained myself to the person intent on twisting my words into weapons or ascribing to me an opinion or intention I never had, I could reason with them. We could sort this out, surely. Like adults. This so rarely happens as to make it statistically irrelevant. I've come to understand and accept that there are some people who are heavily invested in hating me (and others) for reasons best understood by them. Whatever is the opposite of the benefit of the doubt, that's what they give me because they want to believe I'm a terrible person.

While strange and disturbing, this realisation has been a relief frankly, because it's freed me from even trying to placate them. That's not what they're seeking. It's a futile exercise.

The feedback you receive online as a public figure exists on a spectrum of delightful to frightening and it's unfortunate that you can't expose yourself to one without the other. You have to shut out the commentary about yourself entirely because it's impossible not to be detrimentally affected by both the bad and the good.

This often surprises people and it took me years to appreciate; reading about yourself makes you become attached and addicted to the praise while being eviscerated by the criticism and abuse which sounds much louder and lingers far longer. Neither is healthy. Neither helps me do my job or live my life or be a sane person in the world who isn't twitching and dribbling in the foetal position under my desk.

That's why many years ago I stopped reading my mentions on Twitter. Then I stopped going to Twitter at all except during breaking news or to search the names of people, journalists usually, whose tweets I specifically wanted to read in a batch. I miss the opportunity to interact with people who are genuinely interested and interesting but I cannot allow my sanity to be collateral damage.

There are many tremendous things about the Internet. Trolling and the incessant, vicious abuse of women online is not one of them[25].

Whenever I speak to groups of women, I'm always asked about this. 'How do you cope with the criticism?' My answer is: very carefully.

Here's what I can tell you after a long time on the frontline of the Internet: you need to keep a laser-like focus on whose opinions matter to you and do your best to filter out the rest.

All opinions are not created equal even though online they can appear to be. Make a list, in your head, in your phone or on a t-shirt. On it, put the names of everyone whose opinions you value.

---

25 In my experience, the three most common words of abuse hurled at women online are 'fat' 'ugly' and 'old'. Imagine any of those words being used to attack a man.

For me, this includes my family, my friends, my colleagues, my peers in the media, tech and business worlds and people in other fields I admire or respect.

They do not include egg avatars or anyone who wishes to pass commentary on my appearance, age, religion, family, sex life, weight, gender or identity as a feminist.

Those people are not on my who-matters list and not in my life. Writing this book has been an exercise in banishing them from my head. A fear of being attacked, ridiculed or abused on social media is a real but ultimately fruitless thing to be governed by. It's happened to me many times and I survived it.

Many people will tell you not to feed the trolls. I'd add you shouldn't even make eye contact.

FUTURE LESSONS FOR MY DAUGHTER

IN THE FIRST part of my career in magazines, I was always the youngest person in the room, including when I became the editor of *Cosmopolitan*. From about the time I turned 30 though, I've been steadily becoming the oldest. I'm okay with that. Wisdom comes with age. Fuck-ups and age. With that in mind, there are a few Life Lessons I want to pass on to my daughter that I suspect she will be more inclined to absorb if they're in book form rather than delivered in my usual manner: while she's captive in my car on the way to soccer training.

1. *Don't do anything to permanently remove your pubic hair.* Bald may be popular right now but that's because of porn and like most things about women's bodies, trends change with infuriating frequency. Wax all you like (shaving can give you ingrowns) but permanently changing anything about your appearance is high-risk, including pubes. You don't want to be one of those women forced to buy a merkin (pubic wig) when the bush comes back. Which it probably will by the time you read this.

2. *Be proud to say you're a feminist.* Some people will tell you that feminism is redundant. 'We're all equal now! You should be a humanist or an equalist instead!' Slap them. Then remind them that women are paid less than men for doing the same jobs, being killed (by men) thousands of times more often than men, don't have the right to drive or vote or choose who they marry or have control over their own bodies or literally show their faces in many countries and that we most definitely are *not yet equal*. You need to call yourself a feminist and urge all your friends to do the same – male and female – because you can't fight for something if there's no word for it. Feminism is that organising, uniting word. Imagine if someone decided they didn't like the label 'tree' and they wanted to call it a leaf-holder. That is some confusing bullshit right there. The word is feminist. Use it. Be it.

3. *Don't take nude selfies.* Find another way to express your sexuality. It's not because nudity is shameful; I'm not ashamed of the tampon string hanging out of me but I don't want a picture of it out in the world. Not shameful, just private. Your body is a beautiful thing and you should inhabit it with love and pride. I understand that you might feel powerful by claiming your body with a nude photo and sharing it with someone by choice. If only you could guarantee who saw it. The moment a nude photo exists on your phone – let alone is sent out into the world – you've lost control of it forever.

   The cloud is not perfect and neither is technology. You know what else isn't perfect? People.

   There are arseholes out there who will try to objectify or humiliate you by sharing or posting your nude photo. There are small men who will use it to try and impress their mates or strangers. All of this – while not your fault *ever and obviously* –

robs you of any power that photo may give you and hands it to someone – everyone – else. Ask yourself: would I be happy for my nana, my teachers, my boss, my brother and my next Uber driver to see this photo? If you do ever take a photo of yourself that you wouldn't want Nana to see, *for the love of God,* crop out your head and anything that could identify you. But not doing it in the first place is definitely the better option.

4. *If someone ever betrays your trust by sharing a nude selfie of you, it's not your fault.* It's theirs. Everyone will know this. You will be okay. You will have nothing to feel ashamed of. PS: this is another reason we need feminism – to call out this kind of crap and work towards laws that protect women from crimes like this.

5. *If a man you love ever calls you a slut, even in the heat of an argument – especially in the heat of an argument – run far and fast in the opposite direction.* Any man who uses that word about any woman (let alone one he purports to love) is a misogynist and has some deeply messed-up ideas about women. Your sexual history has no bearing on who you are and it should be as benign as which school you went to or what your star sign is. Insecure, damaged men will sometimes try and use the word 'slut' or 'slutty' to make you feel humiliated or ashamed and these men do not respect women. If anyone tries to use these words as a weapon against you, even if he claims to be 'joking', get out. Get away. It cannot and will not end well if you stay, I promise.

6. *Surround yourself with women.* Women you know and women you admire. Seek them out. Foster a close circle of girlfriends who have your back and love you fiercely. Love them fiercely back. Listen when they tell you things. Ask them for advice. Reveal your vulnerabilities to them so they will feel safe enough to do the same. If you see a woman being attacked online reach

out to offer her some words of support. Even if you don't know her. I have made many lifelong friends this way.

7. *Every hour you spend gazing at yourself in selfie mode is an hour you're not looking out at the world.* The camera on your phone can act as a window or a mirror. Consider how much time you're looking into that mirror each day.

 The act of posting images of yourself on social media invites judgement and appraisal in the form of likes and comments. This is a trap. You are not your likes. Your value as a person is not related to what anyone else thinks of the photo you posted. Don't be thirsty for external validation of your appearance or your life. By indexing your self-esteem against the number of likes and 'So beautiful!' comments you get, you are creating a bottomless pit of need in yourself, one that will never be filled and will leave you as dependent and edgy as a crackhead looking for your next fix. This is no way to live. By all means express yourself through social media but don't attach your self-worth to how these images are received.

8. *Get piercings if you want, although be aware that they hurt and will probably get repeatedly infected if they're anywhere other than your earlobes.* I did my bellybutton when I was 21 and it never healed. My friend came with me to get the top of her ear pierced and ended up in hospital for two weeks with a raging staph infection; literally a fashion victim. With facial piercings, be aware that future employers may be put off. Take them out before an interview. And don't get those awful 10-cent-piece sized things that stretch out your earlobes because you can't reverse it.

9. *Tattoos are fine.* You can always get them removed, although it's incredibly expensive and even more painful than a tattoo which

feels like getting 1000 hot needles in your skin. So don't ever get inked on a whim or on a hens' night. I waited until my 30th birthday for this reason. Try drawing it with a permanent marker for a few weeks first to see how it looks. Also be wary of getting them in places you can't cover like your arms, hands, chest, neck and legs. Don't do that. You want to keep your options open. I know people say a lower back tattoo is cheap and tacky but I've always found mine is easily hidden and I never see it which can be either a plus or a minus. You certainly don't get sick of a tattoo you can't see.

10. *Wear clothes that lift your spirits.* The clothes you choose can affect the way you feel as well as the way the world sees you. Don't 'save' your best, favourite or most expensive clothes, wear them until they disintegrate.

11. *If someone shows you who they are, believe them (I learned this from American poet Maya Angelou and I'm stealing it to give to you).* Both the good and more importantly, the bad. Your romantic partner and your friends should add value to your life, not subtract from it. Fundamentally, people don't change. Be wary of men or women with 'potential'. Be more than wary. Know deep in your heart that very few people live up to their potential. Damaged people can damage people. They don't mean to but sometimes they do. You can't fix someone and you can't save them, even if you love them romantically; especially if you do. And you will hurt yourself trying.

12. *Don't ever expect your romantic partner to complete you.* Gah. That's a crock. A healthy relationship will not meet all your emotional needs so don't ever put that pressure on someone unless you want to suffocate love with the weight of unrealistic expectations. Girlfriends are a vital source of emotional inti-

macy and family can be too, both the one you came from and the one you may create.

13. *Most of the women you see on social media and in the media are not real.* They exist, just not like that. Their images are face-tuned or Photoshopped and they've used filters and all manner of trickery to make themselves look thinner and taller and thigh-gappier and more flawless than any human woman could biologically be. Almost all the female celebrities you see on TV have had injections in their faces; Botox, fillers or both. They have extensions clipped into their hair to make it longer, thicker. They have professionally applied makeup and contouring and professional lighting. It's all artifice. This is their choice, of course, but you need to remind yourself not to compare your real-life face or body to digitally altered, surgically modified ones.

14. *Walk in her shoes.* Go out of your way to learn about the experiences of others, particularly other women. Women of colour, refugee women, disadvantaged women, women with disabilities, gay women, trans women, women from different backgrounds and political points of view. Intersectional feminism means where being a feminist intersects with other types of minority like any of the categories above. If, like me, you remain a white, privileged, non-intersectional feminist, we must use our privilege and our power to pull other less privileged, less powerful women up along with us and help give them a voice whenever we can.

15. *You don't have to support every woman just because she has a vagina.* That's not what feminism is. Loving every other human regardless of their actions or beliefs is possibly Buddhism, I'm not sure, but it's certainly not feminism. The only 'rule' of feminism is that you believe women should have the same social,

economic and political rights as men – which includes having rights over our own bodies. Beyond that, feminism is a broad umbrella with many different opinions sitting comfortably underneath it. Roll your eyes at any self-proclaimed feminist who gets outraged on social media about who can and can't call herself a feminist. These women are tiresome and burn a lot of time and energy fighting petty battles. There's a place for angry feminism but it does not define the movement and you should never be silenced by it.

16. *Technically, what we call a vagina is actually called a vulva.* A 'vagina' is the inside bit. I know this. You know this. You should know this. But for the purposes of daily life and general conversation, the term vagina is perfectly fine. The people who bang on about this are known as the Vulva Police. I like to think they drive Volvos and eat Iced VoVos. They mean well. Onwards.

17. *Being interested in fashion or beauty or celebrities doesn't make you less intelligent than someone who isn't.* Just like NOT being interested in those things does not make you *more* intelligent. Your interests, hobbies and the music you like have no bearing on your IQ or your feminism. Don't ever apologise for the pop culture you love.

18. *In the immediate aftermath of any sickening tragedy, like terrorism, when you're feeling despondent about the state of the world and fearing for humanity, look for the helpers.* There will always be people running to help, queueing up to donate blood, taking care of victims, hunting down criminals, looking after each other because fundamentally, people are good.

Similarly, when people are being persecuted, there will always be people standing up for them even if they don't have skin in the game. Be one of those people.

19. *Your body is yours alone.* Don't let anyone try to tell you how it should look or how you should feel about it. Your body is capable of great things. It carries you through every day and is the vehicle for all your ambitions. Treat it with love and respect even when society tries to tell you not to.

20. *Have an epidural.* Or whatever drugs are available. Have them. Some people will try to convince you that it's more 'natural' to give birth without drugs. Tell them to go insert a swivel chair into an orifice, any orifice. That won't hurt them a fraction as much as giving birth without drugs. They are monstrous hypocrites who probably take cocaine on weekends. As feminist Jessi Klein points out, it's funny how society never wants women to be natural except when we are experiencing excruciating pain. Body hair? Gross. Periods? Disgusting. Wrinkles? Yuck. No makeup? Nasty. But during the most physically agonising experience of our lives, natural is suddenly preferred. This is hogwash. Don't buy it. Take the drugs. It will make you more present when you meet your baby, less traumatised afterwards and it won't harm either of you even a jot. Science has proved this.

21. *Remember that men can be our allies.* Seek out men who love women, who identify as feminists, who aren't afraid of a woman's strength or beauty or power. Seek out partners who celebrate your success as if it's their own and who are willing to lean in and out of family and work as you do the same, complementing and facilitating a true partnership. It's the only way you can succeed. Feminism does not exclude men. Hell no. We need all the soldiers available to help us fight for equality. Also: without men we can't make more feminists.

22. *When you go to someone's house for a BBQ or a dinner party, don't take a bunch of flowers as a gift.* It's annoying for your host to have to find a vase and dick around with water and stems while she's trying to greet her guests and get shit done. Chocolate is better. She can eat it after she's stacked the dishwasher when everyone's gone home. Nobody in history has ever been sad to receive chocolate. If your host has quit sugar, bring a potted plant: it's a better symbol of your relationship – constantly growing. Also better for the environment.

23. *Have sex on your terms.* Always. Every single time. If you don't want to try something, don't. Or if you start trying something and change your mind, stop. Just because you did something once with one person doesn't mean you have to do it again with them or anyone else. Just because you had sex with someone, even if it was last night or an hour ago, doesn't mean you have to do it with them again. Your consent must be non-negotiable for anything sex related, even kissing. Don't ever let a man make you feel like you wanted something if you didn't. Honesty, trust and mutual consent are the most crucial aspects of good sex – of any sex. Don't settle for anything less.

24. *Porn is bullshit.* I know some women who are porn stars and they have confirmed to me that women rarely enjoy the things they have to do in porn. Don't get any ideas from porn about what you should enjoy, what's considered 'normal' or how you should behave during sex. The women – and the men – in porn are paid money just like actors in any other kind of movie. The women are paid more because it's less enjoyable for them. Their 'pleasure' is faked to make the men watching feel good. Remember that. (Although there is little porn out there that shows how to pleasure a woman, women *are* now making porn

for women. If a man insists you watch porn with him, suggest he watch something that shows how women reach orgasm.)

25. *If a man ever seriously tries to tell you what to wear, run fast in the other direction.* By this I don't mean if there are types of clothes he does or doesn't like because we all have preferences (just as you may prefer he burn his reefer sandals or those cargo pants with zips that convert into shorts). But he should never make you deliberately feel bad about any way in which you wish to present yourself to the world. Be aware that a man buying clothes for a woman can be a form of control (a woman buying clothes for a man is just a public service). Your body, your clothes, your choices.

26. *Work.* Work for money and hopefully work for enjoyment as well. You won't enjoy it every day and there may be periods of weeks or even months when you hate your job. If it lasts longer than that, find a job you don't hate. If you're lucky enough to love your job, try not to define yourself by it. Jobs end. People get sacked and made redundant. Your job is not who you are, it's what you do.

27. *Don't squeeze your pimples.* I know this is really hypocritical advice because I squeeze mine and have been known to offer my children money to let me squeeze theirs. Cough. But it's a bad habit even though it's the best fun you will ever have in your life. I'm just saying.

28. *Wear sunscreen on your face, neck and chest every single day, even in winter.* And take off your makeup before you go to bed. Neither of these ideas are original but they're bang-on.

29. *Don't ever complain or lie about your age.* There are people who are sick or have lost loved ones who would give anything

for more birthdays, more years. Having a birthday is a privilege. Celebrate it.

30. *If you're keeping secrets about the state of your relationship from your closest girlfriends, it's a red flag and probably means the relationship is not a healthy one.* Friends are an excellent filter of duds and danger.

31. *If someone you know offers to walk you home or accompany you to your car or put you in an Uber at night, always say yes.* This does not make you weak or helpless. There will always be bad people in the world who want to hurt women. There are lots of us working on trying to make the world a safer place for women and it is never, ever a woman's fault if she is attacked. At the same time, you must be vigilant about your personal safety. Always look out for your girlfriends, be as street smart as you can and remember that every drink you have, every drug you take makes it harder to recognise danger when it crosses your path.

32. *Sometimes music with sexist lyrics is really great to sing along or dance to.* I know. This is confusing. I have no good answer for this. Being a woman and a feminist is about knowing that sometimes you will have to sit with that discomfort.

33. *Be wary of adult men who play video games.* It suggests they're having some trouble growing up. Imagine if adult women still played with Barbies. Just to relax. And at 1 am, our partners said, 'Come to bed, Babe,' and we said, 'I will soon, I'm just up to a really good bit where the prince comes along on the horse.'

34. *The most important decision you will make in your career is the romantic partner you choose.* Male or female, choose someone who supports your ambitions and is willing to work with you as a team if and when you have children. This is crucial.

BALANCE IS BULLSHIT

THERE HAS NEVER been more pressure on women to be everything. At work, at home, on social media, in the mirror. And always, *always* in our own heads where the pressure feels at times unbearable. If you're single, you're constantly asked why. If you don't have kids, people want to know what's wrong with you; are you infertile or are you just a child-hating shrew? What about donor eggs, have you considered it? If you take time out of your career to have a baby, everyone wants to know when you'll be back. If you return to work in less than six months, people wonder, 'But how can you leave the baby?'. If you stay away for longer, people ask, 'But what about your career?'. And any time you win a promotion, grab an opportunity for more responsibility or take a new job, people express concern about how you'll find work–life balance.

THE FIRST YEAR AFTER HAVING A BABY

WORK

LIFE

Then there's the incessant pressure to be thin and beautiful and young even when you're pregnant or a new mum or sick

THE FIRST FEW YEARS
OF A START UP

or depressed or hungover or old or have cancer or cystitis or are caring for your elderly father or you just woke up with the flu. Be hot 24/7 and document your hotness regularly via multiple social media platforms and associated hashtags or #fail. Don't be thirsty. Remember to be blessed. How many followers you got? Don't retweet praise but if you do, remember to have #gratitude.

As we silently internalise all this societal pressure to be and do everything, it constricts and tortures us in a way that's uniquely female. *Men do not do this*. They don't. They divert precious little mental energy to questioning whether they're being a bloke in exactly the way society deems correct at this particular moment. Men are rarely judged by society or by each other and especially not by themselves.

Not like we are, not like we do.

They just bloody get on with it.

How good does that sound?

Because when, as women, we can't fulfil society's absurdly long list of impossible demands – and nobody can – we sadly yank on our hair shirt and flagellate ourselves with the big three: shame, guilt and the pervading anxiety that we're failing. At life. At being women. Mothers. At our careers. And we pile these feelings on top of the already challenging circumstances that pushed us to this point.

TRYING (& FAILING) TO
CONCEIVE MY DAUGHTER

Rinse, repeat, angst, infinity.

No wonder the boundless, manic pursuit of a 'balanced' state makes us feel inadequate and wretched.

Work–life balance is like thigh gaps. It's yet another rotten external pressure women are putting on ourselves. Another impossible standard against which we're measuring ourselves and our lives. And for what?

Ambition ebbs and flows and so do your needs or the needs of those around you. I've had periods in my life, usually in the 12 months after giving birth, when my ambition goes AWOL and I've honestly wondered if it would ever return.

At other times it's roared deafeningly in my ear and I've gone without sleep or food just to get more work done. Writing this book has been one of those times. There are times when I want to rule the world and many moments when all I want is to walk away from my career and have a different life, maybe go back to being a

THE YEAR AFTER
HAVING A MISCARRIAGE

LIFE

WORK

waitress like I was when I was 19. Something where I could just go home at the end of the day instead of lumbering around with the weight of work in my head.

Most days, though, most years, I live somewhere in the middle. I don't think I'd necessarily describe this as balance though because that implies some kind of impossible perfection. It feels finite and finished. And life never is, until it is.

I'm not sure how much of my realisation that my feelings about work and family are constantly shifting is due to having kids and how much is just getting older, more reflective and more nuanced in my view of the world and of myself. I think you have less to prove as you age out of the career angst of your twenties and thirties and grow more comfortable with the idea that who you are isn't what you do. Because it's really not.

Not everyone has the luxury of stepping away from work

even for a short time. Many, many new mothers must return to work earlier or for more days per week than they'd like. Many women can't afford to take time out at all. They can't risk losing their jobs. Many workplaces don't offer flexibility and not all jobs are compatible with part-time hours. Do *women* really need to

INTERVIEWING THE PM AND MISSING MY SON'S 2ND BIRTHDAY

LIFE

WORK

feel guilty about this? It matters not a jot what's logical or fair, any woman who cares about doing a good job at work and at home will feel guilty until society as a whole takes a good hard look at itself and puts some viable solutions in place to ease our burdens.

MY SON'S HSC YEAR

WORK

LIFE

Of course, I hold myself to that standard as I should. At Mamamia we employ over 100 women who make up 99 per cent of our work force. Those with little kids rarely work full-time in the office. Some work reduced hours, others work a nine-day fortnight. Some work four days over five, others work a day or two from home. And as an employer of so many women, it can be both enlightening and challenging when you're faced with this desire for flexibility en masse. But it's worth it. Because I've also seen the toll, both physical and existential, that it takes on a huge group of women bashing themselves up because they don't feel they're attaining sustainable work–life balance.

And it's not just mothers who need flexible working conditions.

Women do the vast majority of caring in our community whether it's for children, the elderly or the disabled. Behind every person who needs care is a woman – usually several – who are stepping up to ensure it gets done. Often at enormous personal cost. These regular interruptions to our work lives are one of the reasons women have significantly less superannuation than men, which can be disastrous and is one of the reasons the fastest growing group of homeless people are women over 65.

In the space of 12 months recently, I watched two young women forced to move interstate to care for ailing parents. One had to take long stretches of leave before continuing to work for us in another state, something that hampered her ability to progress within the company in the way she'd hoped.

The other attempted to go part-time for several months before resigning due to the impracticality of trying to hold down her job while she struggled to meet the unpredictable demands of her parent's illness.

A third young woman, also an only child, had to take multiple days off work to help one of her parents navigate a health crisis that lasted for six months.

Yet another woman we employed could only work part-time because of her obligations caring for her kids, one of whom had special needs. Three days per week in the office was already a big step for her after putting her highly successful career on hold a decade earlier to care for her 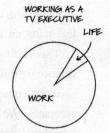 children full-time. Soon after she started with us, her mother became ill and she struggled through the next few months in a state of permanent panic, guilt, fear, grief and a pervading sense of overwhelm that only deepened when her mother died.

After battling for months to manage work under such anguished, stressful circumstances, she reluctantly resigned.

3:20PM–3:25PM ON A
TUESDAY IN MARCH 2013

WORK | LIFE

'Nobody is coping,' she told me. 'Especially not me.'

Several staff have resigned so they could follow their partners interstate or overseas as a 'trailing spouse', a term that describes the person in a relationship (almost always the woman) who sacrifices her own ambitions to move for a partner's job. Others have scaled down their careers or changed them to accommodate lives in new cities.

The women I've described above range in age from 20 to 50. I'll reiterate, this isn't an issue for a particular generation or even just for women with kids. It's an issue for all women.

It's not that balance on some level isn't worthwhile pursuing. It is. But without exception, each one of these women I've mentioned has spoken to me in hushed tones of their concern, their fear, their frustration and their reluctance to step back from work, even for a while. They talk about feeling deflated and defeated. They feel guilty, anxious and sad.

The feeling that they are failing to balance their lives is crushing them.

It all comes back to that impulse to compare. We need to stop measuring ourselves against an impossible ideal. By all

WRITING THIS BOOK

LIFE

WORK

means make changes to your life if it's not working for you. But don't let the pursuit of some mythical idea of balance push you over the edge, because think about how ironic that is.

Plus, balance is overrated. And often boring.

Of course, I like to cruise as much as the next person. But the times in your life you remember most vividly – the highs and the lows – are rarely those for which 'balanced' would be your adjective of choice.

Tell life you want balance and watch it throw up in your face by way of a sick relative, a bout of anxiety or infertility, a job opportunity, falling in love, an unexpected pregnancy, divorce, getting sacked, a needy rescue dog, a miscarriage, a financial challenge, the painful realisation your kids are growing up way too fast, grief, infidelity, childbirth, getting engaged, getting herpes, a friend with cancer, finding a bag of pills, a wad of cash and three mobile phones under your kid's bed . . .

As I wrote this book I started flicking back through a few conversations with friends in my phone. I found a text from a girlfriend who was struggling through a difficult pregnancy with her third child and working in a high pressure job.

> Feel like shit. Physically obv but mentally too. I just want to be able to do my job like I used to. The other girls at work don't have kids so . . . . . . ugh. I hate this. 😕

See how quick she was to compare herself to something that she just couldn't be?

She wanted me to say, YOU'VE GOT THIS.

I said, YOU HAVE NOT GOT THIS.

> Babe, this is not the time to be climbing the ladder. You can't compete with those girls right now. You can't put your hand up for a promotion or even a change. It's not the time to lean it, it's the time to lie down. Chill out. Recalibrate your expectations of yourself. Work at a more moderate level as you grow a human inside your body and try to make peace with it. Not forever but for a bit.

Her reply:

Whoops.

Genuinely, I *was* trying to make her feel better. I wanted to reassure her that taking a step back isn't the same as giving up. Sometimes the best thing you can do for your friends is give them permission to do what they secretly know they must (and might even want) to do but are resisting because they feel guilty about it. They're worried they're letting someone down and so they continue to battle their way through the impossible pits of hell.

Sometimes we need emotional permission.

And for full disclosure, I got another text from my friend later that evening:

*

So now we come to the end. I really hope that you're feeling a bit better about yourself, or just smug because you had already thrown off the shackles of the unattainable. Either way, it's grist to my mill, because I really worry about this stuff. In my job I see, daily, the way that the language and imagery of a certain constant pernicious sexism in society can creep in even to the seemingly 'democratic' new media. #DonaldTrump. When I think about my life and how much these unattainable standards have contributed to my anxiety over the years, and coloured my enjoyment of living, working, parenting, loving . . . I really worry for my friends, I worry for my daughter, I worry for my colleagues. I could fill a book with that worry. Instead I'll just state, once more, for the record:

Life likes to give balance the middle finger.

And every time you are overwhelmed by the fear that you're doing life wrong? You should do the same.